THE EGYPTIAN REVOLUTION OF 1919

THE EGYPTIAN REVOLUTION OF 1919

Legacies and Consequences of the Fight for Independence

Edited by
H. A. Hellyer and Robert Springborg

I.B. TAURIS
LONDON • NEW YORK • OXFORD • NEW DELHI • SYDNEY

I.B. TAURIS
Bloomsbury Publishing Plc
50 Bedford Square, London, WC1B 3DP, UK
1385 Broadway, New York, NY 10018, USA
29 Earlsfort Terrace, Dublin 2, Ireland

BLOOMSBURY, I.B. TAURIS and the I.B. Tauris logo are trademarks of Bloomsbury Publishing Plc

First published in Great Britain 2023
This paperback edition published 2024

Copyright © H. A. Hellyer, Robert Springborg and contributors 2023

H. A. Hellyer, Robert Springborg and contributors have asserted their right under the Copyright, Designs and Patents Act, 1988, to be identified as Authors and Editors of this work.

For legal purposes the Acknowledgments on p. viii constitute an extension of this copyright page.

Series design by Adriana Brioso
Cover images: [top] Cairo, Egypt, 1919 © Bettmann/Getty Images; [bottom] Cairo, Egypt, 2011 © Corentin Fohlen/Sipa Press/Alamy Stock Photo

All rights reserved. No part of this publication may be reproduced or transmitted in any form or by any means, electronic or mechanical, including photocopying, recording, or any information storage or retrieval system, without prior permission in writing from the publishers.

Bloomsbury Publishing Plc does not have any control over, or responsibility for, any third-party websites referred to or in this book. All internet addresses given in this book were correct at the time of going to press. The author and publisher regret any inconvenience caused if addresses have changed or sites have ceased to exist, but can accept no responsibility for any such changes.

A catalogue record for this book is available from the British Library.

A catalog record for this book is available from the Library of Congress.

ISBN: HB: 978-0-7556-4361-5
PB: 978-0-7556-4365-3
ePDF: 978-0-7556-4362-2
eBook: 978-0-7556-4363-9

Typeset by Deanta Global Publishing Services, Chennai, India

To find out more about our authors and books visit www.bloomsbury.com and sign up for our newsletters.

CONTENTS

Figures · vii
Acknowledgments · viii

REVOLUTION AND REVOLUTIONS: 1919 TO 2011
AND BEYOND IN EGYPT
H. A. Hellyer · 1

1 MEDICAL DOCTORS, MATERNAL HEALTH, AND THE
REVOLUTION OF 1919
Beth Baron · 9

2 ARABI AND HIS COMRADES: WORKERS ON THE CANAL AND
THE 1919 REVOLUTION
Mohamed Elsayed · 29

3 MUSLIM AND CHRISTIAN EGYPTIAN IDENTITIES AND THE
NARRATIVE OF THE 1919 REVOLUTION
Mark Bebawi · 53

4 FROM NATIONALISM TO ISLAMISM: REVOLUTION, THE WAFD,
AND THE RISE OF THE MUSLIM BROTHERHOOD
Philip Marfleet · 73

5 BRITISH RESPONSES TO THE 1919 REVOLUTION
James Whidden · 93

6 LORD ALLENBY AND THE 1919 REVOLUTION: AN AMBIVALENT
COLONIZER
Zeinab Abul-Magd · 113

7 CROSSING THE GLOBAL COLOR LINE: 1919 AND
COLONIAL RACISM
Kyle J. Anderson · 135

8 POLITICS FROM AFAR: EGYPTIANS IN EXILE DURING TWO
REVOLUTIONS (1919 AND 2011)
Taqadum Al-Khatib · 159

9   THE GREAT THEFT OF HISTORY: THE EGYPTIAN ARMY, THE
    FIRST WORLD WAR, AND THE 1919 REVOLUTION
    Khaled Fahmy   183

    CONCLUSION
    Robert D. Springborg   203

List of Contributors   209
Index   212

FIGURES

2.1	A section of the petition (written in French) that the SCC's representative workers sent to the British High Commissioner during the 1919 strike	36
2.2	A list of demands written (in Arabic) by the SCC workers, May 1919	37
2.3	A photo showing Al Masry club's flag as an adjusted copy of the independence flag	45
2.4	A photo of graffiti art on a building wall in Port Said that reads (as translated to English): "1919, the story of a revolution that created a club." March 2019	45
7.1	Petition from Abu Shadi	136
7.2	Shepheard's Hotel main dining hall, 1920	143
7.3	Flyer for Minstrel Show at the Cairo YMCA	144
7.4	"Al-Shughul fi-l-Sulta" (Working for the Government)	151

ACKNOWLEDGMENTS

We're grateful to the British Egyptian Society and its members for hosting and organizing the original conference dedicated to the 1919 Revolution; the conference provided a substantial part of the impetus for this book. We particularly thank Noel Brehony, Magdy Ishak, and Noel Rands for their assistance. Peter Mackenzie-Smith, who played a key role in organizing the conference, passed away while this volume was being prepared. The editors would also like to show their gratitude to Sophie Rudland, senior editor of the Middle East Studies & Islamic Studies section at I.B. Tauris; her efforts in ensuring a smooth transition from our ideas to this volume, that the reader holds in their hands, were invaluable. Transliteration decisions were generally left to the individual authors' discretion. With all that said, responsibility for the positive contributions, and any mistakes, belongs to the individual authors alone.

REVOLUTION AND REVOLUTIONS

1919 TO 2011 AND BEYOND IN EGYPT

H. A. Hellyer

* * *

On December 1, 2010, I left my home in Oxford with my family to travel to Cairo, Egypt. Our reasons for relocating were rather mundane, and, looking back, rather counter-intuitive. Oxford is hardly the busiest place in the United Kingdom, let alone more generally, but I think after having recently had our first child, my wife and I were keen to go to a place we generally found stable, quiet, not particularly expensive, and where we both had family ties. Of course, we soon found that "quiet" was not the word that would characterize our immediate future. A few weeks after arriving in Cairo, Tunisia's president was forced from power and into exile. A few weeks after that, the protests in Cairo began against then Egyptian president Hosni Mubarak. And days later, I found myself in the "Square of Liberation"—Tahrir Square, in downtown Cairo.

I have gone into some depth about my own views and experiences pertaining to that revolutionary uprising of 2011; what preceded it; what followed it; the main themes around it; and this is not the place to rehearse or repeat those discussions. What I thought important about those experiences is that they ought to be written and analyzed, so that in the future we might be able, as historians and as political scientists, to understand what happened and why. Particularly against the backdrop of so much historical revisionism, in such a short period of time, I wrote *A Revolution Undone: Egypt's Road beyond Revolt*.

There are other books as well, with excellent points made, that take on aspects of the years following the uprising, and there is little doubt in my mind that the discussions around that period will continue for years to come. But one question continues to occupy the scene when the revolutionary uprising of 2011 in Egypt is raised: Was the revolution successful?

* * *

Of course, the easy answer to that question relies purely on what one might mean by "revolution." If one defines it as the removal of the top echelon of power in any given political dispensation, then one could argue that 2011 was successful, because it led to the departure of Mubarak from the presidency. On the other hand, if, like for this author, the definition of "revolution" is far more expansive than that, then the assessment might differ quite substantially.

Those are items we consider only a few short years after the uprising itself took place in 2011; and if one separates the eleven days of uprising from the revolution itself, which many in Egypt considered to outlast the uprising itself, then we come to yet more questions. And perhaps fewer and fewer answers. When did the revolution begin; when did it end? Did it ever end? What were its impacts? Did it succeed, or fail? Or both?

The unpopular view, one suspects, is that it's far too early to answer those questions. Any historian who looks at events considered to have been "revolutions" in the annals of the stories of mankind is unlikely to have come to much of an accurate assessment about those events, until decades later. Indeed, in many cases, much longer than that.

Historians looking at the events of the French Revolutionary period, which stretched over a decade in the eighteenth century, would have no doubt disagreed as to the nature of that revolution, if they'd been looking at it in the late eighteenth or early nineteenth centuries. They probably differed tremendously as to the causes: when it ended, what could be "counted" as part of the revolution, and so on. It would take decades before historians would come to even a majority opinion of one sort or the other on the success or failure of the French Revolution, because the impacts of it were not necessarily so clear at the time.

For centuries thereafter, there continued, and continues, to be a vivid debate about the French Revolution. Alexis de Tocqueville had a much more positive viewpoint of the period, as compared to Edmund Burke, for example. Marxist thinkers emphasized certain aspects over others and so on. But one thing is relatively clear, and agreed upon, largely, by historians: that the French Revolution was a milestone event that separated the premodern and modern eras of particularly European history. It's humbling to recognize that such a near consensus assessment took many decades, if not centuries, to arrive at; and even so, there's no majority paradigm today that explains, interpretatively, the reasons behind the French Revolution, let alone its final impacts.

That example ought to instill within us a kind of humility that relates to the assessment of such tumultuous periods. That would apply to the French Revolution; and it would most certainly apply to Egypt's revolutionary uprising of 2011 and its aftermath.

* * *

What, then, of an event that takes place in between, which is precisely the subject of this volume. Egypt's revolution of 1919 is significant less because of the event itself, and more because of where it happened. The country traces its heritage along the Nile back to the sixth millennia BCE, making it one of the few in the world that has a specific national history that spans 8,000 years. Alongside Mesopotamia, India, and China, Egypt is recognized as one of the cradles of civilization in the so-called "Old World" of Africa, Europe, and Asia; and in the modern period, Egypt continued to be an important country. It was a prized part of the Ottoman domain from the sixteenth to the nineteenth century, and was important enough at the crossroads of Europe, Africa, and Asia, that the French military leader Napoleon Bonaparte engaged in a lengthy campaign to occupy Egypt during his own country's revolutionary period. The expulsion of French forces was followed by the establishment of a new Egyptian authority, the Khedivate of Egypt, which began with the dynasty of Muhammad Ali in 1805. During its existence, this new Egyptian entity controlled the present-day Arab territories of Sudan, the northwest of present-day Saudi Arabia, part of Yemen, Palestine, Jordan, Syria, and Libya, in addition to southern and central Turkey, Greece, Cyprus, and elsewhere in Africa, including Chad, the Central African Republic, and the Democratic Republic of the Congo. It is against that background that we ought to consider the Egyptian Revolution of 1919.

By the time the revolution came about, Egypt's glorious Khedival period had already come to an end; the British Empire had invaded in 1882, and while there would continue to be a Khedive in Cairo for many years thereafter, the reality of a British occupation remained from 1882 for decades thereafter. In 1914, even the title of Khedive was abolished, and the Sultanate of Egypt was established.

Par excellence, the 1919 Revolution was an anti-colonial one; the British colonial enterprise had not yet come to an end, and it was far too early to speak of post-colonialism in any way. The full consequences of the colonial enterprise had not yet been entirely understood; whether in terms of their effects on the educational system for Egyptians, the disastrous impacts on the trusts (*awqaf*) that had characterized so much of Egyptian society, or many other deleterious results.

But there was more than enough resentment to external interference in Egypt that brought about a sense of anger and hostility to its continuation. Egyptians had seen that during the First World War, the British occupation had exploited Egyptians for conscription, its economy for below-market purchases, and its land, as a base for foreign troops fighting alongside Britain. The end of the war did not mean the end of those effects; the economic repercussions continued, and they were painful for Egyptians across the country.

This was all happening in an age where national self-determination was not some kind of distant myth, but a concept that had been gaining ground for decades and had been publicly upheld by powerful international figures such as the Soviet Premier Vladimir Lenin and the president of the United States, Woodrow

Wilson. The later declared, in comments that would have been noted far beyond American borders, on February 11, 1918: "National aspirations must be respected; people may now be dominated and governed only by their own consent. 'Self-determination' is not a mere phrase; it is an imperative principle of action."

* * *

But empires seldom see the writing on the wall. Had the British occupation recognized that history was against them, it might have realized that the best course of action would have been to establish a settlement between itself, as the occupier, and the Egyptians, as the occupied: that would have meant a new sustainable relationship. Indeed, it might have been able to arrange one that would have meant a new ally in the region for London, as opposed to inadvertently encouraging a post-colonial elite that would be suspicious of Britain for a century to come.

Naturally enough, significant Egyptian figures, including the likes of Saad Zaghloul, petitioned the then British high commissioner to allow them to go to London to put their case for Egyptian independence in front of the British government. Their delegation, which means "*al-Wafd*" in Arabic, formed the basis of one of Egypt's most prominent political parties of the twentieth century—but at the time of this petition it was far from being a party. Rather, Zaghloul recognized that the moment had called for a coalition, representing various political and social elements of the Egypt that he saw and wished to make independent.

It was an interesting coalition, to say the least; Zaghloul, the most prominent leader among them, was a graduate of the Azhar, Egypt's pre-eminent religious seminary institution, and imbibed that traditional Egyptian Muslim outlook. Other members of the Wafd included the likes of Wasif Ghali, who was the head of the most prominent Coptic family in Upper Egypt, and deeply loyal to Zaghloul, as was another noted Coptic figure, Sinut Hanna. Egypt's independence movement was deeply indebted to this Muslim-Christian solidarity; if the leadership of the movement, and later the party, was an Azhari like Zaghloul, Christians would note that the secretary of the Wafd Party that would later emerge was a middle-class Egyptian Copt, Makram Ebeid. In advance of the famous delegation that would visit the British High Commission, Zaghloul declared to a meeting of Coptic notables: "Copts have the same rights and duties as Muslims and are on the same footing." At the same time, there were tensions between religion, ethnicity, and identity within Egyptian nationalism of the day, which Mark Bebawi explores in his chapter in this volume.

Again, had the British occupation been imbued with much foresight, they might have considered this an immense opportunity to shape relations with a wide consensus of the most influential members of Egyptian society. It's not terribly surprising that they did not see it in that fashion; as historians will note, authoritarianism's own logic is to promote and widen its own power as the natural imperative, as unbridled as it can, because there is no accountability mechanism that will halt it. When accountability is ensured, authoritarianism ends; and colonial enterprises are nothing if not authoritarian. The British occupation was, by its very essence, incapable of seeing any other route than the continuation of the occupation.

The foretelling of this kind of rulership mentality in Egypt and the region, at the hands of far too many rulers who were left to engage without proper accountability, is obvious to anyone with the slightest degree of honesty. In this case, there was undoubtedly a racialized sense of superiority at work; Kyle Anderson, in one of the contributions to this volume, explores the racism that Britons felt toward Egyptians, and how this was expressed at the time. Zeinab Abul-Magd discusses further the role of one Briton in particular, Lord Allenby, who served as the British special high commissioner for Egypt from March 1919 till June 1925. Ironically, Allenby was one of the few senior British figures who supported at least partially Egyptian independence. James Whidden, in another chapter, looks at the impact of the 1919 Revolution on the British from another angle, one that forced the imperial entity of the time to reconsider their relations with their colonies in the early part of the twentieth century.

Zaghloul and other prominent members of the Wafd were never allowed to go to London. They continued to agitate at home, which meant their movement only gained more and more currency among Egyptians across the country. I remember in 2011, following the revolutionary uprising, the Gallup Organisation carried out surveys to see the makeup of the protesters. The research showed that while participants weren't proportionally representative of all sectors of society, they were, undeniably, drawn from all sectors of society. One of the chapters in this volume, written by Mohamed Elsayed, focuses on the engagement of the working class, particularly those who were working on the Suez Canal or dockworkers in the city's port—the attraction of the promise of the revolution went far beyond the elite. Philip Marfleet, in another chapter, examines the uprising as a mass movement that brought new forms of public activism, raising expectations of radical change in both political and social affairs—expectations that were never fulfilled.

From 1918 to March 1919, the nationalist movement of the Wafd engaged further and further, eventually becoming such a thorn in the side of the occupation, Zaghloul and others were arrested, and then exiled.

Again, that is the logic of the authoritarian; faced with rebellion, he does not consider if the rebellion has widespread support or touches a nerve that the broad majority feels. Rather, he attempts to stamp it out. Invariably, it has a counterproductive result. One of the chapters in this volume, by Taqadum al-Khatib, looks at the dynamics of exile when it applies to Egyptian political activists, comparing those who left Egypt in the years leading up to the 1919 Revolution, and those who left many decades later.

Egyptians of all social classes, of all religions, of both genders, the young and the old responded to the deportation of their most noted nationalist leaders, with an uprising. The country was brought to a halt—there were student demonstrations; strikes across the country; and violence in Cairo, in Tanta, and in other cities in Lower Egypt and Upper Egypt. The uprising proved that support for Zaghloul and his campaign for independence was across all sectors of Egyptian society.

Beth Baron, in a unique contribution for this volume, looks beyond the apparent, to retrieve resistances to the British colonial encounter through medical practices, particularly how inequities in a colonial health-care system were challenged. That focus on women's rights via sexual and reproductive health would be mirrored in another way via the famed "Women's March" of March 16, which was led by a small group of Egyptian women. That included the likes of Safiya Zaghloul, wife of the noted nationalist leader, illustrating the activity of scores of women who were demonstrating across the country, participating in revolutionary activities, and organizing strikes and boycotts. The following day, Egyptians writ large responded to that march; tens of thousands began marching in Cairo, Alexandria, Tanta, Damanhur, Mansurah, and Fayyum. The revolution had begun.

* * *

If we return for a moment to the French Revolution, it may be noted that historians today focus a good deal more on social history; in that regard, analyzing the impact of the French Revolution on individual lives. The point is to document structural changes as the result of those events, understand the experiences of the ordinary, "average" individual during those events, and connecting the two.

This volume is meant to provide not a plethora of answers, but to raise further questions. The Revolution of 1919 had impacts on Egyptian social consciousness for decades afterward. In his 1998 book on Saad Zaghloul, the famed Egyptian judge Tariq al-Bishri declared: "Those who ask me who I am, I tell them I am a son of Egypt's nationalist movement. I hail from the generation which was raised in the embrace of the 1919 Revolution."[1] Bishri wasn't even born until fourteen years after 1919, but the impact of that period remained significant and substantial upon him.

He wasn't the only one. Bishri notes in his own work:

> Popular mobilisation against the British occupation and the monarchy's tyranny was very powerful. Ideas on social justice, socialism, labour rights and the

---

1. "Egypt's 1919 Revolution: The Nation in 100 Years" by Amira Howeidy, Ahram, March 7, 2019, https://english.ahram.org.eg/NewsContent/1/1199/327744/Egypt/-Revolution/Egypts--Revolution-The-nation-in--years--.aspx, accessed July 15, 2021.

working class evolved ... For us, the notion of a fully independent democratic state was the definition of Utopia, so powerful it moved all emotions towards betterment and self-improvement. That's why you will find adroit writers, men of law and artists associated with that period. It was a complete renaissance.[2]

Of course, later writers might take issue with how far that renaissance went. For while the British occupation eventually departed, the damage done to the fabric of Egypt was not so short-lived. The enduring legacies in that regard are not easily understood, and reinvention via historiography is a temptation that nationalist writers can often fall into. Khaled Fahmy's chapter in this volume recognizes that the 1919 Revolution was a multifaceted historical event: one that lacks a detailed account of the ideas and actions of the multitudes who participated in it. Fahmy turns his attention to the sacrifices of thousands of peasants who were recruited to serve in the First World War, and the activism of many more Egyptians in cities and in the countryside.

The chapters in this volume are not meant to come to final conclusions about the 1919 Revolution. Rather, this book is meant to urge us all to scrutinize, inspect, and analyze that history, with the respect it warrants. More than a century since that revolution, the country of Egypt and the peoples of this historic land remain of great importance for many reasons regionally and internationally. One hopes that this collection will help to inspire a new generation of historians to forensically understand the relevance and impact of 1919, so that one day, we might do justice to the complexity of it.

2. Ibid.

Chapter 1

MEDICAL DOCTORS, MATERNAL HEALTH, AND THE REVOLUTION OF 1919

Beth Baron*

In 1902, Department of Public Health authorities in British colonial Egypt sent the then medical student Naguib Mahfouz (not to be confused with the Nobel laureate of the same name) to Alexandria to help fight an outbreak of cholera after he had successfully located the source of infection in a village in Upper Egypt. One evening, Dr. Shukry Bey, a doctor of Turkish origin and assistant director of the government hospital, asked Mahfouz to assist in a difficult labor in his private clinic by administering an anesthesia. Shukry had been trying to deliver the fetus with forceps, but it would not budge. After Mahfouz reassured the patient and gave her the anesthesia, the doctor and his assistant attempted to pull the fetus down for two more hours, at which point Shukry suggested that Mahfouz, who had thin arms and hands, try. But Mahfouz declined, having seen few deliveries and having no experience in this field. Shukry continued attempting delivery for an hour and was able to bring the body out, but in the process, its head was severed and remained in its mother's uterus. When Mahfouz suggested that they call in an obstetric surgeon or take the patient to the government hospital, Shukry told him that there was no obstetrician—Egyptian or foreign—in Alexandria. The unnamed woman died that night. Afterwards, images from the incident haunted Mahfouz, who wrote later that at that moment he "resolved to do everything in my power to study obstetrics and gynaecology and to dedicate my life to help women suffering from difficult labour."[1]

---

*I would like to thank Rebecca Irvine, Fadi Kafeety, Hratch Kestanian, and Tamara Maatouk for research assistance and help in thinking about the arguments in this chapter.

1. Naguib Mahfouz, *The Life of an Egyptian Doctor* (Edinburgh: E. & S. Livingstone, Ltd, 1966), 52–3; Najib Mahfuz, *Hayat Tabib* (1966; repr. Cairo: al-Hay'a al-Misriyya al-'Amma li-l-Kitab, 2013), 88–9. The Arabic and English versions of Mahfouz's memoir both appeared in 1966, with some variations in the text and different forwards. The Arabic version was translated into English by Mahfouz's grandson, Dr. Samir Mahfouz Simaiki. The Arabic version features a forward by Taha Hussein, and the English version has one by the president of the British Royal College of Surgeons.

In the decades leading up to 1919, there were few maternity hospitals and specialists to deal with difficult labors in Egypt. British health officials were much more concerned with infectious diseases like syphilis and gonorrhea, which could easily spread to imperial troops, than to indigenous women's reproductive health, difficult labors, and maternal and infant mortality. To keep imperial troops safe, Egyptian prostitutes came under a strict regime of weekly inspections and when found to be infected with venereal diseases were incarcerated in lock hospitals until they were ostensibly cured. When it came to women's health, the main priority of the colonial government was the smooth functioning of the regulatory regime and lock hospitals rather than significantly improving maternal care.[2]

While the history of Egyptian women's active involvement in the Revolution of 1919 has been mapped and become part of the collective memory, the story of their gaining greater access to health care with the help of Mahfouz and his Egyptian colleagues has gotten much less attention.[3] In *Gender and the Making of Modern Medicine in Colonial Egypt*, Hibba Abugideiri argues that doctors in Egypt were "instrumental mediators between the state and society," who were not only "disseminating a medico-nationalist discourse that supported Egyptian nationhood"—a medicalizing discourse that often targeted women—but "also participated in political events, published articles, joined nationalist parties, and assumed political positions."[4] This chapter looks beyond the street, press, and political parties to retrieve everyday resistances to colonial encounters through medical practices and lived experiences. Mahfouz, who was one of the leading Egyptian medical authorities of his time, was much less concerned with disseminating a medical discourse on women's health and hygiene to the larger public than delivering healthy babies, healing women's bodies, and fixing the medical system. He led the struggle against British administrators at the Qasr al-`Aini Hospital and Medical School complex and colonial officials within the Department of Public Health to expand provisions for women's maternal health in the two decades leading up to the Revolution of 1919. The revolution itself provided a significant opening and golden opportunity to improve maternal health services.

---

2. See Beth Baron, "A Fraught Regulatory Regime: Prostitutes, Soldiers, and Venereal Diseases in Colonial Egypt," in *Bulletin of the History of Medicine* (June 2022); idem, "Perilous Beginnings: Infant Mortality, Public Health, and the State in Egypt," in *Gendering Global Humanitarianism in the Twentieth Century: Practice, Politics, and the Power of Representation*, ed. Esther Moller, Johannes Paulmann, and Katharna Stornig (Cham: Palgrave Macmillan, 2020), 195–219.

3. On women in the Revolution of 1919, see for example Margot Badran, *Feminists, Islam, and Nation: Gender and the Making of Modern Egypt* (Princeton: Princeton University Press, 1995); Beth Baron, *Egypt as a Woman: Nationalism, Gender, and Politics* (Berkeley: University of California Press, 2005).

4. Hibba Abugideiri, *Gender and the Making of Modern Medicine in Colonial Egypt* (Surrey: Ashgate, 2010), 230.

A pioneer in Egyptian obstetrics and gynecology, Mahfouz challenged inequities in a colonial health-care system that ignored women's sexual and reproductive health. While constantly working to perfect his own surgical skills, Mahfouz pushed for more wards and beds for female obstetrical and gynecological patients, greater access to health care, and better training for midwifery and medical students. While the British sought to undermine the standing of *hakimas* (midwives) trained at Qasr al-ʿAini by Mahfouz and his colleagues, he championed *hakimas* and promoted a domiciliary model of delivery in which female practitioners would continue to attend normal deliveries. In Mahfouz's model for domiciliary delivery, which proceeded that implemented in Great Britain, specialists would only be called in for difficult deliveries.

We can tell this story because Mahfouz was a prolific writer. From the early 1900s through the 1960s, he authored articles for scientific journals on gynecology, obstetrics, and other topics in Arabic, English, and French; textbooks and a medical Atlas; *History of Medical Education in Egypt*; and memoirs in Arabic and English.[5] His works acknowledged the influence of the imperial doctors who taught him and at the same time illuminated the structural constraints he and other Egyptian doctors faced under British rule. Mahfouz's writings also show the debt he owed, and often acknowledged, to his patients, whom he attempted to heal and from whom he learned and drew inspiration, including the unnamed woman who died in a private clinic one night in Alexandria. His writings can be read in conversation with documents from the British National Archives as well as with the papers of imperial doctors such as Roy Dobbin, an Irish medical doctor who became Mahfouz's supervisor, and Bonté Elgood, an English physician who worked in Egypt in the decades leading up to the revolution, first for the Sanitary, Maritime, and Quarantine Board of Egypt and subsequently as a health inspector for Egyptian girls' schools.

From Student to Young Doctor under British Rule

In his memoir, Mahfouz tells the story of his mother's labor and his own birth in the Delta town of Mansura in the winter of 1882, the year the British occupied Egypt. His mother, who was forty-five at the time and had already bore seven children, "had a long and tedious labour" that lasted for three days, resulting in fetal distress. The attending midwife, Bahana, thought he was stillborn and placed him with the placenta on a copper tray near an open window. When half an hour later an aunt noticed that the baby was "breathing feebly every few minutes," the

---

5. Naguib Bey Mahfouz, *The History of Medical Education in Egypt* (Cairo: Government Press, 1935); Naguib Pacha Mahfouz, *Atlas of Mahfouz's Obstetrics and Gynaecological Museum*, three volumes (Altrincham: John Sherratt and Son, 1949); Mahfouz, *The Life of an Egyptian Doctor*; Mahfuz, *Hayat Tabib*.

midwife cut the umbilical cord, wrapped him up, and resuscitated him.[6] That the wife of a well-to-do merchant was attended at home in childbirth by a midwife and a doctor—Bahana's husband Dr. Mansour was also on hand—was not surprising. Nor was the fact that the medical pair were married, as it was the practice of the state to arrange marriages between the graduates of the School of Midwifery and School of Medicine.

Mahfouz was a precocious child who decided at an early age that he wanted to study medicine. Growing up with a view of the Nile, he had a great love of nature and science, and read widely in his father's big library, which included subscriptions to a number of magazines and newspapers. He attributed his interest in medicine to articles he read in the monthly periodical *al-Muqtataf* on Koch's discovery of the tuberculosis bacillus as well as essays on Darwin's theory of evolution and the origins of the species. He also read books in Arabic by Dr. Van Dyke and Dr. Wartbat, teachers at the Protestant College in Beirut (later renamed the American University of Beirut). He grew up at an exciting time in medicine, with Louis Pasteur and Robert Koch competing to identify the micro-organisms causing diseases and Lister making breakthroughs in antiseptic surgery.[7]

Arriving at the School of Medicine in Cairo in 1898, Mahfouz began his course of training just as the British made English-language instruction mandatory. This was part of an imperial project of using medicine to colonize Egypt and colonizing medicine in Egypt. Within two years of the occupation, the British had taken over the Sanitary Department, transforming it into a Department of Public Health that would open a laboratory, collect statistics, and monitor the population. The new language requirement at the School of Medicine led to the appointment of British (and a few German) instructors, as Egyptian medical men were transferred, eased out, or pushed out. (As one example, the oculist `Ali Bey Haydar was forced to work in the skin department.) Mahfouz studied surgery with Frank Cole Madden and Frank Milton but had no opportunity to study abroad, as had Egyptians when the medical school was under French influence and graduating medical students had traveled to France or elsewhere for specialization. The British stopped foreign medical missions, preferring to keep Egyptians as generalists who would work as medical officers under the supervision of British and other foreign doctors of higher rank, and in the process sought to replace French influence with British models.[8]

---

6. Mahfouz, *The Life of an Egyptian Doctor*, 3; Mahfuz, *Hayat Tabib*, 21; Mahfouz, *Medical Education*, 75.

7. Mahfouz, *The Life of an Egyptian Doctor*, 11–15; Mahfuz, *Hayat Tabib*, 33–7. See "Akhbar wa-Iktishafat wa-Ikhtira`at," *al-Muqtataf* 15, no. 5 (1891): 347–8, 389.

8. Ahmad Jamil al-Sharqawi, *al-Tibb wa al-Jiraha fi Misr* (Cairo: Maktabat Dar al-Kutub wa al-Watha'iq al-Qawmiyya al-Qahira, 2017); Abugideiri, *Gender and the Making of Modern Medicine in Colonial Egypt*; Mahfouz, *The Life of an Egyptian Doctor*, 22; Mahfuz, *Hayat Tabib*, 47; Amira El-Azhary Sonbol, *The Creation of a Medical Profession in Egypt 1800–1922* (Syracuse: Syracuse University Press, 1991); Robert L. Tignor, "Public Health

Qasr al-`Aini Hospital had only recently started wards for women, which were superintended by English nurses; but at the turn of the century the hospital had no beds for maternity patients, no section of gynecology or obstetrics in the hospital, and no outpatient clinic for maternal care. Any gynecological cases that happened to come to the hospital were turned over to the assistant surgeon in the surgical outpatient section. In training at the School of Medicine, Mahfouz had taken a course in midwifery offered by Mahmoud Shoukry Pasha, who due to illness gave only a small fraction of the forty theoretical lectures he was meant to deliver. The students made do by memorizing the two books in the field by Dr. Henry Jellett, an Irish physician who was known for his textbooks on midwifery and gynecology, which had worldwide circulation.[9] Mahfouz and his classmates had virtually no clinical training in the subject and saw only one or two labor cases, both conducted by the resident surgeon, who knew little of obstetrics: the first ended in rupture of the uterus and death of the mother and child, and the second, in which the fetus presented in transverse, ended in a "tug of war" as the surgeon and his assistants pulled on the fetus's arms and shoulders.[10] At turn of the century, maternal mortality for urban women was estimated to be 3 percent, which meant that over the course of her childbearing years, an individual woman faced an increasing risk of dying during or after childbirth due to complications.[11]

After graduation and a short stint in Suez Hospital as a medical officer, Mahfouz returned to Qasr al-`Aini as an anesthesiologist in 1904. When he asked his former teacher, the head surgeon Madden, why there was no gynecological outpatient department and why so few operations or cases of labor were admitted to the hospital, Madden replied that attempts had been made, but "Egyptian men refused to send their wives to a teaching hospital like Kasr El Aini where young students had to look after them."[12] The answer, a stock British response when it came to maternal health, absolved the British of expanding services to women and legitimized their staffing the hospital with British matrons and nurses. The young Egyptian doctor proposed that he be allowed to start a gynecology outpatient section before his work in the operating theater started. With pressure and

Administration in Egypt under British Rule, 1882–1914" (PhD dissertation, Yale University, 1960).

9. Mahfouz, *The Life of an Egyptian Doctor*, 35; Mahfuz, *Hayat Tabib*, 65; Mahfouz, *Medical Education*, 76–7; H.S., "Obituary: Henry Jellett, M.D., F.R.C.P.I.," *British Medical Journal* (June 26, 1948): 1262. See Henry Jellett, *A Short Practice of Midwifery* (London, 1897). At one time Jellett advocated pre-emptive pubiotomy, an operation to divide the pubic bone near the front midline where the left and right pubic bones meet to increase the size of an abnormally small pelvis. Fortunately, the operation never caught on.

10. Mahfouz, *Medical Education*, 77.

11. Qasim Amin, *al-Mar'a al-Jadida* (Cairo: Matba`at al-Sha`b, 1900), 158; see Beth Baron, *The Women's Awakening in Egypt: Culture, Society, and the Press* (New Haven: Yale University Press, 1994), 159.

12. Mahfouz, *The Life of an Egyptian Doctor*, 70; Mahfuz, *Hayat Tabib*, 114.

persuasion, the British director of the Hospital and School of Medicine, Dr. Henry Keatinge, approved a two-month trial. "The result was more encouraging than I ever anticipated," wrote Mahfouz.[13] In spite of the skepticism of the British staff, Egyptian women came in numbers: during the first twelve months, the outpatient clinic recorded the visits of 850 patients; the next year, close to 500 more arrived. This led to the reservation of ten beds in the hospital for obstetrics and gynecology, with Mahfouz attached to the surgical department as an assistant and assigned all the obstetrical cases, most of which were emergencies requiring instrumental delivery.[14]

After two years of running the gynecological section, Mahfouz authored a report with Madden's help, an abstract of which was published in *The Lancet*, the pre-eminent English-language medical journal of the day.[15] According to hospital records, 154 operations were performed in the first year: 72 by Madden, 39 by Milton, and 43 by Mahfouz. Of these, 6 died, and the balance—148—were "cured." The deaths included a "very feeble old woman" with tuberculosis who died of shock shortly after an operation to remove an ovary. Mahfouz pointed out that the number of cesarean sections was approximately five a year. "This operation was always done as a last resort in cases of severe contraction of pelvis admitted to hospital after fruitless attempts at delivery outside it."[16] Rather than over-medicalizing childbirth, Mahfouz and his colleagues tried to keep surgical interventions to a minimum.

Due to the demands of the outpatient clinic and its success, Keatinge authorized Mahfouz to relinquish his work as anesthesiologist and assistant surgeon to focus on obstetrics and gynecology, requesting that he also give clinical demonstrations to medical students and come up with a plan for reorganizing the School of Nursing. Mahfouz consented but asked to go abroad to observe the surgery of specialists at maternity hospitals because he never had specialized training as a student. Keatinge denied Mahfouz's request, arguing that the progress in the field of gynecology and obstetrics that had been made would erode in Mahfouz's absence and agreed instead to bring a specialist in gynecology and obstetrics to Qasr al-ʿAini.[17]

---

13. Mahfouz, *Medical Education*, 78.

14. Ibid.

15. Madden and Mahfouz, "Two Years of Gynaecology and Obstetrics in Egypt," *The Lancet* (August 11, 1906): 383; Mahfouz, *The Life of an Egyptian Doctor*, 72; *Hayat Tabib*, 117.

16. Mahfouz, *Medical Education*, 78. This attitude toward cesarean sections as a last resort can be compared to the 2020 rate in the United States of 32 percent (or one in three), according to the Centers for Disease Control and Prevention, or the rate in Egypt, estimated at 52 percent. See *Caesarean Section Deliveries in Egypt: Trends, Practices, Perceptions, and Costs* (Cairo: Population Council Report, 2018), 3.

17. Mahfouz, *Medical Education*, 79; Mahfouz, *The Life of an Egyptian Doctor*, 72; Mahfuz, *Hayat Tabib*, 117–18.

Negotiating Colonial Hierarchies

The man selected for the job of professor at the School of Medicine and senior obstetric surgeon and gynecologist at the hospital was Dr. Roy Dobbin (1873–1939). Dobbin was hardly a seasoned specialist: he had worked from 1899 as a resident surgeon, resident assistant, and pathologist in Dublin hospitals and was then named assistant master at the famed Rotunda Hospital in Dublin, one of the oldest maternity hospitals in the world. Within a year of his taking up work in the Rotunda, the post at Qasr al-ʿAini was advertised. Dobbin applied and was selected for the job, which he attributed not so much to his medical experience—he had relatively little—but to his language skills, which in addition to English included French and German.[18] It was in part through its language requirements or language preferences that the British were able to exclude Egyptian doctors from attaining higher posts. Dobbin arrived in Cairo in late 1906, joining those white male and a few female doctors who came from throughout the British Empire, including the British Isles, Australia, and New Zealand, to benefit from the British occupation of Egypt, and enjoying a rank, status, and pay that might have taken years to achieve at home.

Dobbin had read Madden and Mahfouz's article in *The Lancet* and thought that "there was wide scope for useful work to be done."[19] Yet unlike some of the other imperial doctors of his generation, such as the Australian Madden, Dobbin did not use the resources of his post—including the bodies under his care—to conduct research and produce medical knowledge. Rather, he accumulated manuscripts and books, amassing a large collection of invaluable works in languages such as Arabic and Persian on midwifery and other medical subjects. Toward the end of his life, he worked very hard to get the "oriental items" and other collectors' pieces out of Cairo to London, trying to keep this transfer unknown to colleagues who may have objected. He sent twelve early printed books plus thirty Arabic manuscripts to the library of the Royal College of Physicians in London. Among the manuscripts were a pharmacopoeia of the ninth century, Mansur's Anatomy of the thirteenth century, and Ibn al-Nafis' account of the lesser circulation, also of the thirteenth century.[20] He also donated rare works to the Royal College of Obstetrics and Gynaecology.[21] In short, benefiting from his salaried imperial

---

18. Royal College of Physicians (RCP), "Roy Samuel Dobbin," https://history.rcplondon.ac.uk/inspiring-physicians/roy-samuel-dobbin, accessed March 7, 2021; T. P. C. Kirkpatrick, "Obituary: Roy Samuel Dobbin," *British Journal of Obstetrics and Gynaecology* 46, no. 3 (June 1939): 569–74.

19. Mahfouz, *The Life of an Egyptian Doctor*, 72; Mahfuz, *Hayat Tabib*, 118.

20. Royal College of Physicians (RCP), MS 687, Arnold Chaplin to Dobbin, January 16, 1938; Harveian Librarian to R.F. Parker, April 24, 1939, "Facts Concerning the Gifts of Professor Roy Dobbin to the College Library."

21. Royal College of Obstetrics and Gynaecology (RCOG), Dr. Dobbin Correspondence, S3/3-S3/6.

position, Dobbin amassed a large collection of medical texts and transferred knowledge produced in Egypt or the greater Middle East to England.

When he arrived in Egypt, Dobbin joined his assistant (Mahfouz) in the outpatient clinic that had been set up, which at that point was a small room on the ground floor of the hospital, enforcing discipline and order on the whole project. According to Mahfouz, he taught patients in the waiting room—a dark corridor to which a few benches were added—how to stand in a line "in an orderly fashion." As more and more patients came to avail themselves of the services offered, Dobbin and Mahfouz took careful case histories, with the two working from early in the morning to early afternoon every day.[22] Dobbin introduced aseptic techniques in the operating theaters, including use of gloves, masks, and special clothes, and, as Mahfouz relates, "forcibly impressed upon the students that patients were not 'cases' but human beings suffering from pain and poverty that awaken feelings of pity and sympathy."[23] Qasr al-'Aini was, after all, a public teaching hospital that served the poor; wealthier patients received private care at home, or if need be, in a private hospital. Mahfouz acknowledged learning a great deal from Dobbin, particularly to examine the patient only twice, once upon entry to the hospital and once when the amniotic sac broke, and to be patient and relaxed in delivering babies in normal and abnormal cases.[24]

Yet Dobbin was less of a guide when it came to pushing the boundaries of the field and left the difficult labors to his assistant. Mahfouz began performing special operations and developing his own techniques, such as ones for retroflexion of the uterus and tears of the perineum, which Dobbin labeled "Mahfouz's techniques." The student quickly passed the teacher, with Dobbin giving Mahfouz license to conduct certain specialized surgeries, such as urinary fistula repairs, which set the groundwork for his earning an international reputation for his work in this field.[25] At the same time, it was Dobbin who held the professorial chair in obstetrics and gynecology at the School of Medicine in spite of his lack of research and writing, and Dobbin who during his long tenure in Egypt headed the department in Qasr al-'Aini Hospital. Egyptians were meant to serve under imperial doctors, not supervise them, which would have inverted the colonial hierarchy.

Mahfouz clearly had a complicated relationship with the imperial doctors who ran Qasr al-'Aini and the Department of Public Health, cognizant of their deficiencies and at the same time appreciating the opportunity to learn from them. Of Dobbin, he and Shafiq noted: "In his operating he was bold but

---

22. Mahfouz, *The Life of an Egyptian Doctor*, 72–3; Mahfuz, *Hayat Tabib*, 119–20; Naguib Mahfouz Pasha and Ahmed Shafeek Bey, "Obituary: Roy Samuel Dobbin," *British Journal of Obstetrics and Gynaecology* 46, no. 3 (June 1939): 574–77.

23. Mahfouz, *Medical Education*, 79.

24. Mahfouz, *The Life of an Egyptian Doctor*, 73; Mahfuz, *Hayat Tabib*, 119.

25. Mahfouz, *The Life of an Egyptian Doctor*, 73; Mahfuz, *Hayat Tabib*, 119–20; Beth Baron, "Of Fistulas, Sutures, and Silences," *International Journal of Middle East Studies* 53, no. 1 (February 2021): 133–7.

extremely careful about details, and from those early days he was a true apostle of conservative surgery."[26] Mahfouz defended Dobbin in the face of accusations by a colleague that the senior surgeon had refused to operate on a patient with fistulas who had gonorrhea for fear of becoming infected, leaving the surgery to Mahfouz (the colleague said that Dobbin himself had admitted this in a lecture). Of Madden and Frank Milton, Mahfouz wrote: "I learned much from watching the two professors, who were first-rate surgeons, at work," noting that while the former clearly explained the steps of an operation and gave good instructions during rounds, the latter "was a quicker and to a certain extent a more brilliant surgeon."[27] Frank Milton also introduced Mahfouz to his brother Herbert, a famous surgeon who after directing Qasr al-'Aini had opened a private clinic.

Despite his gratitude to some of his teachers, Mahfouz's memoirs demonstrate how living with colonialism impacted the quotidian life of the hospital and its Egyptian staff. Mahfouz points out that the British doctors blocked suggestions to expand maternity and childcare, which would have benefited the poor of Cairo. He also shows how British and foreign doctors tried repeatedly to humiliate him, which he invariably responded to by showing that his diagnoses were the correct ones. Mahfouz relates one case in which Dr. Sandwith, an internist with a "sharp tongue," had made a wrong diagnosis; Mahfouz (then still a student) had attempted to correct him to no avail; the patient died, and in the autopsy, Sandwith blamed Mahfouz for the mistake. Mahfouz also shared the story of how during the cholera epidemic of 1902 he had painstakingly mapped houses and wells in the infected Upper Egyptian village of Mousha and located the source of the disease, only to have one of the British experts sign his own name to the map, thus appropriating his work. Outside the hospital in private work, the pattern continued. He related the story of a consultation in which he diagnosed an ectopic pregnancy that had ruptured, a diagnosis which one of the foreign doctors dismissed quite rudely, but his assessment proved correct.[28]

As a doctor, Mahfouz seemed less concerned with the everyday slights that were part of the colonial order than with the structural problems in the hospital, lack of adequate space for maternal care, especially in difficult labors, and lack of support for midwifery students. Teaching clearly meant a great deal to Mahfouz, who had always looked for ways to improve the training of midwives and medical students. Unlike the male medical students, the female midwifery students studied in Arabic. Realizing that his midwifery students lacked suitable textbooks, he wrote two, one on gynecology *Amrad al-Nisa'* (Diseases of Women), the other on obstetrics, *Fann al-Wilada* (The Art of Childbirth), both of which went through

26. Mahfouz and Shafeek, "Obituary: Roy Samuel Dobbin," 575.
27. Mahfouz, *The Life of an Egyptian Doctor*, quote from 69; see 73; Mahfuz, *Hayat Tabib*, 113–14.
28. Mahfouz, *The Life of an Egyptian Doctor*, 29, 47, 89–91.

multiple printings.[29] He also started a specimen collection to help illustrate anatomy and diseases in classroom lectures that later became a medical museum.[30] Yet he recognized that one of the biggest obstacles to midwifery training, and to the training of male students in obstetrics, was the lack of a sufficient number of maternity beds in Qasr al-`Aini Hospital.

Despite the formation of an outpatient clinic and new wards, the number of hospital beds for obstetrics and gynecology at the hospital remained limited. Most women, whether their pregnancies were high risk or not and whether their labors were difficult or not, continued to deliver their babies at home. Eager to learn and perfect his skills early on in his career, Mahfouz arranged with medical officers in the Department of Public Health to call him to attend difficult cases in patients' homes. He had a male nurse prepare equipment and accompany him on these calls. Among those in distress who called Mahfouz to their home in December 1911 was a woman so appreciative of his services that she named her new-born son after him: that son became the author and Nobel Prize winner Naguib Mahfouz.[31] The young medical doctor attended roughly two thousand difficult deliveries in and around Cairo over the course of a decade and a half, never charging patients for his services. As his reputation grew, he also began attending wealthier Egyptian and foreign patients, which would give him leverage to pursue his dream of expanding services for women in the hospital.[32] In this he would be helped by the arrival of a new colleague, Dr. Ahmad Shafiq, a fellow of the Royal College of Surgeons, who joined the staff right before the war as a resident and quickly became an assistant surgeon specializing in obstetrics.[33]

At the outset of the First World War, British medical staff at Qasr al-`Aini and in the Department of Public Health enlisted or were drafted in large numbers into the imperial war effort. Dobbin, for example, joined the Royal Army Medical Corps and served as an officer and surgical specialist with the British Expeditionary Force in France. The absence of imperial doctors and the internment or exile of German and Austrian doctors created vacancies inside the teaching hospital, which Egyptian staff filled, providing the bulk of the care. Throughout the war, Qasr al-`Aini acted as a military hospital, treating Turkish prisoners of war and thousands of injured soldiers from the Gallipoli and Palestine campaigns.[34] Mahfouz was among those

---

29. Najib Mahfuz, *Fann al-Wilada*, 4th ed. (Cairo: Dar al-Ma`arif, 1957) and *Amrad al-Nisa`* (Cairo: Matba`at al-Tawfiq, n.d.).

30. See https://obgynmuseum.com/, accessed April 20, 2021.

31. Raja al-Naqqash, *Safahat min Mudhakirat Najib Mahfuz* (Cairo: Dar al-Shuruq, 2011), 174–5; Samia Ayad, "If You Give Not of Yourself, You Have Given Nothing," *Watani International*, July 22, 2015.

32. Mahfouz, *Medical Education*, 78; *The Life of an Egyptian Doctor*, 71–2, 82–96; *Hayat Tabib*.

33. Mahfouz, *Medical Education*, 80.

34. al-Sharqawi, *al-Tibb wa al-Jiraha fi Misr*; Mahfouz, *The History of Medical Education in Egypt*, 56.

who received recognition for their services during the war, in his case a medal for service at the rank of doctor in the Egyptian Expeditionary Force at Qasr al-`Aini.[35] The war raised expectations among those who helped the British war effort about independence in the wake of the war.

Midwives, Medical Sovereignty, and the 1918 Commission

At the end of the war, the British moved to reinforce their medical authority in Egypt, convening the Commission to Advise as Regards the Future Organization and Work of the Department of Public Health. The man selected to head the commission, Dr. Andrew Balfour, was an Edinburgh native and specialist in tropical medicine who had been the first director of the Wellcome Tropical Research Laboratories in Khartoum and sanitary adviser to the Anglo-Egyptian Sudanese government from 1902 to 1913.[36] The commission called over sixty men to share their expertise, the overwhelming majority of whom—more than 80 percent—were British or other non-Egyptian experts. The School of Medicine was represented by six foreign doctors, including Keatinge, the director of the school and hospital, and Madden, the head of surgery.[37] Mahfouz, whose input on women's sexual and reproductive health could have been invaluable, was not on the list of those asked to prepare reports or testify. Instead, the commission turned for advisement to Bonté Elgood, a medical doctor who trained at the College of Medicine for Women in London and who appears to be the only female health practitioner or woman called to appear before the commission (midwives were not listed as a category among those unnamed Egyptian officials interviewed during commissioners' inspections).

Elgood's family had deep connections to the colonial state: her father, Sheldon Amos, had worked on the Native Court of Appeals; her brother, Maurice Amos, also a lawyer, had risen quickly up the ranks in the Ministry of Justice; and her husband, Percival Elgood, had served with Lord Herbert Kitchener in the Sudan, headed the Police School under Cromer, and had returned to service in the army

---

35. United Kingdom, The National Archives (TNA), War Office (WO) 372/14/173157, Naguib Bey Mahfouz, Medal for service at the rank of Doctor in the Egyptian Expeditionary Force at Qasr al-`Aini.

36. Heather Bell, *Frontiers of Medicine in the Anglo-Egyptian Sudan, 1899–1940* (New York: Oxford University Press, 1999), ch.3: Ahmed A. A. Adeel, "A Pioneer of Tropical Medicine Worldwide: Andrew Balfour, of Khartoum," *Sudanese Journal of Paediatrics* 13, no. 1 (2013): 63–74.

37. Wellcome Institute, Private Papers (PP)/ Bonté Elgood (ELG)/D3, Ministry of Interior, *Report of a Commission to Advise as Regards the Future Organization and Work of the Department of Public Health* (Cairo: Government Press, 1918), Appendix 1: List of Witnesses, vi.

during the war.[38] But Bonté Elgood was a force in her own right. Having started her career as a research doctor for the Quarantine Board, working in laboratories and hospitals in Suez and Alexandria, she took up an appointment in 1906 in Cairo with the Department of Education as medical inspector for girls' schools. She was tapped in 1913 by Kitchener, British high commissioner, to set up a training school for *dayas*—local and village midwives who delivered the bulk of Egypt's babies in homebirths—to set higher standards for licensing. The result was the launching of the Cairo Maternity House, which offered *dayas* a three-month training course. In its first year, the examining medical board, which included Mahfouz and Elgood, certified 118 *dayas* for practice. The Maternity House became the model for a network of provincial maternity schools paid for by local governments that continued to operate even when war broke out. At the same time, British officials closed the Cairo Maternity House to cut wartime expenses, dealing a blow to those women who sought training and those who benefited from its midwifery services. When asked by the commission about the training of *dayas*, Elgood noted that she had already seen improvement and credited the Cairo Maternity House and those patterned after it with good work.[39]

Elgood did not have kind words for *hakimas* or "lady doctors." As she testified, "They are given at Kasr el Aini what one might call a good nurses' and midwives' training, but the trouble is that they are called hakimas, and from this title they get the idea that they are certificated doctors." She asserted, "Of course they are not."[40] When Clot Bey launched the School of Midwifery in 1832, the women had been given a training akin to that of male students in the School of Medicine and the title of *hakima* or female doctor. British policy was to recast the Egyptian medical landscape in the image of the metropole, which meant changing titles, roles, and curriculums both inside the School of Midwifery and outside of it. Under British administrators, the School of Midwifery added nursing to its title. Aspiring midwives followed the same three-year training course as nurses, specializing in an additional fourth year in midwifery.[41] Elgood admitted that some midwifery

---

38. PP/ELG/A2, "Manuscript of Maurice Sheldon Amos Memoir"; PP/ELG/D6, Reginald Wingate, "Obituary: Colonel George Elgood," reprinted from the *Journal of the Royal Central Asian Society* 29 (April 1942): 157; "Death of Lt.-Col. P.G. Elgood: Soldier-author Friend of Egypt," December 21, 1941; in PP/ELG/ Bonté Elgood Scrapbook, 66.

39. TNA, Foreign Office (FO) 371/3202/177595, Bonté Elgood, July 1918, "Appendix 11: Medical Aid for Women and Children"; PP/ELG/D3, Commission, Bonté Elgood, July 1918, "Appendix 11: Medical Aid for Women and Children."

40. PP/ELG/D3, Elgood, Appendix 11, 4.

41. There is a large historiography on the School of Midwifery. See Abugideiri, *Gender and the Making of Modern Medicine in Colonial Egypt*, ch. 5; Khaled Fahmy, "Women, Medicine, and Power in Nineteenth-Century Egypt," in Lila Abu-Lughod, ed. *Remaking Women* (Princeton: Princeton University Press, 1998, 35–71); Nancy Gallagher, "Writing Women Medical Practitioners into the History of Modern Egypt," in *Re-Envisioning Egypt 1919–1952*, ed. Arthur Goldschmidt, Amy J. Johnson, and Barak A. Salmoni (Cairo: American

trainees resented being forced to follow a curriculum that taught them bandaging and bed-making rather than the more scientific curriculum of the past. Yet she was pleased that the Ministry of Education had changed the title on midwives' certificates, calling them *mumaridda* (female sick nurses). "The woman till recently known as hakimas (women doctors), but now rightfully called mumarridas, receive an excellent training in nursing and midwifery at Kasr el Aini."[42]

The problem in Elgood's eyes was now not one of training but rather of comportment and practice of the midwives. "The tragedy is that the hakimas are excellently trained as nurses and midwives but they will not nurse," Elgood continued. She asserted that they "always wanted to diagnose the case and do work which properly belongs to the doctor." She did not think they were trained to diagnose "even in the living, much less in the dead."[43] While British matrons in the hospital supervised midwives during their training, once graduated, the midwives had a degree of freedom, much to the chagrin of Elgood. "On leaving the hospital scarcely any of them consent to nurse: they prefer to practice midwifery privately or to occupy Government posts, where they diagnose deaths from infections and other diseases, treat prostitutes and generally make themselves useful at the kisms [departments] and hospitals to which they are attached."[44] These women, she claimed, are not supervised by the kism doctors: "My experience is that the kism doctor is much too busy to do so: moreover these women are very haughty and consider that they title of hakima confers on them an equality with the kism hakim in matters affecting women."[45]

Elgood's characterization of the midwives as "haughty" and her critique of them suggest that these women were confident in their abilities, enjoyed autonomy as state agents, and ran flourishing private practices. "Most of these women go in for general practice as doctors and gynaecological specialists and charge fees as high as those charged by certificated men and women doctors." Bonté, who did not think that *hakimas* attached to Cairo kisms should even be allowed to set up private practices, blamed them for cases of puerperal fever. "They are usually very busy and often rush from a case of death or infectious disease to a midwifery case without taking any precautions whatever." She wanted to see their duties restricted in the kisms of giving first aid, attend simple midwifery cases, perform nursing

---

University in Cairo, 2005), 351-70; Mervat F. Hatem, "The Professionalization of Health and the Control of Women's Bodies as Modern Governmentalities in Nineteenth-Century Egypt," in *Women in the Ottoman Empire*, ed. Madeleine C. Zilfi (Leiden: Brill, 1997), 66-80; Liat Kozma, *Policing Egyptian Women: Sex, Law, and Medicine in Khedival Egypt* (Syracuse: Syracuse University Press, 2011), ch.2; Laverne Kuhnke, "The 'Doctoress' on a Donkey: Women Health Officers in Nineteenth Century Egypt," *Clio Medica* 9, no. 3 (1974): 193-205.

42. PP/ELG/D3, Elgood Appendix 11, 4.
43. PP/ELG/D3, Interview: Mrs. Elgood, 5-6.
44. PP/ELG/D3, Elgood, Appendix 11, 4.
45. Ibid.

duties; in addition, they should be supervised in their practices and punished for prescribing.⁴⁶ What most galled Elgood, then, was the competition that *hakimas* presented to foreign women doctors who had their own private practices. The latter "have taken refuge in the title of 'Doctora' which conveys to the public a correct conception of our knowledge and our ideals."⁴⁷

Elgood supported a plan to downgrade the *hakimas* into specialized nurses and to start training Egyptian women doctors. "Nothing would raise the repute of women in medicine in Egypt, but a number of young women coming from abroad with foreign diplomas."⁴⁸ Yet her recommendation to the commission for the training of women doctors met with a cold reception. "The training of Egyptian women doctors proposed by Dr. Elgood is a matter for consideration; other witnesses [all male and almost all British] have informed us that the need for such is small, that the right class for training would not be forthcoming, and that the prejudice against men doctors is rapidly disappearing."⁴⁹ The commission preferred to safeguard the privileges of foreign doctors and Egyptian male practitioners. Elgood's call for a central maternity hospital in Cairo with full training for nurses and midwives met with a warmer reception, perhaps because it was endorsed by British officials in the Department of Public Health, who saw this as a project they could launch, staff, and control.⁵⁰

The commission report showed that the British were heavily invested in micromanaging medicine and public health in Egypt and had clear ideas about who should be included and excluded from medical professions in Egypt. British matrons and nurses would continue to play a central role in imperial medicine, and imperial doctors would sit at the apex of departments, schools, hospitals, and laboratories. At the same time, Egyptians like Mahfouz and the *hakimas* he trained resisted exclusion, seeing the boundaries of the medical profession as sites where resistance against the colonial authority played out. The revolution provided Egyptian doctors with an opportunity to chip away at British sovereignty.

The Revolution of 1919 and Its Aftermath

When demonstrations broke out in 1919, Egyptian medical students rushed to join them and, in the process, fought with the director of the Qasr al-'Aini Hospital and School of Medicine, Keatinge. This was not the first time that Egyptian medical students had confronted the director over politics. Over a decade earlier, Ahmad Fu'ad, a student in the School of Medicine who had joined a group of anarchists, plotted his assassination. Fu'ad alleged that Keatinge had failed him three times

---

46. PP/ELG/D3, Interview: Mrs. Elgood, 5–6.
47. PP/ELG/D3, Elgood Appendix 11, 4.
48. Ibid, 5.
49. PP/ELG/D3, *Report of a Commission*, 26.
50. Ibid., 21.

for his involvement in politics and inciting demonstrations. Before he could carry out his plan, the police apprehended him in a sweep that followed the assassination in 1910 of Prime Minister Butrus Ghali by a pharmacology graduate.[51] In 1919, when Keatinge tried to prevent medical students from joining demonstrations, the students confronted him, and he was thrown to the ground in the encounter. Having lost his balance and authority, he resigned, retiring after thirty years of work in Egypt, during twenty-six of which he had served as the director of the hospital and medical school.[52] He would be replaced by Mr. Owen Richards, a surgeon who had served in the war as a colonel.

As the protests continued, the doctors debated their next steps, forming a committee and electing the senior Egyptian medical officer at the Cairo Department of Public Health, Dr. Muhammad Bey Izzat, as president. The students and senior doctors had differences of opinion as to the best strategies to pursue, with the students advocating a boycott of government institutions and the senior doctors preferring a more moderated approach. At a meeting at the end of March at the home of Dr. ʻAli Bey Ibrahim, an Qasr al-ʻAini surgeon who had taken the lead in launching the medical journal *al-Majalla al-Tibbiyya al-Misriyya* (Egyptian Medical Review) in 1917, they agreed "it was the duty of all medical men to attend even gratuitously all sick and wounded in the streets or other public places where disturbances may occur."[53] But they disagreed on whether or not doctors should strike and treat the sick and wounded protesters in private homes rather than in Qasr al-ʻAini or other government buildings. The senior doctors pointed to emergencies—women in labor, strangulated hernias, and other operations needed urgently—as well as the imperative to register births and give burials permits as rationales to stay at their posts.

After a long discussion, during which strikes and paralyzing government hospitals were proposed as potential actions, those assembled agreed to form a council of eleven leading doctors, including Mahfouz, Ibrahim, and Izzat, as well as men from the Ministry of Endowments, Central Laboratories, Forensic Medicine/Criminal Investigation, Ministry of Public Instruction, and private practices. The senior doctors on the council persuaded the younger ones to allow

---

51. Shihab Fakhri Ismaʻil, "al-Tajammud fi al-Zaman: Ziyarat ila Mathaf Najib Pasha Mahfuz li-Wilada," https://www.medinaportal.com/naj/, accessed January 23, 2019.

52. al-Sharqawi, *al-Tibb wa al-Jiraha fi Misr*, 148; Abugideiri, *Gender and the Making of Modern Medicine in Colonial Egypt*, 95.

53. FO 371/3716/65055, Wingate to Curzon, Cairo, April 8, 1919, 1; Donald M. Reid, "The Rise of Professions and Professional Organizations in Modern Egypt," *Comparative Studies in Society and* History 16, no. 1 (Jan. 1974): 32–3, 45–8. The periodical appeared ten months a year, publishing scholarly articles on a range of medical issues. Its founding helped spawn the Egyptian Medical Association, with Ibrahim serving as vice president than president of the organization, which subsequently took over the journal. In choosing Arabic as the language of the journal, Egyptian doctors were making a statement against the forced Anglicization of medical instruction under the British.

the daily work of the hospitals, dispensaries, public health offices, and medical government institutions to continue but met their demand that those doctors who were not needed would be allowed to leave work to protest.[54]

With Keatinge out of the picture and Dobbin gone—he was not demobilized until the end of 1919—Mahfouz and his colleagues had the opportunity "to accomplish our long-cherished plan of converting into a maternity hospital the small hospital, built in memory of the late Lady Cromer, that adjoined Kasr El Aini."[55] Part of the problem in serving pregnant Egyptian women and training obstetricians and midwives was the absence of maternity hospitals and dearth of beds in hospitals and centers for difficult maternity cases. This was so even in Cairo, where only a few beds each were available at the Waqfs Hospital at Bab al-Luq and Qasr al-'Aini. Public Health officials had called repeatedly for the establishment of a maternity hospital and training school in Cairo but had in mind a British-designed and run institution.[56] Mahfouz and Shafiq were able to convince Owens "that the only chance of getting in, ordinary decent women before their confinement, was to get them a place apart from the general wards."[57]

The story of the home is representative of the ways in which the British sought to inscribe the occupation and occupiers in the memory of Egyptians and narrate the history of the occupation as one of benevolence. By erecting foundling homes, hospitals, and clinics, the imperial power sought to reshape its image, focusing on its contributions in the field of health and medicine. What better way to do this than through honoring the first wife of the proconsul? Yet the story was not so simple. The Lady Cromer Memorial Home had been built in 1898 with money subscribed by British residents, according to British officials, and public subscription, according to Mahfouz, to serve as a home for foundlings. It had subsequently been handed over to the Department of Public Health to run with the understanding that a British nurse would supervise the work, reporting to the matron at Qasr al-'Aini. The inscription in stone over the ornamental doorway made clear that the home was in memory of Lady Cromer, as did the detailing on the sheets in the early days of the home. But since no endowment had been made to run it, the Egyptian state took over the expenses of the foundling home, running it the through the Department of Public Health. This reality was marked by changes in the bedding: when sheets marked Lady Cromer Memorial became worn out, they were replaced by Department of Public Health sheets. In short, the Egyptian state—that is Egyptian taxes—funded the enterprise as part of the government grant to Qasr al-'Aini. Years later, the British could find no record of the initial agreement about management and suggested that it may not have been

---

54. FO 371/3716/65055, Wingate to Curzon, Cairo, April 8, 1919, 1–2.

55. Mahfouz, *The Life of an Egyptian Doctor*, 74; Mahfuz, *Hayat Tabib*, 121.

56. Ministry of the Interior, Egypt, Department of Public Health, *Annual Statistical Report for 1915* (Cairo: Government Press, 1917), 25.

57. Quote from Mahfouz, *Medical Education*, 80; Mahfouz, *The Life of an Egyptian Doctor*, 105–7; Mahfuz, *Hayat Tabib*, 168–9.

thought necessary at the time to commit the understanding to paper, "the Public Health Dept. being in those days an almost entirely British concern."[58]

Mahfouz and his Egyptian colleagues found the home underutilized given the high mortality of foundlings, who were often overexposed to the elements before they were brought in and died of pneumonia. Mahfouz's report suggesting that some of the space could be used by a new maternity department convinced Richards to apply to the trustees of the Lady Cromer's Home to see if they would agree to the transformation of part of it into a maternity unit. As it turned out, many of the members of this "ladies' committee" were Mahfouz's private patients, and so the proposal met with approval. In November 1919, the ground floor of the Lady Cromer Memorial Home became an outpatient clinic for gynecology and the first floor a maternity ward, with the second (upper) floor reserved for the foundlings. To placate the British and conform to the unwritten agreement about staffing, a sister from St. Thomas's Hospital in London was specially appointed to the new maternity service.[59]

Dobbin would return to Egypt to find a fait accompli, that the repurposing of the building had taken place without his input and imprinting on his memory, and he would later be at a loss to reconstruct the events or their timing. Nor could British officials find a paper trail in the colonial archives approving this transformation. All they could locate were the record books of the matron of Qasr al-`Aini Hospital noting November 23, 1919, as the day midwifery work was started in the Home.[60] In the process of repurposing the foundling home in the wake of the revolution, the Egyptian doctors who pushed the plan also nationalized what was intended as a British memorial. When the Egyptian journalist Balsam `Abd al-Malik, editor of *al-Mar'a al-Misriyya*, visited the institution a year later, she found that the maternity section had fifty-four beds, with two Egyptian doctors—presumably Mahfouz and Shafiq—and three "English" ones—presumably Dobbin and two others—rotating rounds. She noted that the Refuge for Babies (Malga' al-Atfal) "had been previously known as the Lady Cromer Home. The truth is that there is no connection between the home and that name, for it is part of Qasr al-`Aini Hospital and is funded by the Egyptian government."[61]

---

58. FO 141/709/18, quote from RHH, Minute, Lady Cromer Memorial, February 17, 1931; Dobbin to Hoare, January 13, 1931; Hoare to Dobbin, January 29, 1931; Dobbin to Hoare, February 1, 1931; Hoare to Dobbin, February 21, 1931; Mahfouz, *Medical Education*, 80; Mahfouz, *The Life of an Egyptian Doctor*, 106; Mahfuz, *Hayat Tabib*, 168–9; Muhammad Fawzi al-Minawi and Husni Muhammad Nuwaysar, *Tarikh al-Nahda al-Tibbiyya al-Misriyya: Mathaf Qasr al-`Aini* (Cairo: Nahdat Misr, 1938), 190–2.

59. FO 141/709/18, Dobbin to Hoare, "Cromer (Lady) Memorial," January 13, 1931; Mahfouz, *Medical Education*, 80; Mahfouz, *The Life of an Egyptian Doctor*, 106; Mahfuz, *Hayat Tabib*, 168–9.

60. FO 141/709/18, Dobbin to Hoare, "Cromer (Lady) Memorial," January 13, 1931.

61. Balsam 'Abd al-Malik, "Malja' al-Atfal wa al-Wilada," *al-Mar'a al-Misriyya* 1, no. 10 (Dec. 1920): 353–7; quoted in Beth Baron, *The Orphan Scandal: Christian Missionaries and*

While the "takeover" of the Lady Cromer Memorial Home and its transformation into a maternity hospital had been a great success, the new space still proved inadequate for the needs of the city and its surroundings. Mahfouz came up with a new plan: starting centers for external midwifery service in poorer neighborhoods. Under the plan, one or two rooms would be rented, furnished with the necessary medical supplies and instruments, and staffed by a qualified midwife or student to handle calls from anyone desiring to deliver at home free of charge. The plan met with a lack of enthusiasm from the British matron and director at Qasr al-`Aini and with clear opposition from British officials in the Department of Public Health, who threatened to stop the salaries of the midwives working in the centers. Undaunted, Mahfouz launched the project, setting up two ante-natal centers and initially paying the midwives himself. Within two months of opening, the centers were swamped with women wanting home deliveries at the hands of qualified midwives.[62]

Mahfouz described how the maternity unit and centers had been set up on a new footing: a pregnant woman presenting herself at the ante-natal unit or center would get a ticket that entitled her to be delivered at home by a trained midwife. Accompanied by a student from Qasr al-`Aini's School of Midwifery, the midwife took all necessary aseptic precautions and gave patients needed dressings and medications for free. In the case of a difficult labor or complications, the midwife immediately sent the laboring woman to the hospital. Mahfouz regularly inspected the centers and admitted his pleasure with the success of the operation, which helped Cairene women and gave the school a way "for training the pupils in the management of normal labours."[63] Under this model, pregnancy and delivery were still seen as "normal," which meant that obstetric specialists did not intervene in a childbirth unless necessary. Home, not the hospital, was still considered the proper place to give birth.

Aside from the opposition from Qasr al-`Aini administrators, who in time came around, and Department of Public Health officials, who eventually saw the benefits of the system and replicated it elsewhere, Mahfouz faced attacks in the daily press. These attacks criticized him for allowing male medical students, who joined the program when it was inundated with requests, to cooperate in the project with female midwifery students. To counteract these attacks, Mahfouz asked the parents of the female students to sign waivers allowing their daughters to continue their training at these centers.[64] The reaction in the press to the new external midwifery service pointed to a public interest in the goings on inside Qasr al-`Aini and in its community projects and their nationalist ramifications.

the Rise of the Muslim Brotherhood (Stanford: Stanford University Press, 2014), 34.
    62. Mahfouz, *The Life of an Egyptian Doctor*, 106; Mahfuz, *Hayat Tabib*, 169–70.
    63. Mahfouz, *Medical Education*, 80–1.
    64. Mahfouz, *The Life of an Egyptian Doctor*, 107–8; Mahfuz, *Hayat Tabib*, 169–71.

Conclusion

The takeover of the Lady Cromer Memorial Home and the establishment of midwifery centers in the wake of the Revolution of 1919 provided new opportunities to train students and at the same time raise the level of care and aseptic conditions in delivery. If opening a maternity ward meant that poorer patients with difficult labors would have access to trained medical professionals, then this was a victory for parturient women as well as for the doctors and midwives trained in these centers. It was these difficult deliveries and the marks they left on women's bodies—fistulas, ruptured uteruses, and life-threatening infections—as well as physical impediments to fertility in the first place—blockages, cysts, and cancers—that concerned Mahfouz most. Rather than run around Cairo to the homes of poor patients who had difficult deliveries, which he had done for fifteen years, he realized that opening a maternity unit attached to Qasr al-`Aini would give poor women with difficult labors greater access to life-saving care.

This was also a victory for trained midwives, who despite the erosion of their autonomy under the British continued to deliver babies in Cairo and across the country. The midwives' role was to attend normal labors, and to call in obstetricians, who were trained as surgeons, in difficult deliveries that might require surgical or other interventions. Mahfouz saw a need for skilled hands and taught women in the School of Midwifery and men in the School of Medicine, creating opportunities for them to see childbirth and practice before they went out in government or private work to deliver babies. Over the course of his career, he educated more than 1,000 midwives in addition to the many medical students he instructed and mentored. Mahfouz may not have been able to prevent changes to the midwifery curriculum and attempts to change their title, but he succeeded in creating a model for domiciliary midwifery delivery that relied on them.

Imperial medicine in Egypt was contested at many stages and translated by Egyptian doctors for local contingencies. Weathering the daily indignities of the occupation, these medical practitioners and their midwifery counterparts proved that Egypt was not just a laboratory for the British, but a space in which new models in the delivery of health care could be tried. The Revolution of 1919 provided an opening for Mahfouz and his Egyptian colleagues in obstetrics and gynecology to realize a vision they had to improve maternal health care. Moreover, Egyptians taught the British a thing or two. As Mahfouz noted, the formula devised for training midwives in the new maternity home and dispatching them to centers in poorer neighborhoods to attend normal labors became a model for centers throughout the country, and preceded a similar project started in England twelve months later.[65]

---

65. Mahfouz, *The Life of an Egyptian Doctor*, 107; Mahfuz, *Hayat Tabib*, 170.

Chapter 2

ARABI AND HIS COMRADES

WORKERS ON THE CANAL AND THE 1919 REVOLUTION

Mohamed Elsayed

This is our Canal and our sea
This is our good and our fortune
Those who dug it before us,
They are our grandfathers and our people
Oh our Canal, your days are festivals
No more masters and slaves
Long live your people, Port Said
This is our Canal and our sea
   —A song associated with the nationalization of the Suez Canal[1]

Introduction

This song played on the Simsimeyya, an instrument local to the Suez Canal Zone and Red Sea area, was written and sung in the commemoration of the 1956 nationalization of the Suez Canal Company (referred to as SCC or "the Company" hereafter), and the following national epic, known as the Tripartite Aggression in Egypt or the Suez crisis in the Western world. It refers to nationalization not just as an economic turning point but radical change in the dynamics in the city of Port Said. Masters and slaves are the words to describe the relationship between the inhabitants of the Isthmus cities. The master and the slaves in the song are describing the two categories of Canal inhabitants, Natives and Europeans. Port Said, Ismailia, and to a lesser extent Suez were known for hosting these two groups of people. This classification was not subtle; it was explicitly used in the Company records, British colonial documents, and Egyptian sources.

---

1. The lyrics were translated to English by the author. The song can be accessed here: https://www.youtube.com/watch?v=6GiggAkbC9o.

The title "Arabi and His Companions" refers to the Egyptian workers who worked for the SCC before nationalization. "Arabi" is associated in Egyptian culture with the city of Port Said. A cogent explanation of this is that since foreigners in the city were the dominant group and Arabs were menial workers, servants, and, to a lesser extent, functionaries, foreigners used the title "Arabi" to refer to the faceless, nameless Arab servants and workers. It was a racial classist term referring to the natives working in the Canal or dockworkers in the city's port. Hence this chapter is trying to reframe the 1919 Revolution experience of those "Arabis" who lived, worked, and experienced it in the Canal cities and were agents in deciding its destiny.

The 1919 Révolution in "L'Etat du Canal de Suez"

On March 21st [1919], a tremendous demonstration started in Port Said on Eugénie street in the Arab Quarter marching toward Mohamed Ali street and the European quarter that the British army dealt with brutally—killing at least 8 people and injuring 17 persons.

—Abdelrahman Fahmy[2]

Once the news reached Port Said on March 8, 1919, that the nationalist leader Saad Zaghloul was about to be deported from Port Said, the Egyptians in the city acted instantly. They started to gather mainly in the Arab quarter as a starting point for demonstrating against British rule, seeking to reach the port. However, the English police commissioner there, Grant Bey, shut the streets leading to the European neighborhood and the port down. This is one of the key events of the buildup toward the 1919 Revolution.

Two weeks later on March 21, after Friday prayers took place in major mosques in the Arab quarter, two large demonstrations moved toward the European neighborhood. They were joined by a third demonstration coming from the Virgin Mary Orthodox Church on Mohamed Ali Street. There is little doubt that SCC workers were involved as individuals in such sweeping momentum. In Mohamed Ali Street, which separates the Arab and European neighborhoods, the British forces fired at the demonstrators, killing eight men and wounding seventeen people.[3]

Multilingual pamphlets secretly printed by revolutionaries were disseminated in the city. They were not only meant for the city's European population but also for those onboard ships crossing the canal. *Bambouties*[4] and Pashas in Paris, London,

---

2. Abd El Rahman Fahmy, *Diaries of Political Life in Egypt* (Cairo: General Egyptian Book Organization, 1988), 166.

3. Al-Qadi, Diaa'al-Din Hussain, *Mawsucat Tarikh Bur Said (Historical Encyclopaedia of Port Said)*, Vol. 2 (3 vols.) (Port Said: Al-Rashidi lil-Tibaʻa wal-Nashr, 2010), 212.

4. Petit merchants that sell their goods in the Canal to passing ships using boats.

and New York exerted effort to raise international attention to the Egyptian cause. It was a cross-class endeavor. High-ranking judges and native workers both worked to advance the cause.[5] The Arab quarter also included another workers' group, the SCC workers, who besides being part of the nationalist milieu had their economic grievances and comrades on the other side of the city with whom to form alliances.

Less than ten weeks after the first demonstration in Port Said, Arab workers of the SCC united with European comrades for the first time in Egypt and made the headlines by carrying out the largest and longest strike against the SCC in May 1919. This strike was a turning point in the history of both Egyptian nationalism and workers' movement. It was an international strike driven by both economic grievances and the seemingly contradictory ideologies of nationalism and communism. The events of the 1919 strike, the historical opportunities it offered, and its long-term consequences are the topic of this chapter. But first, it is necessary to address key issues in the literature about nationalism and workers in Egypt.

Histories of a Nation and Its Workers

Historicizing nationalism was one of the major topics in Middle East Studies since its rise as an academic discipline. Egyptian nationalism specifically has been studied primarily through the lens of Cairo-based intelligentsia. Contributors such as Jamal Mohammed Ahmed,[6] Albert Hourani,[7] Nadav Safran,[8] Charles Wendell,[9] Charles D. Smith,[10] and Donald Malcolm Reid[11] all traced the emergence of European nationalism and its influence on these Egyptian intellectual elites.[12] Some studies took a more inclusive perspective, focusing on street politics, primarily drawing upon sources on the workers' movement and labor activism to place the emerging nationalism in a broader socioeconomic context. This endeavor

---

5. El Kady 2015, 33.

6. Mu ammad A mad Jamāl, *The Intellectual Origins of Egyptian Nationalism* (New York: Oxford University Press, 1960).

7. Albert Habib Hourani, *Arabic Thought in the Liberal Age: 1798–1939* (Oxford: Oxford University Press, 1962).

8. Nadav Safran, *Egypt in Search of Political Community: An Analysis of the Intellectual and Political Evolution of Egypt, 1804–1952* (Cambridge, MA: Harvard University Press, 1981).

9. Charles Wendell, *The Evolution of the Egyptian National Image: From Its Origins to Aḥmad Luṭfī Al-Sayyid* (Berkeley: University of California Press, 1972).

10. Charles D. Smith, *Islam and the Search for Social Order in Modern Egypt a Biography of Muhammad Husayn Haykal* (New York: State University of New York Press, 1984).

11. Donald Malcolm Reid, *Cairo University and the Making of Modern Egypt* (Cambridge: Cambridge University Press, 2002).

12. Ziad Fahmy, *Ordinary Egyptians: Creating the Modern Nation through Popular Culture* (Stanford: Stanford University Press, 2011).

can be best illustrated by the works of Zachary Lockman, Joel Beinin, Juan Cole, and, later, John Chalcraft.[13] While these studies have broadened the scope of our understanding of the emergence of Egyptian nationalism, they, however, focus too much on a specific class context in Cairo rather than providing a more holistic and decentralized account, which this chapter is aiming to do.[14]

Unlike the nation's story, narrating the story of the workers' movement in Egypt had to wait till the 1960s, when literature on labor history was produced by Egyptian historians including most importantly Raouf Abbas[15] and Amin Izz al-Din.[16] Their foundational work on the labor movement was taken up in the classic "Workers on the Nile" by Joel Beinin and Zachary Lockman.[17] Despite their pioneering character and huge impact, these works had two main characteristics: overemphasizing nationalism and Marxism. The emphasis on the nationalist character of the labor movement was explicitly stated. Abbas, for example, emphasized the labor activists' role in the nationalist struggle and the entangled relationship between nationalist and labor movements. Similarly, the leftist Egyptian historian Amin Izz al-Din argues that the Egyptian working class has been "a nationalist social force honing its anti-imperialist and anti-capitalist consciousness ever since its birth in the late nineteenth century."[18]

This overemphasis on nationalism and Marxism can be explained by understanding the particular historical context. Influence of worker movements by nationalism is attributable to the relative congruence of class and national identity in state-owned or state-protected enterprises such as the transport sector under British colonialism. "The foreign nationality of supervisors, owners, and skilled workers helped Egyptian workers link abusive treatment in the workplace to their

---

13. Joel Beinin, "Will the Real Egyptian Working Class Please Stand Up?" in *Workers and Working Classes in the Middle East: Struggles, Histories, Historiographies*, ed. Zachary Lockman (New York: State University of New York Press, 1993), 247–70; John T. Chalcraft, *The Striking Cabbies of Cairo and Other Stories: Crafts and Guilds in Egypt, 1863–1914* (Albany: State University of New York Press, 2005); J. Cole, *Colonialism and Revolution in the Middle East* (Princeton: Princeton University Press, 1999).

14. H. Hammad, "Daily Encounters That Make History: History from Below and Archival Collaboration," *International Journal of Middle East Studies* 53, no. 1 (2021): 139–43. https://doi.org/10.1017/s0020743821000076.

15. Raouf Abbas, *al-Haraka al-'ummaliya fi Misr, 1899–1952* (Cairo. Dar al-katib al-'Arabi lil-tiba'ah wa al-nashr, 1967).

16. Amin Izz al-Din, *History of Egyptian Working Class (1919–1929)* (Cairo: Al Shaa'b Publishing, 1969). [translated from Arabic by the author].

17. Joel Beinin and Zachary Lockman, *Workers on the Nile Nationalism, Communism, Islam, and the Egyptian Working Class, 1882–1954* (Cairo: The American University in Cairo Press, 1998).

18. Izz al-Din, *History of Egyptian Working Class (1919–1929)*, 31.

humiliation as Egyptians subject to foreign rule."[19] However, such emphasis on the nationalist movement has been criticized for overlooking the role of foreign labor as agents in the workers' movement.[20] This led to neglecting class-based solidarity and the transcendence of national division between Egyptian and foreign workers or, more broadly, between the local and the international.

Concerning orthodox Marxism, it can be explained by labor inevitably adopting socialism in opposition to colonial capitalism.[21] However, this fixation on Marxism overlooks the workers' entanglement in a dense web of social relations composed of their families, villages, and urban centers among other components. Workers' communities were not one-dimensional. They were part of complex webs that contributed to and re-formed the structures of neighborhoods and popular culture.[22] Joel Beinin and Zachary Lockman had a similar approach to the one adopted by nationalist historians. By only focusing on strikes and politics, scant attention is paid to questions of identity, lived experience, and gender.[23] Beinin himself said, "we only considered workers when they were politically active."[24] Hammad states, "the exclusive focus in historical writings on revolutionary conflicts based in nationalist and class causes misses the rich drama of ordinary and everyday life."[25]

Focusing on protests does not answer the question: "What do we know of how the social, emotional, and intellectual life of laboring men and women fit into larger patterns of social, emotional, and intellectual life in Egypt as a whole?"[26] In the case of the Suez Canal Zone, thousands of peasants had been impacted by the capitalist structure of the SCC and the new urban life of the cities. Labor history examined through strikes and protests would provide little knowledge of the social lives of workers inside and outside their workplaces, their sense of belonging to

---

19. Nancy Y. Reynolds, "Entangled Communities: Interethnic Relationships among Urban Salesclerks and Domestic Workers in Egypt, 1927–1961," *European Review of History: Revue europeenne d'histoire* 19, no. 1 (2012): 3. https://doi.org/10.1080/13507486.2012.643669.

20. Zachary Lockman, "Notes on Egyptian Workers' History," *International Labor and Working-Class History* 18 (1980): 3. https://doi.org/10.1017/s0147547900006670.

21. Hanan Hammad, *Industrial Sexuality: Gender, Urbanization, and Social Transformation in Egypt* (Austin: University of Texas Press, 2016), 9.

22. Beinin and Lockman, *Workers on the Nile Nationalism, Communism, Islam, and the Egyptian Working Class, 1882–1954*, 23.

23. Zachary Lockman, "Reflection on Labor and Working-Class History in the Middle East and North Africa," in *Global Labour History: A State of the Art* (Bern: Peter Lang, 2008), 130.

24. Beinin, "Will the Real Egyptian Working Class Please Stand Up?" 267.

25. Hammad, *Industrial Sexuality*, 9.

26. Ellis Goldberg, *Tinker, Tailor, and Textile Worker: Class and Politics in Egypt, 1930–1952* (Berkeley: University of California Press, 1986), 164.

social groups and communities, and the times and places they shared with the rest of the urban population.[27]

The events of the 1919 Revolution in the Suez Canal region provide a new and paradoxical, broader setting for understanding the emergence of nationalism among workers and their wider networks in the Suez Canal area. Despite being a symbol of colonial presence in Egypt, unintentionally, the Company provided fertile ground for cross-national class-based alliance among its workers to form and grow. Racial work hierarchies, the sense of "family" and the spread of imported European radical ideologies fostered moments of class-based solidarity among workers from diverse backgrounds during the peak of Egyptian nationalism. Shedding light on this massive strike reveals a more nuanced account of history than a simplistic nationalist epic. It tells a story of at least temporal comradeship and class awareness along the Suez Canal. Highlighting the unique case of Canal cities as company towns modeled on urban apartheid is a cornerstone to understanding the revolutionary moment in the region. Through investigating the moment of the 1919 Revolution in Port Said and Ismailia, the chapter illustrates how camaraderie was fostered in part by apartheid. Using the strike of the SCC workers in May 1919 as a starting point, the chapter shows a more complex picture of nationalism that did not emerge in effendis' cafés in Cairo but rather in the alleys and huts of Arab towns of the Suez Canal Isthmus.

Suez Canal Company (SCC) and Its Workers

In 1919, the Company's workforce, comprised of 3,000 workers, was divided into the following main categories: clerical workers, technical staff (including engineers, pilots, and maritime workers such as seamen, shipmen and foremen) and manual workers. Manual workers were divided into company registered workers (*inscrit*[28]) and non-registered workers (*du tâcheron*[29]). Non-registered laborers represented 30 to 35 percent of the Company's labor force until the First World War. They were mainly Egyptian workers, but there were European workers among them as well. By contrast, two-thirds of inscrit workers were Europeans. Initially, most foremen were recruited in France and constituted the workers' elite later, in the interwar period; such positions were gradually taken over by Italians and Greeks. Inscrit workers had been directly employed by the Company guaranteeing job security, social benefits, and better work conditions in general unlike the non-registered workers. The Company's recruitment and training policies were designed to exclude Egyptians from skilled and technical positions (especially those of pilot

---

27. Hammad, *Industrial Sexuality*, 11.

28. Inscrit is a French term (used by the Company) which translates to "enrolled" or "registered."

29. Temporary or seasonal laborers recruited by local middlemen mainly for construction works.

and foreman) and tended to favor the sons and family members of European personnel. Such policy continued till nationalization in 1956.³⁰

The 1919 Revolution and Workers Strike

A few months after the March uprising in 1919 though the situation was starting to calm down in the country, it was escalating in the Canal Zone. On May 13, 1919, the workers of the Company started a strike that lasted for almost a month and spread to other companies operating in the Canal Zone. The strikers demanded increased wages, an eight-hour workday, and other requests related to work compensation.³¹ The main body behind this strike was "Le Phenix," a group founded by Greek workers in the Company. Greek was the most common ethnicity within the permanent cadre of foreign workers.

Strikes were organized in three different cities of the Canal Zone: Port Said, Ismailia, and Suez. Despite being initiated by a Greek workers' association, the participants were a diverse mix of races and nationalities. The committee for the strike was composed of two Greeks, two Italians, an Austrian, and an Egyptian in Port Said; three Greeks, a Serb, a Frenchman, an Italian, and an Egyptian in Ismailia; and eight Greeks, three Egyptians, two Italians, a Maltese, and an Armenian in Suez.³²

A petition sent to the British High Commissioner by the Company workers included the signature of the European representative of workers and the representative of native workers, a certain Mr. Mohamed El Ayat. The petition was written in French to the British High Commissioner and signed by Italians, Greeks, and one Egyptian. This diverse participation reflects the unique events of the Canal Zone in a moment that was considered the birth of Egyptian nationalism. Moreover, such militant spirit extended to the rest of the workers across cities, ethnicities, and specialties across the Canal. This strike encouraged workers of other companies in the Canal cities whether native or European to seize the moment and express their grievances. The strikes seeped deeper into the three cities, with workers in worker groups such as cigarette-makers, the Suez electric lightworkers, and ice factory workers gradually joining in. Egyptian coal heavers also joined in a few days after the main strike. The total number of workers striking was about 4,500 including 3,000 SCC workers.³³

---

30. Carolin Piquet, *La Compagnie Du Canal De Suez Une Concession française En Égypte, 1888–1956* (Paris: PUPS, 2008), 326.

31. FO 141/781/8915.

32. I. Leropoulos, "I apergia ton eraton tis diorygas tou Suez" [The strike of the Suez Canal workers], in C.N. Fragoulis, *Imerologion ton dodeka* [The diary of twelve] (Port Said, 1936), 412.

33. Diplomatic and Historical Archives of the Hellenic Ministry of Foreign Affairs (hereafter AYE), 1919/A/5/II, 269, Suez, May 2, 1919, Vice-consul of Suez to the Ministry

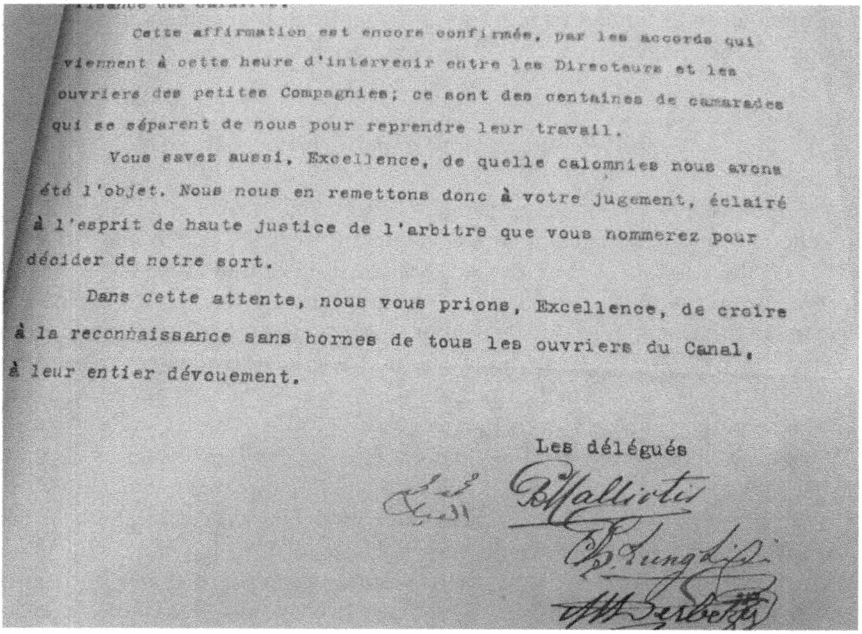

36 The Egyptian Revolution of 1919

> Cette affirmation est encore confirmée, par les accords qui viennent à cette heure d'intervenir entre les Directeurs et les ouvriers des petites Compagnies; ce sont des centaines de camarades qui se séparent de nous pour reprendre leur travail.
>
> Vous savez aussi, Excellence, de quelle calomnies nous avons été l'objet. Nous nous en remettons donc à votre jugement, éclairé à l'esprit de haute justice de l'arbitre que vous nommerez pour décider de notre sort.
>
> Dans cette attente, nous vous prions, Excellence, de croire à la reconnaissance sans bornes de tous les ouvriers du Canal, à leur entier dévouement.
>
> Les délégués

Figure 2.1 A section of the petition (written in French) that the SCC's representative workers sent to the British High Commissioner during the 1919 strike. FO 141/487/1.

Although the strike lasted for a month, the Canal did not stop running due to another form of transnational cooperation between the British army and the French Company. The British army had positioned its naval personnel to support the French company to prevent the stoppage of the Canal. This weakened the impact of the strikers. The strikes ended with partial success and acceptance of few but not all their demands by the Company.[34]

Transnational Solidarity in the Age of Nationalism

This strike was a turning point in the history of both the region and the workers' movement in Egypt. Before 1919, the strikes in the Canal Zone were mainly of a social nature. Strikes were divided across ethnic lines such as the strike of Egyptian coal heavers in 1882 and the series of strikes in the 1890s led mainly by Greek workers. Most of the Egyptian workers were excluded from the only workers'

---

of Foreign Affairs.
34. FO 141/ 487 / 7392/23.

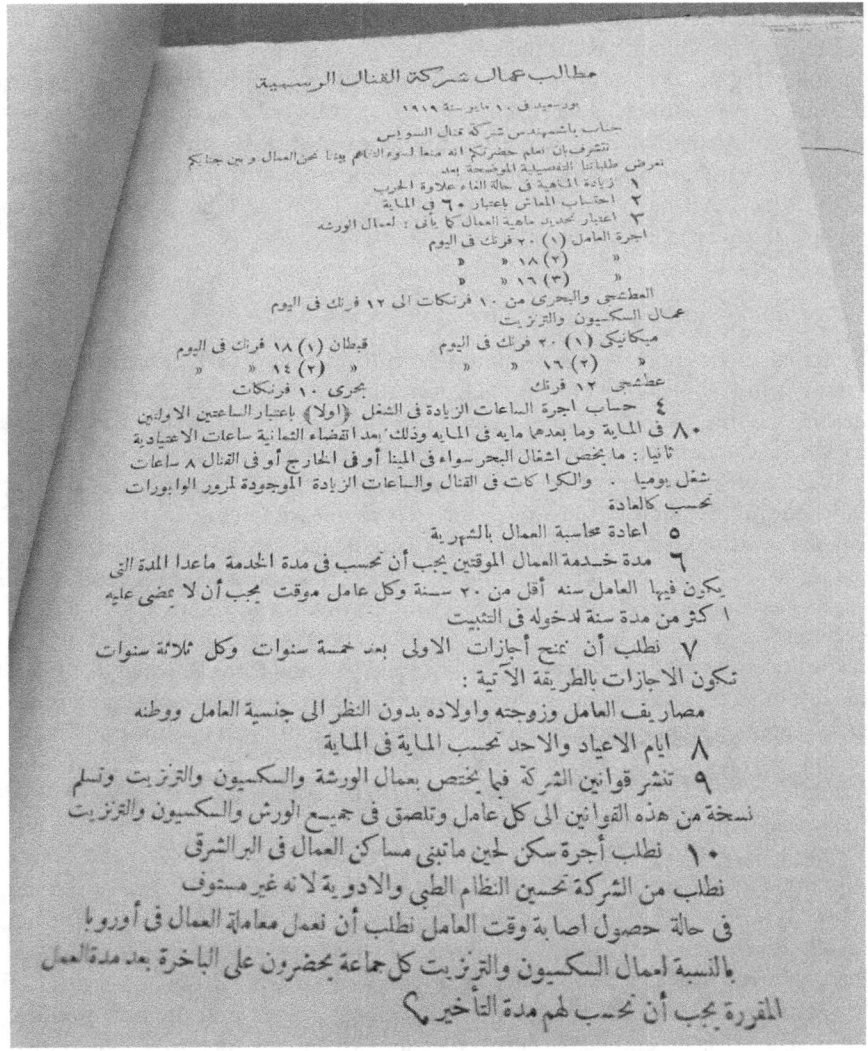

Figure 2.2 A list of demands written (in Arabic) by the SCC workers, May 1919. *Source*: The National Archive, Kew Gardens, London.

syndicate in the region as it was only for inscrit workers.[35] However, the strikes that took place in April 1919 were mainly led by blue- and white-collar Egyptians. Participants included transportation workers, government employees, and ulama

---

35. Piquet, *La Compagnie Du Canal De Suez Une Concession française En Égypte, 1888–1956*, 324.

and lawyers. Conversely, the May strikes ushered a new era of cross-national collaboration amid nationalist peaks.

Following the May strike in the Suez Canal region, a new wave of strikes began in August 1919. This new wave was co-organized by both Egyptian and foreign workers (particularly Italian workers). This upheaval created significant challenges for the British authorities after a brief moment of tranquility.[36] Thus, the May strike in the Suez Canal was a unique turning point; the following four factors shed light on how this turn of events came to be.

Nationalism a Precursor for Internationalism

Nationalism emerged as the dominant form of identity in the aftermath of the First World War over other forms of identities such as Caliphate and Empire. Thus, despite the international organization committees and its cross-ethnic solidarity, nationalism was still a major driving force behind the strike. This was the case for Italians, Greeks, and Egyptians. For example, the Greek community was neither satisfied with the First World War peace accords nor with being unable to capture Istanbul in the Greek-Turkish war. This heightened sense of nationalism and dissatisfaction with the French among the Greek community led to the formation of a Greek nationalist committee in Port Said led by George Malititos.[37] This sense of bitterness in addition to economic hardship converged to justify strike action. As for Italian workers, it was not only class solidarity and labor activism that made them join forces with Egyptians; rather, many of them felt bitter at Britain for not giving Italy its share of war spoils. The unjust peace or "La Paix injustice" made Italian workers actively militant against the British authorities on many fronts, not only the Suez Canal one, but they were also the spearhead of the second wave strike that happened in August.[38]

As for Egyptian workers, the strike was collaboratively organized and highly supported the nationalist movement in Port Said represented by Aly Bey Lehita and other local notables. Aly Bey and his brother were already involved in organizing revolutionary activities against the British. In fact, his brother was arrested by British forces. Aly Bey Lahita was already in contact with Zizania, the head of the "Phenix," and pressured him to allow native workers into the organization. Zizania also was in contact with other nationalist leaders such as Helmi Housri who encouraged the native coalers in Port Said to strike. This occurred after many militant events in Port Said took place against the British after March 8 when Saad Zaghloul was deported to Malta from there. The nationalist movement must have discovered that the stoppage of the Canal, even by an economically driven strike, would give great momentum to the revolution which at that point in time had

36. FO 407/185/57 Allenby to Curzon, July 22, 1919.
37. CADN, ambassade du caire, 511/512, note de service d'informations de la marine au levant, May 6, 1919.
38. MAE, Afrique, 1918–1929, Egypt, 4, rapport 1919.

started to slow down. Such an alliance made British High Commissioner in Egypt, Lord Edmund Allenby, comment in July 1919, "the foreign and native working class have apparently identified in their own minds with the syndicalist movement and extremist agitation."[39]

Suez Family: Corporate/Urban Identity

One of the main reasons for such solidarity among workers was the sense of belonging to "the family of the Suez Canal," a concept that rarely developed anywhere else in Egypt. Acting as a state within a state, the SCC played a paternal benevolent role. It created towns, provided a welfare infrastructure such as housing, water, electricity, health, and churches, and was rarely being checked by the government or even the British army which was an exceptional case in Egypt.[40] The Company provided for its employees what can be called welfare capitalism. It performed social patronage for its employees following the philanthropic philosophy spread in the enlightened circles of Paris at the time.

As Bonin mentions, "the Spirit of 'Suez large family' was conceived in the Isthmus either in Port-Said, Port-Fouad or Ismailia,"[41] creating a feeling of belonging that cannot be easily created in any other company in Egypt, even in Cairo or Alexandria. Hence, the spirit of one family, though a hierarchical one, contributed to forming a common bond among workers. The theme of the Suez Canal family happened to be common not only among European but also Egyptian workers. In several reports by Ian Malcolm, one of the British directors in the Company, about his visits to the Canal Zone, he highlighted the familial atmosphere among everyone working in the Canal Zone. In his visit in 1925, he stated that the Company provided this welfare status to all of its employees and workers (those who were permanent and mostly European), and they were grateful to be part of this harmonious family.[42]

The workers and their syndicate used family rhetoric to claim more rights. In the petition of 1919, the workers stressed being part of the family of the Suez Canal and held the Company responsible for welfare services such as the education of their children and trips to their home countries. The existence of a paternal state established by providing services to its employees and workers or causing them to aspire to have it one day, especially as in the case of non-registered workers, created a certain common identity, a corporate identity in today's terms, among the workers who shared the same parent: the Company. This sense of shared

---

39. FO 407/185/57 Allenby to Curzon, July 22, 1919.

40. Piquet, *La Compagnie Du Canal De Suez Une Concession française En Égypte, 1888–1956*, 411.

41. Hubert Bonin, *History of the Suez Canal Company: 1858–1960 I.e. 1858–2008: between Controversy and Utility* (Genève: Droz, 2010), 274.

42. FO 141/812/16.

identity and belonging, especially among workers, helped to shape the historical events that were described earlier.

This sense of specific urban/corporate identity of belonging to the Suez Canal family, be it Company or Isthmus, was the main reason the strike spread across other companies. Port Said and Ismailia are small towns where everyday contact between people of different ethnic backgrounds who lived in the same streets and resided in the same blocks of flats. This was especially the case for the Europeans. Additionally, working together whether directly for the SCC or other companies working in the Isthmus facilitated that sense of belonging to a "family"—the Suez Canal family—"that had to improve its common fate," as the flyers of the International Workers Union of the Isthmus of Suez stated in August 1919.[43] Such a sense of belonging made the populations of these cities very sympathetic with the workers during their strikes. The collective sympathy also facilitated community fundraising efforts, especially by European residents. This solidarity was consolidating despite the fact that a propaganda campaign attempting to convince foreigners across Egypt that the revolution is xenophobic was taking place simultaneously.

Workers versus Employees

The dichotomy of workers versus employees was influential in the relationship between the workers and the Company, as well as their relationship with one another. The Western/Mediterranean European division-based hierarchy of the Company structure made the Western European employees far more removed from their Mediterranean European workers as foremen or technicians. Such a schism created more commonalities between European workers and native workers. The Company elite had been structured racially as such: a French board, Anglo-French management, and majority Western European pilots of English, French, and Dutch origin.

The worker-employee schism was intensified by the various measures in place for cutting wages or reducing workdays for both registered and non-registered workers. Tensions were exacerbated by the fact that these measures rarely affected employees. For example, the last time the pilots of the SCC ever went on strike was in 1918, and it did not take long for the Company to reach an agreement with them in a "spirit of mutual trust."[44] Even hospitals, accommodation, and recreational places for predominantly Anglo-French employees were different from those of the workers.[45] The inequalities between employees and workers including racial and capitalistic division played a decisive role in creating common cause among workers transcending nationality and religion.

43. ACUCMS, 1345, greves, notes de 1921.
44. Captain Paul Parfond, *Pilotes de Suez* (Paris: France-Empire editions, 1957).
45. Piquet, *La Compagnie Du Canal De Suez Une Concession française En Égypte, 1888–1956*, 483.

This division overshadowed the division between registered and non-registered workers. The inscrit workers and foremen commonly originated from Greek Islands, Italy, and other Mediterranean countries. However, by the beginning of the twentieth century, Egyptians constituted around 30 percent of this category.[46] The non-registered workers were majority Egyptians but also included European workers who also sought job security as their Egyptian colleagues. Beinin argues that Greek workers thought of the surplus of cheap Egyptian workers as a threat that may lead to their substitution, so they included them in the strike as a survival mechanism. Equal wages and status for all workers would have kept the Greek workers and other Europeans as more favorable options to the Company.[47] However, Piquet counterargued this by stating that both categories included Egyptians and Europeans. The latter category was not job secured and fought for job security for long periods in the 1890s strikes. Additionally, the economic and social situation was ruthless on both categories of workers, unlike employees who enjoyed much higher salaries.[48]

Notably, it was the lack of a workers' majority from one nation that made it difficult for any independent worker association, the Greek (Le Phenix) or the Italian (Margherita), to challenge the Company alone. Thus, a common cause among the workers, both registered and non-registered, European and Egyptians, was necessary to have any leverage on the Anglo-French elite governing body.

Radical Ideologies Within the Isthmus

Class solidarity in the Canal Zone can also be attributed to the diffusion of ideas of anarchism, syndicalism, and communism which had a presence early in the Isthmus. The workers were aware of these ideologies, and a group of them were already activists in their countries of origin, especially Italians and Greeks. They saw themselves as European working class and thus contrasted their conditions with European conditions and also those of their peers in labor movements throughout Europe and Revolutionary Russia. They basically worked in a company of French-British shareholders, thus they naturally looked up to European working conditions, not to Egyptian workshops on the other side of the town.[49]

---

46. Piquet, *La Compagnie Du Canal De Suez Une Concession française En Égypte, 1888–1956*, 326.

47. Beinin and Lockman, *Workers on the Nile Nationalism, Communism, Islam, and the Egyptian Working Class, 1882–1954*, 107.

48. Piquet, *La Compagnie Du Canal De Suez Une Concession française En Égypte, 1888–1956*, 326.

49. Angelos Dalachanis, "Internationalism vs. Nationalism? The Suez Canal Company Strike of 1919 and the Formation of the International Workers' Union of the Isthmus of Suez" Essay, in *Social Transformation and Mass Mobilisation in the Balkan and Eastern Mediterranean Cities: 1900–1923* (Heraklion: Crete University Press, 2013), 4.

The rise of communism and anarchism in Europe in the 1850s and 1860s spread across borders including the ports in the Mediterranean. Port Said and Ismailia were among the four cities which had anarchist organizations in 1860 other than the capital and Alexandria.[50] In her book, Ilham Khuri argues the movement of radical ideas and individuals between Eastern Mediterranean cities such as Beirut, Izmir, and Alexandria created the Eastern Mediterranean hub for radicalism and socialism.[51] Port Said is not an exception in that case. Ideas such as anarchism had a strong footing, at least among foreign workers, in Egypt in the wake of the twentieth century. The establishment of the free popular university in Alexandria in 1901 and its strong enrolment and attendance records is evidence of such.

Moving on to the interwar period and the success of the October 1917 revolution, communism had a strong presence in Egypt, not only among foreign workers but also among Egyptian workers. This was particularly the case in the Canal Zone. French reports described the SCC workers as including among them many socialist workers with an anarchist tendency. The French ambassador in Cairo described the situation in Port Said in the wake of the strike as a crisis qualified as a "bolshevik movement."[52] Moreover, Dr. Alexandre Skouphopoulos was the first and longest-serving head of the "International Worker's Union of the Isthmus of Suez," which was formed after the strike.[53] He also was one of the four founders of the Egyptian Socialist Party in the early 1920s along with the famous communist activist Joseph Rosenthal.[54]

The presence of foreign workers and their awareness of the developing labor movement in their countries, as well as the laws protecting workers, was significantly influential. A detailed British report about the reasons for strikes in the beginning months of 1931 in the Canal Zone referred to this point precisely stating, "the existence of Greek and French workers made the Egyptians aware of the laws that protect labor in their countries."[55] This exchange of radical ideas through the Mediterranean affected the dynamics of relations among workers from various backgrounds and created a heightened atmosphere and drive for solidarity.

It is clear that this epic moment did not end with the end of the strike. Rather, it ushered a wave of cross-national strikes in August and kick-started a huge syndicate movement that made La Bourse Egyptienne use the headline "Il pleut

50. Anthony Gorman, "Anarchists in Education: The Free Popular University in Egypt (1901)," *Middle Eastern Studies* 41, no. 3 (2005): 34. https://doi.org/10.1080/00263200500105877.

51. Ilham Khuri-Makdisi, *Eastern Mediterranean and the Making of Global Radicalism, 1860–1914* (Berkeley: University Of California Press, 2013), 13.

52. CADN, ambassade du caire, 511/512, note from February 1919.

53. *Tachydromos*, June 13/May 31, 1919, 2.

54. FO 371/62997, security of the Suez Canal Zone, May 7, 1921.

55. FO 141/ 689/ 3.

des syndicates ['It is Raining Syndicates']."⁵⁶ Regionally, after the partial success of the strike and immense participation of all the workers in the region, not just those of the SCC, it initiated the first multinational labor union in the Canal area and Egypt: International Workers Union of the Isthmus of Suez. This union was meant to unify the working class in the region and Egypt and connect it to the working-class movement in Europe.⁵⁷ This union was presided by Dr. Alexandre Skouphopoulos who later cofounded the Egyptian Socialist Party in 1921 as the first socialist party in the Middle East.

However, the transformation of workers in such unions in the Isthmus into a full transnational class was a dream never actually realized. Despite being active at certain points in time, especially during strikes in the 1930s and 1940s, the workers within the Isthmus were deeply divided by their daily reality. Race, religion, and urban division never allowed such a working class to realize its full destiny.

Urban Experience of Labor and Nationalism

The 1919 Revolution also started a sequence of events that strengthened the nationalist spirit within Canal cities. In such a "cosmopolitan" hub, ideologies such as nationalism and later Islamism had a stronghold. In a few decades after the May strike, more exclusively Egyptian syndicates were founded. Religious movements, especially the Muslim Brotherhood, were founded in the region and were able to exert exceptional influence on labor movements of that area whether on SCC or Shell company workers.⁵⁸ Thus, it is important to step away from the strike and adopt a more comprehensive picture of the workers' lives in these cities and the impact the 1919 Revolution had on such "cosmopolitan" enclaves.

Linking the Canal cities with ideologies such as cosmopolitanism is not uncommon, including but not limited to literary memoirs such as *Port Said Revisited*⁵⁹ and more academic texts in which a full chapter is dedicated to asking if the Canal Zone was a "*Petit France?*"⁶⁰ From the beginning, the region certainly attracted a wide variety of nationalities, starting with western Europeans such as the English, French, and Dutch, as well as Mediterranean Europeans including Greeks, Italians, Maltese, and Spaniards. It also included the Red Sea and the Indian Ocean via seamen from Aden and Somalia, as well as Indian soldiers within the British army who came, fought, and died on the Canal Zone. The

---

56. La Bourse Egyptienne. August 21, 1919.

57. CADN, ambassade du caire, 511/512, note de service d'informations de la marine au levant, July 7, 1919.

58. Beinin and Lockman, *Workers on the Nile Nationalism, Communism, Islam, and the Egyptian Working Class, 1882-1954*, 385.

59. Sylvia Modelski, *Port Said Revisited* (FAROS 2000, 2000).

60. Piquet, *La Compagnie Du Canal De Suez Une Concession française En Égypte, 1888-1956*, 463.

first section in this chapter has already given a sense of its diversity, as well as certain ideologies that transcended nations or religions such as communism and anarchism. However, this is only part of the picture. Taken alone, it would give the impression that the Canal Zone was a melting pot in which different nationalities interacted freely and experienced solidarity and unity that transcended national and religious boundaries.

However, the reality was much more complicated. The story of the Company workers outside the ateliers and shop floors sheds light on a complex history of connectivity but also of antagonism. The cities of Port Said and Ismailia provided a sharp angle to the type of colonial-related cosmopolitanism that prevailed in the interwar period, in Egypt, but greatly took place in these cities. Understanding this phenomenon of the settler colonial "cosmopolitan" cities would help answer the question of how a place characterized by plurality, migration, modernity, and ideologies such as internationalism, communism, and anarchism, can host a significant degree of militant nationalism.

Al Masry, Al-Ismaily, and El Lenby: Nation's Symbolism in the Isthmus

The 1919 Revolution sparked a great sense of nationalism among the Arab inhabitants of the Canal cities. From that point, the 1919 Revolution became the point of departure for a series of actions that represented the fight for a more nationalist spirit in Port Said and Ismailia. The founding of the Al Masry sports club in 1920 and the Al-Ismaily club in Ismailia in 1924 was part of this agenda. The latter was founded based on modest financial contributions from the locals. It is considered to be the first Arab/Egyptian club in the city as a response to exclusive foreign clubs.[61] The sports club "Al Masry," which translates to mean "the Egyptian," was founded in the city of Port Said. It prided itself for being the first club in the Canal region to be completely free of foreigners.[62] Al Masry represented a clear expression of an excluded identity: that of being Egyptian in *L'Etat du Canal de Suez*. The popularity of the team grew dramatically in the 1930s to eventually be praised by Cairo newspaper Al Ahram as being a cornerstone of "Egyptianness" in the Isthmus as this article illustrates:

> The region of Suez Canal was unknown to football fans before the founding of Al-Masry club in Port-Saïd. When Al-Masry was founded, you needed to read the name to know its secret meaning, introducing the Egyptian background of a club in a region surrounded by foreigners. The name was enough to stimulate

---

61. For a brief history of the formation of Al-Ismaily Club: https://www.marefa.org/%D8%A7%D9%84%D9%86%D8%A7%D8%AF%D9%8A_%D8%A7%D9%84%D8%A7%D8%B3%D9%85%D8%A7%D8%B9%D9%8A%D9%84%D9%8A.

62. The official Facebook page of Al Masry club: https://www.facebook.com/Almasryofficial/.

Figure 2.3 A photo showing Al Masry club's flag as an adjusted copy of the independence flag. *Source*: the official website of Al Masry club.

Figure 2.4 A photo of graffiti art on a building wall in Port Said that reads (as translated to English): "1919, the story of a revolution that created a club." March 2019. *Source*: Ahmed ElGezy. The photo, taken by Ahmed ElGezy, was published here: https://picbabun.com/ahmedgezy.

the enthusiasm in Port Saidians' souls. Now, Al-Masry is a football corner stone in Suez Canal region and succeeded to resist the foreign clubs pressure.[63]

The other major manifestation of nationalist spirit displayed in the Isthmus cities was the burning of a dummy figure named "El Lenby" as a symbolic act of

---

63. Al Ahram, August 11, 1934.

resistance against the British High Commissioner of Egypt, Edmund Allenby.[64] Such displays involved the maiming, hanging, and burning of life-size mockups of foreign-looking figures resembling Lord Allenby. This ceremonial act was mainly performed by Egyptians in the native quarter in Port Said and Ismailia, symbolically emphasizing the separation between them and their comrades on the other side of the city. Burning this effigy helped to transcend social hierarchies by mobilizing the rich and the poor in the Arab quarter who chanted lyrics of the colonial experience and social segregation. As Beli states, resistance through the affirmation of national identity targeted not only the colonial authorities and foreign elites but also "estranged native elites, spatially and culturally divorced from them, whom they associated with the occupiers and profiteers."[65] Thus, the subversive celebration was not a subtle act of resistance disguised as a cultural ritual but rather a political feat. The British authorities were aware of its nature, which is why they chased, arrested, and seized both the celebrating crowd and the materials used for the burning in the Arab neighborhood.[66]

Colonial Company Towns as an Urban Apartheid in the Egyptian Periphery

I am tired of searching for the Egyptian Embassy in Port Said without finding it.
—Hamed Adly El Gamil, a character representing an Egyptian ex-employee in the SCC in the famous nationalist drama *Nasser 56*.[67]

The unique nature of the Canal cities, mainly Ismailia and Port Said, resembled cities of urban apartheid. The concept of urban apartheid is related to another French colonial city built at around the same time in Rabat, Morocco. Janet Abu-Lughod describes the status of Rabat, after being totally renovated and heavily inhabited by the French in comparison to the old city of Salé, as urban apartheid.[68] The Suez Canal cities of Port Said and Ismailia were also established based on this separate two-neighborhood concept: the beautiful European/*Afrangi* quarter and the Arab/native quarter. Interestingly, the street separating the two neighborhoods in both cities was named Mohamed Ali Street, after the "founder of Modern Egypt." The categories of native/European were not merely a means for the Company to discriminate against Egyptian workers, but also a daily reality of life. Neighborhoods were divided by race, with great discrepancies in all aspects of

---

64. Mériam N. Belli, *An Incurable Past: Nasser's Egypt Then and Now* (University Press of Florida, 2013), 77.
65. Ibid., 78.
66. Ibid., 89.
67. https://www.imdb.com/title/tt0289355/.
68. Janet Abu-Lughod, *Rabat, Urban Apartheid in Morocco* (Princeton: Princeton University Press, 1980), 40.

daily life such as public spaces, accommodation options, and even basic exigencies such as electricity and sewage systems.[69]

Apartheid as a lived experience was shocking to Egyptians living in Cairo. The situation of apartheid remained unchanged after the 1919 Revolution. In fact, it continued almost until the nationalization of the Canal in 1956. For example, in his visit to Ismailia in 1950, a journalist from Cairo-based Al-Musawwar journal described his experience within the racially divided city. When trying to find accommodation, no hotel accepted him on the claim that they had no rooms. The experience was similar in restaurants; he was told that their tables had been reserved for weeks ahead. He was advised to go to the Arab quarter where he would be served, albeit with an inferior quality of service.[70] The streets in both neighborhoods were designed to prohibit pedestrians intermingling, ending with bottlenecks that were easily controlled, and monitored. Thus, large numbers of pedestrians crossing the street from the Arab quarter to the European one would quickly garner the attention of the authorities: either British colonial or Egyptian. For example, in 1919 a Sufi procession in Port Said tried to cross Mohamed Ali Street to the European neighborhood but was faced by English soldiers who opened fire at them, resulting in several deaths.[71]

The Arab neighborhoods in Ismailia and Port Said were first established as huts and used by the Arab workers remaining in the Zone after the digging of the Canal. Afterward, the Company reorganized both neighborhoods in Ismailia and Port Said by allocating very small land plots to its inhabitants. Port Said was mainly inhabited by those who worked in the lower ranks of manual work, such as small merchandisers and bambouties trading goods with passing ships. These neighborhoods lacked any open spaces or squares suitable for public assembly. Despite their sterile, systematic planning, these neighborhoods were vibrant hubs for public life in comparison to the European ones. In Ismailia, the contrast was much sharper. The Arab quarter was heavily populated, especially after the Second World War, due to massive internal immigration to serve the British military camps during the war.[72] This caused gentrification and pushed the natives further toward the outskirts, to a neighborhood called "Arshyiat El-Abeed," which literally translates to "slave huts" in English. The contrast between this and the European neighborhood was shocking to the aforementioned journalist.

---

69. Céline Frémaux, "Town Planning, Architecture, and Migrations in Suez Canal Port Cities," in *Port Cities: Dynamic Landscapes and Global Networks*, ed. Carola Hein, 156–73 (Abingdon and New York: Routledge, 2011).

70. Al-Musawwar journal, July 21, 1950.

71. 'Aysha Shukr, "Shamm al-nasim fi Bur Sa'id. Dirasa madaniyya fi Bur Sa'id" (Shamm al-Nasim in Port Said: Urban Study of Port Said). Ph.D. diss., University of 'Ayn al-Shams, Cairo. 1995, 131.

72. Rājiyah Ismāʿīl Abū Zayd, *Tārīkh madīnat al-Ismāʿīlīyah: min al-nashʾah ilá muntaṣaf al-qarn al-ʿishrīn* (Cairo: Maktabat al-Ādāb, 2012), 268.

In a picture caption, the journalist from Al-Musawwar journal writes:

> Two views in deep contrast, the view of Afrang neighborhood and a view in Arshyiat El-Abeed. The first is [a] neat heaven with trees and flowers, and the second is hell with clay-built houses not suitable for chickens, roads from clay like village roads, shoeless children, and entrenched poverty. It is called "Arshyiat El Abeed" and it deserves this; it is only suitable for slaves.[73]

He goes on to say that in these places, inhabitants "lost their civility" and were confined to tents and shacks in "conditions not unlike Palestinian camps." He concludes his report with a suggestion from a taxi driver concerning the urban problem in Ismailia: "flatten the Arab quarters. Being homeless is more honorable than living in these shanty towns."[74]

In contrast, the European quarters in both cities were striking for their beauty and glamour. In Port Said, the houses were much larger than their counterparts in the Arab neighborhoods. They had boulevards with trees and arcades, green parks, and sporting clubs. Another type of hierarchy also existed among (mostly French and English) Europeans between the high-level employees and lower-ranked workers. High-level employees enjoyed a more luxurious living experience. They lived in European single-family houses and multi-floor buildings. Lower-ranked European workers lived in semidetached courtyard houses with a pseudo-Moorish style.[75] There were also stark differences between the type of social activities and recreational facilities available in European quarters in contrast to the Arab ones. A detailed childhood memoir of an ex-resident in the Canal region, Sylvia Modelski, reveals a form of social life considered high even by European standards in Port Said. Dance parties, sporting clubs, and mixed-gender socializing in bars and beaches mimicked the lifestyle of beach towns in the South of France.[76]

In Ismailia, the contrast was even deeper. In the words of Lyatuny, a visiting French official, "in the dining hall in a verandah overlooking a veritable botanical garden, complete with Bougainvillea palms, I find myself sitting beside a young lady in pink who was born here eighteen years back, talking to me of tennis, season tickets for music, reading, and comedy"; Lyatuny asked her for tips as he was visiting Cairo, and it turned out that she had not been there. He went on to write, "their entire Egypt consisted of a season's tickets for readings at Port Said and tennis in Ismailia."[77]

---

73. Al-Musawwar journal, July 21, 1950.
74. Ibid.
75. D. ElKerdany, "Port Said: A Cosmopolitan Heritage Under Threat," in *Revitalizing City Districts. The Urban Book Series*, ed. H. Abouelfadl, D. ElKerdany, C. Wessling (Cham: Springer, 2017), 77. https://doi.org/10.1007/978-3-319-46289-9_2.
76. Modelski, *Port Said Revisited*.
77. Bonin, *History of the Suez Canal Company*, 282.

Whose Cosmopolitan City?

Native Egyptian society provided servants, functionaries and prostitutes for the cosmopolitan milieu. They were inferiorized and despised.

—Sami Zubaida[78]

These words were used to describe the port city of Alexandria. Zubaida[79] warned against nostalgia toward the golden age of Cosmopolitan Alexandria. Various scholars have stressed the fact that cosmopolitanism is a phenomenon reserved for the elite, and essentially exclusionary by nature. For example, Hanley states that the European bourgeois cosmopolitanism used in Middle Eastern historiography is "restricted: political, linguistic ... social boundaries are crossed, but only by the elite."[80] Existing cosmopolitanism in the region "is all about wealth and secularism; the poor and the religious, whatever their qualifications of geographical mobility or polyglossia, need not apply."[81]

In the Canal Zone, this applied to a great extent. Highly segregated neighborhoods, hierarchical classification of workers, glaring modernity, exclusive schools, clubs, and leisure time culture were evident in everyday life. "Europeanness," to use Ann Stoler's term, was produced, reproduced, and guarded in everyday life.[82] The communities that lived there could not even be defined by the basic connectivity that characterized other Mediterranean port cities. Rather than connectivity, "apartheid" is the appropriate term. It was a cosmopolitanism in which Arabic-speaking Egyptians and Europeans were encountered not as equals or as comrades but, instead, as servants and owners. This sense of Europeanness, or whiteness as commonly theorized, was used to segregate the inhabitants of these cities. Native workers, especially the non-enrolled who constituted the majority of workers, were living under apartheid every day. It was apartheid defined by racial, cultural-religious differences, and economic disparity. Such a disparity would make these cities easy fodder for nationalism and then Islamism, rather than embracing "cosmopolitan" ideals.

Nancy Reynolds[83] argues in her seminal essay about working-class cosmopolitanism in Egypt during the interwar time that common Mediterranean culture, as well as cultural competencies, such as speaking a foreign language,

---

78. Sami Zubaida, "Middle Eastern Experiences of Cosmopolitanism" Essay, in *Conceiving Cosmopolitanism: Theory, Context, and Practice*, ed. Cohen, Robin and Steven Vertovec (Oxford: Oxford Univ. Press, 2003), 149.

79. Ibid.

80. Will Hanley, "Grieving Cosmopolitanism in Middle East Studies," *History Compass* 6, no. 5 (2008): 13. https://doi.org/10.1111/j.1478-0542.2008.00545.

81. Ibid.

82. Frederick Cooper and Ann Laura Stoler, *Tensions of Empire: Colonial Cultures in a Bourgeois World* (Berkeley: University of California Press, 1997).

83. Reynolds, "Entangled Communities," 113–39.

helped form lower-class cosmopolitanism among service workers in Cairo in the interwar period. Cultural competencies included foreign languages, cultural capital such as knowledge about fashion and modern technologies such as the camera, and leisure culture that included alcohol consumption and mixed-gender socialization. This cultural capital became a claim-staking device to cross class boundaries rather than an exclusionary mechanism. It facilitated forming communities from various national, linguistic, and religious backgrounds. However, foreigners in such communities retained their privileges through legal protection. Reynolds's main research focuses as well on a case study of the city of Cairo which, she argues, shows a less romanticized view of cosmopolitanism than Alexandria.[84]

In the Canal Zone, this image of lower-class cosmopolitanism might have existed but only for a tiny minority. Manual workers such as Company native workers had no use for this kind of cultural competency, and it was not available to them. With rural backgrounds, conservative religious beliefs, economic disparities, and urban exclusivity, it was almost impossible for native workers to attain the education or lifestyle required for such lower-class cosmopolitanism. Literacy rates were low, especially among workers who mainly depended on manual labor for a living. Neither alcohol nor mixed-gender socialization would have ever been acceptable in the native quarter, at least not openly. Even shared social events between Egyptian workers and their European counterparts were rare. Finally, sharing homes or neighborhoods was difficult, even in the case of enrolled workers as the Company always had two separate categories of accommodation: one for Europeans and another for natives. Given that most native workers were non-enrolled, the Company did not provide them with any accommodation, so they remained concentrated in the native quarter. The only shared space that witnessed parity between the Arabs and European workers were the cemeteries, achieving what Beli calls "Cosmo- Necropolitanism."[85]

Conclusion

The strike that happened in 1919 in the Canal Zone sheds light on the intersection of the local and international milieu that Suez Canal workers inhabited. Transnational solidarity shared between native workers and their fellow European co-workers during the strike demonstrates that such moments are more than merely "nationalism" reaching its crescendo in 1919. Workplace relations and dynamics are crucial to understand political subjectivity and refute the overstated and

---

84. Ibid., 34.

85. Mériam N. Belli, "United They Lay: Cemeteries and Community in the. Isthmus Cities of Late 19th-Early 20th Century Egypt" Essay, in *L'Isthme Et L'Égypte Au Temps De La Compagnie Universelle Du Canal Maritime De Suez (1858–1956)* (Le Caire: Institut français d'archéologie orientale, 2016), 195.

superficial arguments that label nuanced living experiences as mere nationalism. The solidarity among Italians, Greeks, French, Maltese, and Egyptians in the Canal Zone contributed to upholding the agency of these workers in front of the fortress of French capitalism and British colonialism. The 1919 Revolution in general and this strike, in particular, were major inflection points in labor history in Egypt.

However, reducing the workers' experience to strike moments conceals more than it reveals. Understanding the workers' larger reality outside the workplace was vital to understand the profound impact the 1919 Revolution had on them. These strikes did not take place in a vacuum; on the contrary, the spatial and urban environment had a great impact on the workers' experiences. The unique nature of the cities as company towns founded on urban apartheid to produce and guard racial division had a decisive impact not only on the Egyptian workers' experiences in the Canal but also across Egypt and the region.

Since the 1990s, the cultural turn in the discipline of history and the "triumph" of postmodernism in academic circles directly affected the centrality of class as a historical category. The 1990s witnessed heated debates between postmodernists and Marxists about the validity of class as a category and collective to be analyzed. However, recent literature argues for fewer polemics and more conciliation between social and cultural history agendas.[86] This conciliation took a decade to affect the agendas of Middle Eastern studies. A review by Beinin of labor historiography in the Middle East reveals the potential for a cultural anthropological lens to examine the labor experience without giving up class-based analysis.[87] This research effort is inspired by these new trends in arguing for the continued relevance and pertinence of class struggle to achieve a nuanced understanding of labor history.

Ultimately, understanding the intimate world of labor and workers' daily lives beyond activism provides us with an enhanced understanding of the role of these colonial enclaves in sowing the seeds of militant nationalism. In the years following the strike, nationalism strengthened its already strong presence in these cities. The city of Ismailia became a symbol of nationalist sacrifice after the police battle on January 25, 1952, followed by "Black Saturday" or "The Cairo Fire" the following day. The two successive events are widely believed to be the last straw before the monarchy's collapse in the coup d'état of July 1952. Four years later, Port Said became a symbol of nationalism and a third-world story of triumph after successfully resisting the Tripartite Aggression.

After many decades of the Canal workers' strike, the radical shift from seemingly "encompassing" identities like anarchism, Communism, and Cosmopolitanism to Nationalism can always be traced back to the journey of Arabi and his comrades on the bank of the Canal.

---

86. Geoff Eley and Keith Nield, "Farewell to the Working Class?" *International Labor and Working-Class History* 57 (2000): 1–30. https://doi.org/10.1017/s0147547900002660.

87. Joel Beinin, "Essential Readings on Labor in the Middle East," Tadween Publishing, https://tadweenpublishing.com/blogs/news/essential-readings-on-labor-in-the-middle-east (accessed June 29, 2021).

Chapter 3

MUSLIM AND CHRISTIAN EGYPTIAN IDENTITIES AND THE NARRATIVE OF THE 1919 REVOLUTION

Mark Bebawi

> But still we are victims of word games, semantics is always a bitch
> Places once called under-developed and backwards are now called mineral rich
> And still it seems the game goes on with unity always just out of reach.
> Libya and Egypt used to be in Africa, but they've been moved to the Middle East.
>
> Gil Scott-Heron, Black History

Introduction

Within four years of the 1919 Revolution, Egypt gained formal recognition of its sovereignty, enshrined a new constitution, and formed its first elected government. From this perspective, the 1919 Revolution was unquestionably a pivotal episode in modern Egyptian history and is often pointed to as a "moment of unity." The narrative is that "the subsequent history of Christian–Muslim relations has had its ups and downs."[1] Another perspective is that Egyptian independence remained nominal until at least 1952, and I argue here that Egyptian Christian-Muslim relations in the years preceding 1919 were turbulent, and that the 1919 Revolution was an episode whose contingent precursors reveal that Egyptian society was less cohesive than the popular images of 1919 would imply. This chapter explores tensions between identity, ethnicity, and religion within Egyptian nationalism with a focus on divergent accounts of Coptic-Muslim relations between 1910 and 1919. My aim is to contextualize the 1919 Revolution by addressing the historiography of Egyptian nationalism's interaction with religious identity, specifically the

---

1. Juan Cole, "Christians, Muslims 'One Hand' in Egypt's Youth Revolution," *Informed Comment*, July 2, 2011. Available online at www.juancole.com/2011/02/christians-muslims-one-hand-in-egypts-youth-revolution.html.

ways scholars have dealt with Egypt's Copts.[2] I contend that opposing binaries have been constructed around Egypt's Copts within historiographies of Egyptian national identity. These binaries buttressed a narrative of Egyptian national unity within which competing discourses of Coptic identity were either subsumed or rejected. Fortunately, a new generation of historians is thwarting previously simplistic notions of Coptic identity to address the role and location of Egypt's Coptic Christians within Egyptian identity. These new historians are complicating what I argue is a false choice between a trope of national unity offered by some and a persecuted minority discourse offered by others.[3] The binary opposition between these narratives oversimplifies tensions between Egyptian and Coptic identities that have been competing for authenticity.

Complicating the Hyphenated Identity of Egypt's Internal "Other"

As Islamic Studies Professor Nelly Van Doorn-Harder points out, being an Arabic-speaking "Christian other" has often meant that Copts have been either ignored, or stereotyped, as objects of study.[4] In addition, there are ongoing politically charged considerations at play. The most significant of these, as noted by historian Paul Sedra, is that both the Egyptian state and the Coptic Church have actively sought to avoid discussion of Coptic identity because of the "political taboo of sectarianism."[5] Because of this taboo, narratives of Copts presented by Egyptians of different backgrounds, even when written decades apart, have tended to reinforce the notion of Egyptian national unity being vulnerable to the diluting

---

2. "Copt" and its adjective "Coptic" are derived from Greek *Aigyptos/Aigyptios* (Egypt/Egyptian). In Arabic, this became *Qibt* (pl. *Aqbat*); and later "Copt" in English. All Egyptians are therefore Copts in the original sense of the word. When the majority of Egyptians became Muslim, Egyptian Christians became "Copts." Today, there are other Christian denominations in Egypt and "Copt" no longer applies as a label for all of Egypt's Christians.

3. Examples of the persecuted minority discourse include John Eibner, *Christians in Egypt: Church under Siege* (Washington: Institute for Religious Minorities in the Islamic World, 1993); Shawky Karas, *The Copts since the Arab Invasion: Strangers in Their Land* (Jersey City: American, Canadian, and Australian Coptic Associations, 1986); Edward Wakin, *A Lonely Minority: The Modern Story of Egypt's Copts* (New York: William Morrow & Co., 1963). Examples of the trope of national unity include Milad Hanna, *Na'am Aqbat, lakin Misriyyun* (Yes Copts, but Egyptians) (Cairo: Maktabat Madbuli, 1980); Milad Hanna, *The Seven Pillars of Egyptian Identity* (Cairo: General Egyptian Book Organization, 1994); Tariq al-Bishri, *Al-Muslimun wa-al-Aqbat fi itar al-jama'a al-wataniyya* (Muslims and Copts in the Framework of a National Society) (Cairo: al-Hay'a al-Misriyya li-al-Kitab, 1980).

4. Nelly Van Doorn-Harder, "Finding a Platform: Studying the Copts in the 19th and 20th Centuries," *International Journal of Middle East Studies* 42 (2010): 479–82, 479.

5. Paul Sedra, "Writing the History of the Modern Copts: From Victims and Symbols to Actors," *History Compass* 7, no. 3 (2009): 1049–63, 1049.

effects of communal identities. We can take journalist and political commentator Mohammed Hasanayn Haykal and historian Mirrit Boutros-Ghali as examples of this. Haykal, a well-known Muslim Egyptian, was the editor-in-chief of *Al-Ahram* newspaper for almost two decades. Mirrit Boutros-Ghali (1908–92) was a Copt and an Ethiopianist historian from a prominent family. Haykal argued that the Copts are not a minority in the ethnic, sectarian, or even ethno-religious sense.[6] He warned that foreign powers could potentially seize upon the "illusion" of a Coptic minority to undermine Egypt's sovereignty and even her armed forces. Boutros-Ghali, writing almost twenty years earlier, said that Egyptian national consciousness had spent decades searching for "the historical and psychological personality that distinguishes" Egyptians from other nations and that no characteristic, whether pharaonic, Arab, Christian, or Muslim, should be ignored.[7] Though nearly two decades separate their work, Haykal and Boutros-Ghali were both bolstering national unity, albeit through very different means—one by trying to paper over differences and the other through the inclusivity of several characteristics into a single national identity. In both cases, national unity excluded religion as an analytical category.

Religion, as an analytical category, is problematic for historians. William Hart contends that Edward Said feared the "exclusionary power of culture" which "constitutes a church-state in which the 'others of culture' (colonized people, the poor and delinquent) are grouped under the rubric of anarchy."[8] Indeed, Said warned that "falsely unifying rubrics" like "the West" and "Islam" create collective identities that belie real diversity and reduce peoples' abilities to mobilize. As a result, in Said's analysis, Orientalism imbued the Orient with a "discursive identity that made it unequal with the West."[9] Said also eschewed imperialism's reductive primordial classifications and their resultant nativism, since accepting nativism was "to accept the consequence of imperialism, the racial, religious, and political divisions imposed by imperialism itself."[10] So powerful was Said's argument against essentializing metaphysical identities that had "the power to turn human beings against each other" that, according to Paul Sedra, it very nearly "vitiated faith as an analytical concept," thus leading many scholars of the Middle East to avoid

---

6. Mohammed Hasanayn Haykal, "Egypt's Copts Are No Minority but Part and Parcel of Egypt's Human and Cultural Fabric," *Al-Ahram Weekly*, April 22, 1994. Haykal wrote his article in the context of a conference on "Minorities in the Middle East." For a discussion of Haykal's article, and the responses to it, see Karim El-Gawhary, "Copts in the Egyptian Fabric," *Middle East Report* 200 (Fall 1996), http://www.merip.org/mer/mer200/copts-egyptian-fabric.

7. Mirrit Boutros-Ghali, "The Egyptian National Consciousness," *Middle East Journal* 32 (1978): 59–77, 59, 60.

8. William Hart, *Edward Said and the Religious Effect of Culture* (Cambridge: Cambridge University Press, 2000), 28.

9. Edward Said, *Orientalism* (New York: Vintage Books, 1979), xxviii, 156.

10. Edward Said, *Culture and Imperialism* (New York: Vintage, 1994), 228.

foregrounding religious identity in historiographical analyses.[11] Not all scholars have sidestepped religious identity's importance, however. Bruce Masters, for example, wrote that while European diplomats "privileged religious difference," and therefore exaggerated its importance, religious identity was "both primary and primordial" within the Ottoman world.[12]

Copts' religion can be used to define them as members of a specific community while excluding them, to some extent at least, as an indigenous minority separate from the Muslim majority. Both the definition and the exclusion can be externally imposed and internally sanctioned, that is by non-Copts and Copts alike. The resulting tension between inclusion as Egyptians and exclusion as non-Muslims is part of the modern Coptic experience of Egyptianness. It is therefore important to acknowledge that nationalism and identity are individually complex phenomena, even more so when one is considering the place of one within the other.

A nation, in this case Egypt, can be defined as an expression of nationalism(s), and the result of shared language, ancestry, culture (even if it is to some extent constructed), and religion. Several somewhat contradictory theories have been put forward to explain nationalism. There is a European historical connection with theories of nationalism and secularism which I discuss later in this chapter. For John Armstrong, nations existed before nationalism and were born out of the impacts of the relationships between centralization, language, and polity on ethnicity.[13] There is significant overlap between Armstrong's work and that of Anthony Smith, who contends that nations have origins derived from an "ethnie," that is based on a shared culture made up of memories, values, and myths that predate the modern nation-state.[14] Benedict Anderson complicates the "ethnie" and ethnicity arguments about nations with his definition of the nation as an "imagined political community" that is objectively modern "to the historians' eye," while simultaneously dating back to time immemorial "in the eyes of nationalists."[15] Anderson's definition has gained favor over the years, in the academic world at least, and the notion of the constructedness of culture and nation is now familiar to many.

While Copts adopted Arabic in the tenth century, and therefore share Arabic with their Muslim co-nationals, Copts clearly do not possess an Islamic religious identity. However, the influence of Islam on Egyptian culture, and therefore

---

11. Ibid., 229; Sedra, "Writing the History of the Modern Copts," 1052.

12. Bruce Masters, *Christians and Jews in the Ottoman Arab World: The Roots of Sectarianism* (Cambridge: Cambridge University Press, 2001), 132.

13. See John Armstrong, *Nations before Nationalism* (Chapel Hill: University of North Carolina Press, 1982).

14. See Anthony Smith, *The Ethnic Origins of Nations* (Oxford: Blackwell, 1998).

15. See Benedict Anderson, *Imagined Communities: Reflections on the Origin and Spread of Nationalism*, rev. ed. (London and New York: Verso, 1991), 5–7.

on Egyptian identity, can also be seen as part of Copts' identity as Egyptians.[16] Given these complexities, defining Coptic identity within the Egyptian nation is a challenging task. In part, the challenge is due to the divergent meanings implied, but rarely explicated, within the word "identity" itself. While the meaning of identity may appear intuitively obvious, sociologist Rogers Brubaker and historian Frederick Cooper have explained that scholars use "identity" in many different ways to discuss race, nation, ethnicity, citizenship, class, tradition, and more.[17] In the Coptic context, identity has been variously seen as the basis for a multitude of phenomena containing an implied essential "Copticness." These phenomena include, at a minimum, a collective political position, an understanding of self in relation to Muslims and non-Coptic Christians, or even responses to socioeconomic and political restrictions defined by the restricted party's "Copticness." All these meanings imply a putative collectivity that may not exist, and this should be kept in mind when examining historians' accounts of the place of Copts in the history of Egyptian nationalism. It is also important to recognize that Coptic identity formation predates the nation-state and our preoccupation with nationalisms and identities informed by the nation-state framework. Significant scholarly works by Stephen Davis, Febe Armanious, and Paul Sedra expound many of the intricacies of Coptic self-definitions. These definitions were themselves a mixture of evolving religious traditions and popular practices, as well as responses to pressures from missionaries and the realities of the Copts' minority status under Ottoman rule.[18]

Copts' interactions with Muslims and other Christians clarified markers of Copticness in relation to Muslims and non-Copts. However, Coptic religious ideas and practices, such as the liturgy or veneration of saints, evolved over time and in response to the combination of Christological developments and local conditions. These developments underscored Coptic religious identity and communal awareness. Coptic church music, for example, is distinct from "the surrounding Islamic musical forms." Some of the markers of Coptic identity were influenced by conditions under Islamic rule. Coptic literature in Arabic adopted Islamic vocabulary to explain Coptic doctrine to Muslims while also offering the hope of salvation to Copts who, by the tenth century, had become a minority in a majority Muslim domain. This apologetic discourse sought to "assimilate itself

16. Exemplified by the secular socialist Copt, Salama Musa, who noted that Islam is the religion of Egypt while Egypt is not Eastern or even Arab. For a detailed discussion of Musa, see Yasir Suleiman, *The Arabic Language and National Identity: A Study in Ideology* (Edinburgh: Edinburgh University Press, 2003), 180–90.

17. See Rogers Brubaker and Frederick Cooper, "Beyond 'Identity,'" *Theory and Society* 29, no. 1 (2000): 1–47, https://www.jstor.org/stable/3108478.

18. Stephen Davis, *Coptic Christology in Practice: Incarnation and Divine Participation in Late Antique and Medieval Egypt* (Oxford: Oxford University Press, 2008); Febe Armanios, *Coptic Christianity in Ottoman Egypt* (Oxford: Oxford University Press, 2011); Paul Sedra, *From Mission to Modernity: Evangelicals, Reformers and Education in Nineteenth-Century Egypt* (London: I.B. Tauris, 2011).

to the language of the dominant culture" while distancing itself from "unpalatable viewpoints within that culture (and thereby to define the boundaries of its own communal identity)."[19]

Following Davis, and agreeing with him on the importance of the "traditions of sainthood, martyrdom, and monasticism," Armanious focuses on "Coptic spirituality and religious practice in relation to processes of identity-formation," but in the later period of Ottoman Egypt. Armanious argues that a "religious worldview grounded in martyrdom" was central to efforts to "protect communal boundaries and maintain a coherent identity." She explores the Coptic response to "heretical" Catholic teachings in the eighteenth century when "an aggressive missionary movement" established a Catholic presence in Egypt. This led to Copts developing "overtly sectarian language and fostered the characterization of an authentic Coptic identity opposed to the perceived depravity of other communities." Armanious also argues that Coptic clerical leaders positioned themselves as defenders of the faith of a marginalized community living within a dominant Muslim culture. In so doing, these leaders fought to protect a coherent identity that was "anti-Chalcedonian, Orthodox, and Coptic," specifically in contrast to imported Catholicism. This was a top-down definition of Coptic "religious and cultural uniqueness" that tied faith and race together by accusing Coptic converts to Catholicism of acquiring a foreign identity and abandoning their Copticness. Using diverse primary sources, including sermons and documents from Coptic monasteries and the Patriarchate library, Armanious pushes back against the secondary importance assigned to religious identity by scholars such as Bernard Heyberger and Molly Greene, who have argued for a "shared mentality" between Christians and their (Muslim) compatriots. That Christian-Muslim relations in the Ottoman context were less violent than contemporaneous Protestant-Catholics relations in Europe does not mean that they were uncomplicated. Armanious therefore challenges the trope of a peaceable *dhimmi*-Muslim binary with a history of clergy who "blamed Catholics and occasionally Muslims for inhibiting their community's potential."[20] Also exploring some aspects of Coptic identity formation is Sedra's *From Mission to Modernity*. Sedra looks at the impact and reception of English Church Missionary Society (CMS) projects in nineteenth-century Egypt. Foucauldian in his framework, Sedra looks not only at how structures of disciplinary power introduced by the CMS were exporting European culture and trying to transform Egyptian culture but also at how those efforts were received, transformed, and resisted.[21] This revisiting of history, with the benefit of new source materials, is a welcome intervention characteristic of a new kind of scholarship, as seen in Marwa Elshakry's exploration of Darwinian thought in the Eastern Mediterranean and Heather Sharkey's examination of American

19. Davis, *Coptic Christology in Practice*, 188, 227–51, 211–12.
20. Armanios, *Coptic Christianity in Ottoman Egypt*, 6, 10, 42, 13, 117–18, 127, 150.
21. Sedra, *From Mission to Modernity*.

missionaries in Egypt.[22] Sedra notes the impact of evangelical efforts to "cultivate the values of industry, discipline and order within the Coptic community" on the Copts' sense of their own "communal identity," and that Pope Cyril VI (r. 1959–71) did not resist evangelical efforts because he hoped to use them to create a "modern Coptic political identity." Once again, Copts are deconstructed into component grouping and subgroupings, as Sedra carefully points to the fractures within Coptic society influenced by class and education. He asks, for example, who it is among the Copts who "merited the 'modern sons of the Pharaohs' label," and shows that there were cleavages between peasants and elites. While Sedra complicates the notion of a singular Coptic identity, he also shows that there was some inter-religious commonality shared by Muslim and Coptic students, who were able to find "creative and complex" ways to resist government efforts to force them into free labor for the state. These students eventually became religious leaders who posited that religious reformation would benefit Egyptian society as a whole and help it fight imperialism, "whether of the Ottoman or British variety."[23] These precursor multifaceted Coptic identities confound the trope of Egyptian unity espoused by Haykal and complicate Boutros-Ghali's notions of multifaceted national identity that downplayed the complexities of early Coptic-Muslim relations. As I shall show, it is possible to deconstruct the trope of a monolithic Egyptian nationalism without resort to the metaphysical essentializing identities Said warned against, while also making the case that Coptic identity was not as simple as implied by the 1919 notion of national unity.

Constructing Egyptian Unity

The pharaonic, Arab, Christian, and Muslim characteristics Mirrit Boutros-Ghali sought to unify into a single Egyptian consciousness were expanded into *The Seven Pillars of Egyptian Identity* by secular Coptic writer Milad Hanna.[24] Hanna's pillars were a civilizational mixture of pharaonic, Greco-Roman, Coptic, and Islamic characteristics residing in a geographical container that was simultaneously part of the Arab World, the Mediterranean and Africa.[25] Hanna's multilayered formulation of Egyptian identity was part of a national project that "mainly seeks to enhance the feelings of national unity in Egypt binding Moslems and Copts together."[26] Hanna, echoing Boutros-Ghali's and Haykal's hopes for national unity, wrote that

---

22. Marwa Elshakry, *Reading Darwin in Arabic 1860–1950* (Chicago: University of Chicago Press, 2013); Heather Sharkey, *American Evangelicals in Egypt: Missionary Encounters in an Age of Empire* (Princeton: Princeton University Press, 2008).

23. Sedra, *From Mission to Modernity*, 63, 106,152–3, 173.

24. Hanna, *The Seven Pillars of Egyptian Identity*, 13.

25. Nadje Al-Ali, *Secularism, Gender and the State in the Middle East: The Egyptian Women's Movement* (Cambridge: Cambridge University Press, 2004), 43.

26. Hanna, *The Seven Pillars of Egyptian Identity*, 10, 188.

it was threatened by religious revivalism: "The more intense Islamic and Coptic religious activities in Egypt become, the stronger the possibility of conflict and strife."[27] Secular Egyptians, be they Copts like Hanna or Muslims like Haykal, are representative of a dominant narrative of Egyptian national unity. These thinkers are not secular in the sense that they propose a secular society; rather they support secular government as a means of sustaining national unity.

One of the most prominent Egyptians writing about national politics, supporting secular governance and not ignoring the Copts, is Tariq al-Bishri. A jurist and judge in the State Council (*Majlis al-Dawla*) under the Nasser regime, Bishri is a Muslim author of multiple books, including the lengthy *Muslims and Copts in the Framework of a National Society*.[28] Meir Hatina argues that Bishri, along with "other liberal writers of a more socialistic persuasion, such as Khalid Muhammad Khalid, Hasan Hanafi, 'Adil Husayn . . . actually reversed their anti-religious position and immersed themselves in Muslim historic research in quest of an authentic heritage."[29] Like many Arab intellectuals, Bishri was provoked into critical reflection by the Arab defeat of 1967, which he felt indicated the need for a civilizational and religious component in Arab efforts to modernize.[30] Within a dominant narrative of an idealized Egyptian national unity, Bishri calls on Egypt's Muslim scholars to return to the Islamic heritage (*turath*) to find a way to grant full and equal rights to Copts so as to overcome any religious obstacles to national unity.[31] Bishri has even gone so far as to say that, while a Coptic head of the Egyptian state is not demographically feasible because of the small number of Copts, national unity is undermined by denying Copts this right, even though they would never be able to exercise it.[32] Like many Egyptians, Bishri sees the 1919 Revolution as the strongest expression of Egyptian national unity, a time when Muslims and Copts were unified by a shared dislike of British colonialism and a

---

27. Ibid., 188.

28. See footnote 3. The State Council (*Majlis al-Dawla*) is a judicial body that gives legal advice to the government, drafts legislation, and exercises jurisdiction over administrative cases. Bishri has modified his views over the years—his earlier views from the 1960s and 1970s are often described as leftist and secular whereas his later work has taken on an Islamic revivalist tone in which he seeks to reconcile Islamic and nationalist notions.

29. See Meir Hatina, *Identity Politics in the Middle East: Liberal Thought and Islamic Challenge in Egypt* (London: I.B. Tauris, 2007), 175. Bishri's earliest works were articles first published in the leftist magazine *Al-Tali'a* (The Vanguard).

30. See Tariq al-Bishri, "Bayn al-'uruba wa-al-islam: Al-mawqif min ghayr al-muslimin wa-min al-'ilmaniyya" (Between Arabism and Islam: The Position regarding Non-Muslims and Secularism), in *Al-Sha'b* (a four-part series of articles published in May and June, 1986). He later expanded the topic into a book, *Bayn al-islam wa-al-'uruba* (Cairo: Dar al-Shuruq, 1997).

31. Bishri, *Al-Muslimun wa-al-Aqbat fi itar al-jama'a al-wataniyya*, 702.

32. See Michaelle Browers, *Political Ideology in the Arab World: Accommodation and Transformation* (Cambridge: Cambridge University Press, 2009), 67.

shared experience of anti-British cooperation.³³ Coptic writer William Sulayman (1924–99) locates national unity in an earlier Muslim-Christian opposition to the crusades. These, argues Sulayman, were an un-Christian comingling of politics with religion and were opposed by Copts and Muslims aligned against foreign invaders. Sulayman was a former vice deputy of the Egyptian State Council, a position also held by Bishri. Sulayman and Bishri co-authored a book in 1982 with Mustafa al-Fiqi called *One People and One Nation*, in which they argued for the authentic patriotism of Egypt's Coptic community.³⁴ This is not to imply that Bishri has ignored complications and tensions in Coptic-Muslim relations. In fact, he describes the period of 1908–11 as the high point in the schism (*shuqaq*) between the "sons of Egypt."³⁵ Even though he juxtaposes sectarian schism with national unity, Bishri still oversimplifies both the schism and the unity, as a deeper examination of 1911 and 1919 reveals.

Diverging Accounts of the 1911 Congresses and the 1919 Revolution

Other historians agree with Bishri that tensions increased between Copts and Muslims between 1908 and 1911 but they differ in their emphasis on the causes of the tension. For example, Umar Ryad points to these years as "one of the most critical moments in Muslim–Christian relations,"³⁶ while Vivian Ibrahim refers to the same period as the "Coptic Question of 1908 to 1911."³⁷ According to both Bishri and Ibrahim, the British were following a classic divide-and-rule policy. Ibrahim supports her assertion with a report by Eldon Gorst (Consul-General in Egypt between 1907 and 1911) declaring that "Copts occupied approximately 45 per cent of the posts and received 40 per cent of the salaries, while Muslims occupied 44 per cent of posts and received only 6 per cent of salaries."³⁸ The report inflamed Muslim opinion because Copts were about "7 per cent of the population in 1907 but occupied nearly half of all the positions in the bureaucracy held by Egyptians."³⁹ Bishri, citing correspondences from Gorst and Edward Grey (British Foreign Minister), lays the blame for Coptic-Muslim tensions at the feet of the

---

33. Bishri, *Al-Muslimun wa-al-Aqbat fi itar al-jama'a al-wataniyya*, 394–5.

34. William Sulayman, Tariq al-Bishri and Mustafa al-Fiqi, *Al-Sha'b al-wahid wa-al-watan al-wahid: Dirasat fi usul al-wahda al-wataniyya* (One People and One Nation: Studies of the Sources of National Unity) (Cairo: Al-Ahram Center for Political and Strategic Studies, 1982).

35. Bishri, *Al-Muslimun wa-al-Aqbat fi itar al-jama'a al-wataniyya*, 63.

36. Umar Ryad, *Islamic Reformism and Christianity: A Critical Reading of the Works of Muḥammad Rashīd Riḍā and His Associates (1898–1935)* (Leiden: Brill, 2009), 103.

37. Vivian Ibrahim, *The Copts of Egypt: Challenges of Modernisation and Identity* (London: I.B. Tauris, 2010).

38. Ibid., 9

39. Ibid., 45.

British and some Copts, most notably Akhnukh Fanus and Kyriakos Mikhail. Bishri argues that Fanus, a wealthy landlord and member of the Legislative Assembly, and Mikhail, a former journalist for the Coptic newspaper *Al-Watan*, who had moved to London, worked together to publicize a proposed Coptic Congress and "Coptic demands" in 1910. In 1911, Mikhail published a book in English about British rule in which he described the Congress and its demands,[40] at which time "the 'Coptic Question' became a hot topic in the British press."[41] Mikhail's book, often through the words of other authors, focused on the idea of British ill-treatment of the Copts. The book's introduction, written by British Anglican A. J. Butler, shares Bishri's discourse of blaming the British for sectarian tensions: "It is sad and humiliating to reflect that the friendly union of Copts and Muslims was practically an achieved result before the British occupation of Egypt, and that it has been destroyed by the policy of the British Government."[42]

Bishri is not alone in pointing blame at Mikhail. Noted historian C. A. Bayly called Mikhail "the major Coptic proponent of racial difference" and part of "constructing the Copts as a separate race" of genuine Egyptians because "they alone trace an unadulterated descent from the race to whom the civilization and culture of the ancients were so largely due."[43] Bayly's evidence for this claim is a "proclamation" he attributes to Mikhail: "Copts have kept their blood pure from admixture with semi-barbarous Arabs and savage Kurds, or other foreign elements whom the licentiousness of Mohammedan family life has introduced into the country."[44] Unfortunately, this quotation, while taken from Mikhail's aforementioned book, is actually from the preface penned by Reverend Archibald Henry Sayce, a British linguist and professor of Assyriology at the University of Oxford from 1891 to 1919. Another quotation Bayly erroneously attributes to Mikhail is: "Copts should take again the high place in the civilized world [occupied by] their pharaonic ancestors."[45] This quotation is from the same preface. The impact of these words that Bayly misattributes to Mikhail distorts the historical figure of Mikhail because a historian of Bayly's prominence tends to be cited in his own right. Thus, we see in Saba Mahmood's *Religious Difference in a Secular Age*, Mikhail's reputation further tarnished as a proponent of Coptic "racial purity" preserved because of

---

40. Bishri, *Al-Muslimun wa-al-Aqbat fi itar al-jama'a al-wataniyya*, 70.

41. Kyriakos Mikhail, *Copts and Moslems under British Control: A Collection of Facts and a Résumé of Authoritative Opinions on the Coptic Question* (London: Smith, Elder, 1911).

42. Ibid., xiv.

43. C. A. Bayly, "Representing Copts and Muhammadans: Empire, Nation, and Community in Egypt and India, 1880–1914," in *Modernity and Culture: From the Mediterranean to the Indian Ocean*, ed. Leila Tarazi Fawaz and C.A. Bayly (New York: Columbia University Press, 2002), 158–203, 173.

44. Ibid.

45. Ibid., 174.

a Coptic "commitment to endogamy."[46] By comparison, Mikhail's own words are less incendiary and do not reflect the racial purity narrative attributed to him by Bayly, and now Mahmood. Mikhail's chapter on "Coptic Grievances and the Coptic Congress," for example, claims that the Copts were "finding it impossible to obtain equality of treatment with their Moslem compatriots."[47] Mikhail describes the Congress as follows:

> The announced aim of the Congress was entirely pacific, it was in no sense to be a Coptic agitation against either the Moslems or the Government of Egypt. That the Coptic delegates were genuine in their desire to preserve order is proved by the fact that there was no disturbance of any kind during the whole sitting of the Congress, and by the moderate tone adopted by the speakers. This orderly attitude was noticed by the local European papers in Egypt, and also by the correspondents of the leading English Press.[48]

To show that Akhnukh Fanus and Kyriakos Mikhail were outliers, Bishri provides numerous examples of Copts and Muslims calling for national unity, especially in reference to the assassination of Coptic prime minister Boutros-Ghali in 1910.[49] Vivian Ibrahim, on the other hand, argues that national unity was less ubiquitous than Bishri claims, and that Muslims did not always take a charitable view of Coptic motivations. She cites the example of Muslim journalist Ali Fahmi Muhammad, who argued in 1911 that Copts gave "nominal support to the nationalist movement" not out of a real sense of national unity with Muslims but out of fear that Muslims would crush them if they did not.[50] Like Bishri, Ibrahim also shows that Coptic positions were not monolithic, but she offers additional evidence beyond Fanus and Mikhail. For example *Al-Watan* newspaper's editorial position was supportive of the British occupation in 1882, while "between 1900 and 1914 [the paper] was a staunch defender of Coptic interests while being highly critical of the nationalists."[51] *Al-Watan* also openly called for Coptic supremacy and reversed positions on the British:

> The Copts are the true Egyptians, they are the real masters of the country. All those who have set foot on Egyptian soil, be they Arabs, Turks, French, or British are nothing but invaders. The originators of this nation are Copts. [. . .] Whoever calls this country an Islamic country means to disregard the rights of the Copts

---

46. Saba Mahmood, *Religious Difference in a Secular Age: A Minority Report* (Princeton: Princeton University Press, 2015), 72.
47. Mikhail, *Copts and Moslems under British Control*, 22.
48. Ibid., 22–3.
49. Bishri, *Al-Muslimun wa-al-Aqbat fi itar al-jama'a al-wataniyya*, 69–72.
50. Ibrahim, *Copts of Egypt*, 66.
51. Ibid, 50.

and to abuse them in their own fatherland. Not one of them would accept such a thing.⁵²

At the opposite end of the political spectrum was Coptic support of, and membership in, nationalist political organizations. One of these was Mustafa Kamil's National Party (*al-Hizb al-Watani*), which used Egypt's pre-Islamic pharaonic past to appeal to Copts.⁵³ Ibrahim points out that some Copts were troubled by Mustafa Kamil's marrying of nationalism and Islam. Nevertheless, *al-Hizb al-Watani* was supported by prominent Copts, at least until Kamil's death, when Coptic support for the party waned considerably. Another party was Hasan 'Abd al-Raziq's Nation's Party (*Hizb al-Umma*), which was regarded by Copts more favorably than any other party because of its "purely Egyptian character," which did not reference Islam.⁵⁴ Juxtaposing *Al-Watan* newspaper with these parties, both of which were led by Muslims, undermines the idea of a single Coptic position in the prelude to the 1919 Revolution.

On the assassination of the Coptic prime minister, Boutros-Ghali, Bishri, without offering evidence, asserts that Boutros-Ghali was against the idea of the Coptic Congress but that his assassination allowed the Congress to go ahead.⁵⁵ Bishri also downplays sectarian tensions as a motive for the assassination. Based on the evidence, this is convincing. Ghali was seen as an anglophile who worked closely with the British who, in turn, were following a classic "divide and rule" model that disproportionately favored Copts over Muslims. In this interpretation, Ghali, who was appointed prime minister in 1908, having already held two ministerial posts in 1893 and 1895 (Finance and Foreign Affairs), was murdered by a nationalist for purely political reasons.⁵⁶ Another view is that the assassin, Ibrahim Nasif al-Wardani was a Muslim Egyptian nationalist who targeted Ghali because of his Coptic identity.⁵⁷ Whatever Wardani's actual motivations were, sectarian tensions were high and formed the backdrop to the holding of two congresses in 1911. One was held by Copts in Asyut to "discuss their sectarian demands," while another "organized by Muslims and some Copts" in Cairo, attempted to find a solution to the violence. The British authorities responded by using the unrest as a pretext to "muzzle the press, ban political meetings, and liquidate the nationalist

---

52. *Al-Watan*, May 22, 1908.

53. Doris Behrens-Abouseif, "The Political Situation of the Copts, 1798–1923," in *Christians and Jews in the Ottoman Empire*, ed. Benjamin Braude and Bernard Lewis, Vol. 2 (New York: Homes & Meier, 1982), 185–205, 195.

54. Yunan Labib Rizq, "Nation's Party," in *The Coptic Encyclopedia*, ed. Aziz Atiya, Vol. 6 (New York: Macmillan, 1991), 1987.

55. Bishri, *Al-Muslimun wa-al-Aqbat fi itar al-jama'a al-wataniyya*, 79–80.

56. Noor-Aiman Khan, *Egyptian-Indian Nationalist Collaboration and the British Empire* (New York: Palgrave Macmillan, 2011), 42–50.

57. Panayiotis Vatikiotis, *The History of Modern Egypt: from Muhammad Ali to Mubarak*, 4th ed. (Baltimore: Johns Hopkins University Press, 1991), 208.

movement."⁵⁸ The idea that the demands of the Coptic Congress were sectarian deserves examination.

Bishri and Mikhail offer summaries of issues discussed at the Congress and the list of demands signed by attendees. These were that the government should: allow Coptic students and civil servants a holiday on Sundays; make ability the only criterion for civil service posts and remove restrictions banning or limiting the number of Coptic employees in certain government posts; set up a system of proportional representation in provincial councils to secure the rights of minorities; make village schools open to all Egyptians (Muslims, Copts, and Jews alike, without discrimination), or allow the 5 percent tax levied for educational funding to be used for private schools for Copts; ensure equal financial treatment by the treasury for Coptic and Muslim amenities.⁵⁹ While these demands reference Coptic and Muslim identity, they do not argue for one group's supremacy over the other. In addition, Bishri notes that the opening day of the Congress saw attendees show their "full commitment to national unity," through the raising of the Egyptian flag and the opening statement of Bishop Macarius of Asyut, wherein he called on attendees to preserve their great relations with their Egyptian brethren.⁶⁰ Was Bishri overstating his position when he described this period as the high point in the schism between the "sons of Egypt"? References to minority rights and the promotion of proportional representation have for decades been depicted as threats to national unity. Yet this is a national unity that historians like Vivian Ibrahim have shown was illusive and fragmented.

Further evidence of division also appeared within Coptic opinion, even within the church, before the idea of the Congress materialized into an event. Both Bishri and Mikhail mention that Pope Cyril VI opposed the Congress. Bishri notes that Cyril cautioned against "building up a huge gathering in Asyut, which could result in agitation and render them liable to criticism" and urged "extreme prudence, wisdom and circumspection."⁶¹ In response, Bishop Macarius of Asyut replied to the Pope's concerns with the assurance that the main objective of the Congress was "the forging of stronger ties among all Egyptians through the safeguarding of the legitimate rights of Copts."⁶² Mikhail points to the Pope's opposition to the Congress in more subtle terms. He quotes Cyril at length to argue that the Pope was not against the Congress but that his opposition was to the Congress being held in Asyut. Striking a conspiratorial tone of papal and government interference, with British acquiescence, Mikhail quotes an article from the *Egyptian Gazette* which included the following: "Of course the idea is that now that the Patriarch

---

58. Fuad Megally, "Abbas Hilmi II, Khedive," in *The Coptic Encyclopedia*, ed. Aziz Atiya, Vol. 6 (New York: Macmillan, 1991), 1693–4.

59. Bishri, *Al-Muslimun wa-al-Aqbat fi itar al-jama'a al-wataniyya*, 81–8; Mikhail, *Copts and Moslems under British Control*, 28–30.

60. Bishri, *Al-Muslimun wa-al-Aqbat fi itar al-jama'a al-wataniyya*, 82.

61. Ibid., 80.

62. Ibid., 81.

has banned the Congress, his attitude will impress the British Government with the idea that the organisers of the Congress are a seditious gang of discredited Copts, who are under the ban of their religious chief and may be looked upon as outlaws."⁶³

Mikhail further supports his contention of British and Egyptian government interference by referring to Eldon Gorst's assessment that "Coptic educational interests everywhere received due consideration from the Provincial Councils."⁶⁴ Several Copts responded to Gorst's assessment with telegrams to national newspapers where they noted that:

> Copts pay about 32 per cent of the taxes, but are compelled to fall back upon private education to satisfy their needs. The Copts have never asked to be considered as a separate community, but only claim equality of opportunity with their compatriots, and that religious belief should not be made a bar to advancement in the public services, a matter which leads to friction between the natives of the country.⁶⁵

It appears, based on the accounts of Bishri, Mikhail, and Ibrahim, that the British and the Egyptian government were in joint opposition to the Congress. Ibrahim offers the attitude of Lord Cromer, the British high commissioner, who regarded all Egyptians with general distain. Where Cromer saw differences between Muslims and Copts, it was in their relative utility to their "masters."⁶⁶

This can explain the British position, even if Ibrahim does not explicitly reference it in this way. British orientalist attitudes toward Egyptians were used to justify both the appointment to senior positions of Copts perceived as pliant, like Boutros-Ghali, and the dismissal of Coptic communal concerns. This orientalist position also facilitated Muslim suspicions of "Coptic collusion with British imperialism."⁶⁷ Bishri and Ibrahim document anti-Congress reactions in the Egyptian press, which accused the Copts of conspiring against Muslims, and engaging in a religious conspiracy and a plot against Egyptian unity.⁶⁸ Mikhail offers more nuance here by exploring the relationship between the press and the government. Whereas Bishri and Ibrahim cite the newspaper *Al-Ahali* and its critical editorial stance toward the Coptic Congress, Mikhail delves into the

---

63. Mikhail, *Copts and Moslems under British Control*, 25.
64. Ibid., 21.
65. Ibid., 22.
66. Cromer wrote: "The modern Copt has become from head to foot, in manners, language, and spirit, a Moslem, however unwilling he may be to recognise the fact." And "his system of accounts is archaic, at the same time it is better to be in a possession of a bad system of accounts than, like the Egyptian Moslem [sic], to have scarcely any system at all." Evelyn Baring Cromer, *Modern Egypt* (London: Macmillan, 1908), 210, 208.
67. Ibrahim, *Copts of Egypt*, 54.
68. Ibid., 57.

connection between that newspaper and the minister of the interior. He cites *The Times* newspaper's observation that *Al-Ahali* is "regarded as the organ of the Minister of the Interior" and quotes its March 19, 1911, piece at length.[69] It is worth reproducing here as a primary source of media coverage:

> The contemptuous and menacing manner in which several of the newspapers daily refer to the Copts and to the Coptic claims amply justifies the ironical references to the Press Law and to the terms of the warning issued to the Watan last December that have appeared in the European and Coptic newspapers. If the Coptic claims are exaggerated, as is the opinion of many persons who are neither Copts nor Mussulmans, the latter have obviously nothing to gain by indulging in a campaign of indiscriminate abuse, which can only produce a deplorable impression of their political capacity both in Egypt and abroad. Happily, there appears to be some reason to hope that the forthcoming Congress will be animated by a more conciliatory spirit and will approach the consideration of the Coptic claims in a calmer and more judicial frame of mind.[70]

Bishri, Mikhail, and Ibrahim all discuss the Egyptian Congress that was held in response to the Coptic Congress but again their emphasis diverges. Ibrahim calls it an "inter-confessional" conference characterized by "moderation and quiet enthusiasm, in direct contrast to the meeting held in Asyut."[71] This directly contradicts Mikhail's claims that there "was no disturbance of any kind during the whole sitting of the Congress" as was "noticed by the local European papers in Egypt, and also by the correspondents of the leading English Press." *The Coptic Encyclopedia* asserts that the Egyptian Congress was "organized by Muslims and some Copts" in Cairo, in an attempt to find a solution to the violence.[72] Bishri notes that, while the Egyptian Congress was indeed inter-confessional, those invited were Muslims, Jews, and, crucially, non-Coptic Christians.[73] Counter to Bishri and Ibrahim, Mikhail cites a newspaper report saying that the "Moslem Congress was 'inspired from a high Government source' to undermine the Coptic Congress and justify government opposition to its demands."[74] These are stark differences in historians' accounts of the same event. Bishri's characterization of the Coptic and Egyptian (Muslim) Congresses as the beginning of the schism is problematic, especially given the numerous violent episodes that occurred in Egypt between 1911 and the publication of his book. Mikhail clearly has an agenda as well but he uses primary sources to support his position and is writing contemporaneously.

69. Mikhail, *Copts and Moslems under British Control*, 33.
70. Ibid.
71. Ibrahim, *Copts of Egypt*, 57.
72. Megally, "Abbas Hilmi II, Khedive."
73. Bishri calls it the Egyptian (Islamic) Congress and actually uses the word "Israelis" rather than "Jews." Bishri, *Al-Muslimun wa-al-Aqbat fi itar al-jama'a al-wataniyya*, 89.
74. Mikhail, *Copts and Moslems under British Control*, 31.

Ibrahim's take is likely the most balanced since she does not attempt to gloss over later Coptic-Muslim tensions and provides more evidence of differences, both between Copts and within Muslim views of Copts.

The 1920s is a period generally depicted as a time when "Copts and Muslims joined in common purpose against the British administration."[75] The fervent nationalism in the narrative of the 1919 Revolution is arguably constructed around "Egyptianness" as a unifying trait based on a shared history, regardless of religious affiliation. As we have seen, there are several narratives of Coptic identity. Nationalists, such as Boutros-Ghali and Haykal, either portrayed Copts as Egyptians who form part of a unified nation or elided differences altogether in favor of an inclusive Egyptian identity. More subtle depictions, like those of Bishri, have explored communal tensions, without labeling them as such, and seemingly as part of an effort to lay them to rest and assert Egyptian unification. However, this effaces episodes of real suffering and oppression that have taken place in more recent decades. As Jim Loewen and Edward Sebesta argue, there is a "reciprocal relationship between truth about the past and justice in the present."[76] Therefore, including Copts as a monolith within Egyptian identity oversimplifies differences within Coptic positions and promotes the minority discourse of an age-old pharaonic Egyptian identity.

As the First World War drew to a close, Egypt was nominally independent under the regime of Tewfik Pasha. In reality, Egypt remained under British control and, by 1919, Egyptians (and Sudanese) revolted against British rule.[77] Sa'ad Zaghloul, the founder of the *Wafd* Party, leader of the revolution in Egypt and Egyptian prime minister in 1924, earned a reputation as a secular nationalist. He was a follower of Mustafa Kamil and Ahmad 'Urābī, who were like-minded in their vision of nationalism as independent of religious identity. When Zaghloul became prime minister he appointed two Copts to his cabinet, double the common practice of just one.[78] The unofficial *Wafd* slogan, credited to Zaghloul, was: "Religion is

---

75. Otto Meinardus, *Two Thousand Years of Coptic Christianity* (Cairo: The American University in Cairo Press, 1999), 76.

76. James W. Loewen and Edward H. Sebesta, *The Confederate and Neo-Confederate Reader: The "Great Truth" about the "Lost Cause"* (Jackson: University Press of Mississippi, 2010), 393.

77. The Condominium of the United Kingdom and the Kingdom of Egypt officially lasted from 1899 to 1956. Sudan was captured by Muhammed 'Ali in 1920. The occupation actually started in 1882 when 'Ali's great grandson Tewfik requested British assistance in putting down a revolt and was the nominal ruler, but British control lasted until 1932. See Kenneth Henderson, *Survey of the Anglo-Egyptian Sudan, 1898–1944* (London: Longmans, Green, 1946).

78. Anthony Gorman, *Historians, State and Politics in Twentieth Century Egypt: Contesting the Nation* (London and New York: Routledge, 2003), 235 n. 12.

for God, but the nation is for all."[79] The dominant narrative of the *Wafd* and the 1919 Revolution is that it was an occasion of Coptic-Muslim anti-British unity, and "the first time in the history of Egypt that cross and crescent appeared on the same flag."[80] As Vivian Ibrahim notes, a "nationalist discourse has supported the idea that the Copts were, and still are, an integral component of the Egyptian state."[81] Even images of the revolution have been deployed to constrict the narrative. The most ubiquitous image of the revolution is of marchers brandishing banners and flags displaying the cross and crescent, and sometimes, a Star of David. Milad Hanna's interpretation was that "March 1919 instilled feelings that are prevalent in the conscience of every Egyptian until today and these are that 'religion is for God, and the nation is for all' [as well as] the slogan 'long live the crescent and the cross.'"[82] There is some evidence that this narrative was carefully cemented after the revolution. Beth Baron's book, *Egypt as a Woman*, shows that pictures of women demonstrators carrying old Egyptian flags (containing a crescent and three stars) published in 1919 were altered in later publications to include the cross and crescent to signal Muslim-Coptic unity.[83] This depiction of Muslim-Coptic unity is often part of a nationalist project and likely, at least in part, as a response to the history of British orientalist imperialism. This is not to assert that there was no such unity. Rather, the evidence suggests that the idea of unity was emphasized in later accounts. The reasons for this are not clear since real examples of unity are available, not the least of which is the case of Qommus Sergius who "delivered speeches for 59 consecutive days at Al-Azhar's pulpit" and was called "Orator of Al-Azhar" and "Orator of Egypt" by Zaghloul.[84] The political taboo of sectarianism has served to reinforce the trope of national unity. In later historical episodes, the discourse of national unity became increasingly emphasized. The 1919 Revolution is a clear example of this.

Conclusion

A minority discourse about an age-old Coptic identity that separates them from Muslims is complicated by British and Egyptian governmental involvement in

---

79. "As Wafd's founder, Zaghloul is often credited for crystallizing in the memory of Egypt's political community the famous statement, 'religion is for God and the nation is for all,' which contemporary defenders of secularism in Egypt still invoke." See Wafd Party, *Ahram Online*, November 18, 2011, http://english.ahram.org.eg/NewsContent/33/104/24940/Elections-/Political-Parties/Wafd-party.aspx.

80. Meinardus, *Two Thousand Years of Coptic Christianity*, 76.

81. Ibrahim, *Copts of Egypt*, 6.

82. Hanna, *Na'am Aqbat, lakin Misriyyun*, 77.

83. Beth Baron, *Egypt as a Woman: Nationalism, Gender and Politics* (Berkley: University of California Press, 2005), 126.

84. Ibrahim, *Copts of Egypt*, 64.

response to so-called threats to national unity. These threats have a history of being deployed as countermeasures to avoid discussions of real grievances. In his review of Edward Wakin's *A Lonely Minority*, prominent historian Albert Hourani writes that Wakin "rightly stresses the good qualities which have been bred or strengthened" by the Copts' destiny. These include the "sharpness of intellect typical of a minority which must live on its wits." Warning against Coptic separatism, Hourani offers this advice:

> The Copts, deeply Egyptian and with the cautious wisdom of minorities, might well prefer their own traditional way of doing things: to try to improve matters by quiet intervention, without drawing too much attention to themselves, with the hope that things may someday be a little better, and the thought that at least they are not likely to grow much worse.[85]

Violent incidents targeting Copts have significantly increased since the time Hourani wrote his review and this had an impact on the historiography, as already noted. The net effect of the fears expressed by Said supports an argument that Coptic identity and agency have been largely marginalized or essentialized, rendering Copts either "passive receptacles for the modern values" espoused by an overemphasized Coptic elite, or "passive victims of state or Islamist violence."[86] A manufactured image of a shared and united past to bolster political unity in the present is not the answer, but neither is the ironic syndrome of Christian Arab nationalists who underplay real grievances to advance a manufactured unified identity. The nationalist narrative that dominated previous accounts has come to define Coptic participation and identity through reducing Copts to mere fragments or stereotypes in critical moments in modern Egyptian history. The reality is that there were real debates, divisions, and choices made, within both the Coptic and larger Egyptian spheres. A clear example can be seen in the diverging narratives of the 1911 Coptic and Egyptian Congresses and the partially constructed national unity discourse of the 1919 Revolution.

Dealing with this period of history in a nuanced way allows us to broach the broader topic of critiques of secular governance as unsuited to Muslim-majority countries. This topic suffers from its own constructed binary opposition between desires for post-colonial states authentically rooted in Islamic tradition and the place of non-Muslims within those states.

Tensions in the 1970s and 1980s, resulting from a growing Islamist wave partially fomented by Sadat's desire to undermine his political opponents, advanced historiographies of Copts as the persecuted minority with a history of dhimmitude. While such minority discourses attempted to take into account Muslim legal supremacy as a structural component of Muslim-majority countries, they also called for the implementation of a secular model of government and

---

85. Albert Hourani, "Review," *Middle East Journal* 17, no. 3 (1963): 323–5, 325.
86. Sedra, "Writing the History of the Modern Copts," 1056.

therefore shared secularity with some prominent nationalists. The European historical experience of the eighteenth and nineteenth centuries, which informed the concept of the secular state, then becomes the next target of criticism.

As Egyptians consider their current political circumstances, some question whether secularism or democracy is viable or sustainable in Egypt, or in the Middle East at large. It is important therefore to understand what the history of those ideas meant in practice because this will explicate the narratives of identity that have defined Egyptian politics for more than a century. Authors such as Talal Asad and Saba Mahmood, among others, have criticized the secular state as inappropriate to Muslim-majority countries, precisely because of its connection to European history.[87] They argue that an imported Western secular tradition is less useful than an Islamic discursive tradition that is authentically rooted in the local histories of Muslim-majority countries. The problem with this rejectionist criticism of secularism in favor of Islamic tradition is that authors such as Asad efface the Copts, and all Middle Eastern Christians, who are clearly neither part of an imported secular Western tradition nor part of an Islamist tradition or discourse. While Mahmood at least gives Copts space in her considerations, she fails to account for the complexity of the issues, and mischaracterizes the debate among Egyptians about the issue of identity and representation. Indigenous Christians in Muslim-majority states cannot be condensed into an Islamic tradition any more than they can be presented as a monolith. This therefore complicates the notion of the binary opposition between the secular and the Islamist. Only by developing a more nuanced understanding of history can we understand questions of identity and address a wider debate over the compatibility of secular government with Islamic societies.

Ongoing socioeconomic and political tensions in Egypt, the Middle East, and Africa are indicative of a history rife with complications. Fear of these tensions, coupled with calls for national unity, should not tempt us to smear stability and sameness over cracks in fluctuating and fragmented identities.

---

87. Talal Asad, *Formations of the Secular: Christianity, Islam, Modernity* (Palo Alto: Stanford University Press, 2003); Saba Mahmood, *The Politics of Piety: The Islamic Revival and the Feminist Subject* (Princeton: Princeton University Press, 2005).

Chapter 4

FROM NATIONALISM TO ISLAMISM

REVOLUTION, THE WAFD, AND THE RISE OF THE MUSLIM BROTHERHOOD

Philip Marfleet

The 1919 uprising has rarely been addressed as a mass popular movement. It has been viewed variously as a phase in the development of Egyptian nationalism, as a chapter in British colonial affairs, and as a moment of sociocultural transition. It has seldom been considered, however, as a movement that engaged millions of people, stimulating new agendas for change that would affect Egyptian society for decades. This chapter examines the uprising as a mass movement that brought new forms of public activism, raising expectations of radical change in both political and social affairs. Neither the British nor successive "independent" governments were able fully to negate its energies, and when nationalist currents collapsed into the colonial regime a new generation of Islamists intervened. The dramatic rise of the Muslim Brotherhood, only a decade after the events of 1919, is closely associated with the uprising and its aftermath, and with Egyptians' continuing aspirations for independence and self-determination.

The Revolution of 1919 was the most significant mass movement in the Arab region during the turbulent period following the First World War. Millions of people engaged in sustained activity to demand independence and to obtain reforms that later would be viewed as basic rights. Egyptians unified across religious and communal divisions and, in an unprecedented development, women engaged actively in public politics. The uprising challenged colonial authorities across the region with the prospect of systemic change: Britain feared social revolution on the Russian model. Within a few years, however, the secular nationalists who dominated events in 1919 faced opposition from a novel political current, as the Muslim Brotherhood grew with startling speed to become the first mass Islamist movement. This chapter addresses the uprising as a key element in these developments—a process initiated in 1919 and followed by a period of frustrated expectations that brought new political forces to the fore.

Hidden History

The 1919 uprising has been addressed primarily as an engagement of local elites with the British state. For almost seventy years there was little sustained research on its popular dimensions. Ziad Fahmy observes that "the existing historiography places Egyptian nationalism primarily within the realm of elite politics."[1] Workers played a leading role but as Joel Beinin and Zachary Lockman note, for decades there was little published material in Egypt on the working class or the labor movement.[2] Peasants were also important participants but as Ellis Goldberg observes in relation to rural society, "the Egyptian Revolt of 1919 has been little studied, and consequently our knowledge of it is not very great."[3] Nabila Ramdani notes that although the contribution of upper-class, aristocratic women to the revolution has been described in detail, "the involvement of poorer, unentitled women has frequently been forgotten."[4] Most accounts of the 1919 Revolution have long neglected its most numerous and energetic participants and the implications of their challenge to the socioeconomic and political iniquities of the established order.

The historiography of the 1919 Revolution reflects a general disinterest among British officials of the period, and among British archivists and professional historians, in the circumstances and experiences of the mass of Egyptians. It also reflects later influences in Egypt during the era of independent government. In his *Philosophy of the Revolution*, published in 1955, Gamal Abdel-Nasser comments that "This 1919 revolution, which was led by Saad Zaghloul, was no more successful than the others in fulfilling the hopes of the people."[5] Taking their cue from the Free Officers regime, most Egyptian writers and academics of the period focused upon what Nasser called "the successful revolution of 1952" and its implications for Egyptian society:[6] with isolated exceptions, events that had taken place thirty years earlier received little attention.[7]

---

1. Ziad Fahmy, *Ordinary Egyptians: Creating the Modern Nation through Popular Culture* (Stanford: Stanford University Press, 2011), x.

2. Joel Beinin and Zachary Lockman, *Workers on the Nile* (Princeton: Princeton University Press, 1987), 19.

3. Ellis Goldberg, "Peasants in Revolt—Egypt 1919," *International Journal of Middle East Studies* 24, (1992): 261–80, 261.

4. Nabila Ramdani, "Women in the 1919 Egyptian Revolution: From Feminist Awakening to Nationalist Political Activism," *Journal of International Women's Studies* 14, no. 2 (2013): 39–52, 46.

5. Gamal-Abdel Nasser, *Egypt's Liberation: Philosophy of the Revolution* (Washington: Public Affairs Press, 1955), 19.

6. Ibid., 19.

7. The most important exception being al-Rifi'i, who had been a witness to events in 1919: 'Abd al-Rahman Al-Rafi'i, *Thawrat Sanat 1919: Tarikh Misr al-Qawmi min Sanat 1914 ila Sanat 1921* [The 1919 Revolution: The National History of Egypt, 1914–1921] (Cairo: Maktabat al-Nahda al-Misriyya, 1955).

British officials who administered colonial rule assumed that Egyptians were unable to undertake effective political change. They presented Britain's invasion of 1882 as an act of altruism and the British presence as benevolent and progressive. Technically still under Ottoman authority, Egypt was administered as if part of the British Empire, mobilizing policies and practices developed in South Asia and Africa. For Alfred (later Viscount) Milner, who in the 1880s directed financial affairs for the colonial authorities in Cairo, Britain had rescued Egypt from "the flame of anarchy" and "inveterate evil."[8] Most important, he proposed, was Britain's role in saving the country from "forces of poverty and fanaticism."[9] In a few brief years, Milner suggested, Britain had succeeded in replacing "almost general ruin and depression" with "a remarkable revolution":

> If the conditions, under which the government of Egypt has to be carried on, seem like a nightmare, the revival of the country during the last few years, under and in spite of these conditions, is almost worthy of a fairy tale.[10]

This account was indeed a "fairy tale"—one sustained by colonial ideologies that embraced a telling paradox. On the one hand, Egyptians were "docile and good tempered," said Milner: they were "a nation of submissive slaves, not only bereft of any vestige of liberal institutions but devoid of any spark of the spirit of liberty."[11] Here, observes Abdeslam Maghraoui, "the indolence and fatalism of the native was the negative shadow of the industriousness and motivation of the European character."[12] Milner also maintained that Egypt was "eternally abnormal": its people were "in the grip of a religion the most intolerant and fanatical," leading them to excesses of conduct including uprisings and "rebellions" such as that of 1882.[13] Egyptians were damned if they protested at subjugation by the British (intolerant, fanatical)—and damned if they did not (passive, submissive).

Evelyn Baring, Lord Cromer, was the senior British official in Egypt for almost twenty-five years from the late 1870s. Architect of the colonial regime, he proposed that Egyptians were *in statu pupillari*—under British guardianship. They were "poor, ignorant, credulous," he said, and required to be raised by "the civilized Englishman" from the abject state in which the latter found them.[14] His *Political and Literary Essays* proposed that Egypt should be shaped by the colonial power—by what "we

---

8. Milner asserted: "We had gone to Egypt professedly with no other object than to 'restore order,' nor can there be the smallest doubt of the absolute *bona fides* of that profession." Alfred Milner, *England in Egypt* (London: Arnold, 1892), 14.

9. Milner, *England in Egypt*, 14.

10. Ibid., 5.

11. Ibid., 178.

12. Abdesalam Maghraoui, *Liberalism without Democracy* (Durham: Duke University Press, 2006), 46.

13. Milner, *England in Egypt*, 4, 12.

14. Cromer [Earl of, Evelyn Baring] *Modern Egypt* (New York: Macmillan, 1908), 130.

consciously think is best for the subject race [sic]."[15] He drew explicitly on models of British rule in India, which he described as a scene of "administrative triumphs of world-wide fame."[16] As in India, the British should seek mediators for their relations with the wider society—a network of Egyptians who could act as the *babus* of the occupation.[17] To this end the colonial authorities established assemblies and councils of Egyptian notables, later described by Cromer as "a mere *décor de theatre*."[18]

On the outbreak of war in 1914 Britain imposed martial law and soon declared a protectorate over Egypt. Using what they called "administrative pressure," colonial officials militarized the economy, undertaking mass conscription of labor and requisitioning crops and animals. According to British records, at least 500,000 men were mobilized and scores of thousands of draft animals secured, with a huge impact on rural society.[19] The mass of Egyptians experienced a significant drop in living standards while a minority, notably specific large landowners favored by British policies, were rapidly enriched. With an expanded garrison of British and Imperial troops and a large police force recruited from army reservists, colonial officials maintained close control in both the cities and the countryside.

By 1917, however, shortages of food and rapidly rising prices brought strikes in Cairo and Alexandria, initially among cigarette workers who had earlier been the most energetic activists among Egypt's small working class. Thomas Russell, Commandant of Police in Cairo, made a personal note of his intervention with strikers who demanded improvements in wages and conditions and announced their intention to march on the 'Abdin Palace—a violation of British restrictions on all forms of public politics:

> We have got very strict laws of course on illegal assembly and this morning about five hundred of the strikers refused to accept the very good terms the Governor had got for them out of the Company ... when I'd got them all in the yard I locked the gate and put a strong guard over them, read the riot act and let them go. I hear they have accepted the terms since![20]

Further police action, including many arrests, brought the dispute to an end but it was to prove a marker of rising discontent and, for the first time since 1914,

---

15. Cromer [Earl of, Evelyn Baring], "The Government of Subject Races," in *Political and Literary Essays, 1908–1913* (London: Macmillan, 1913), 13.

16. Cromer, *Modern Egypt*, 130.

17. Originally a term of respect in much of South Asia, in British usage *babu* was applied to "native" clerks and administrators and later to more senior officials of the Raj who acted as part of the British administration and legal system and who were viewed by colonial officials as loyalists prepared to enact imperial policies vis-à-vis the mass of people.

18. Cromer, *Modern Egypt*, 152.

19. Marius Deeb, *Party Politics in Egypt: The Wafd and Its Rivals, 1919–1938*, St. Antony's Middle East Monographs, No. 9 (London: Ithaca, 1979), 42.

20. Ronald Seth, *Russell Pasha* (London: William Kimber, 1966), 130.

of extensive labor struggles which soon energized the embryonic trade union movement initiated in the pre-war years. In 1918 there were disputes among the Cairo tramwaymen and in early 1919 a revival of union organization in Alexandria. Joel Beinin and Zachary Lockman comment:

> The political, social and economic conditions that characterized the Egypt that emerged from the war were the tinder the spark of nationalist agitation ignited, producing the popular uprising against British rule that came to be known as the 1919 revolution.[21]

These labor struggles were not associated directly with nationalist politicians who approached Britain with demands for a delegation (*wafd*) to represent Egypt at the postwar Peace Conference in France with a view to securing full independence. They were, however, harbingers of a mass popular movement that soon engaged much of Egyptian society, endorsing demands for independence and at the same time undertaking self-organization that extended far beyond the formal nationalist agenda. These were not developments unique to Egypt but part of an international wave of struggles that included revolutionary upheavals in Russia and Germany, and demands for self-determination in India, China, Ireland, and much of the former Ottoman Empire, notably Turkey, Kurdistan, and the Arab East.

After the Russian Revolution of 1917 its Bolshevik leaders had renounced claims to vast territories of the former Tsarist Empire, while US president Woodrow Wilson's "Fourteen Points" for world peace, issued in 1918, included (Point Five) a proposal for "free, open-minded, and absolutely impartial adjustment of all colonial claims."[22] With World War at an end full independence for Egypt became a pressing demand on the colonial power. On November 13, 1918, forty-eight hours after the armistice signed by the main combatants in Europe, a group of Egyptian nationalists including Saad Zaghloul met British officials in Cairo and requested permission to travel to London to press their case. On the same day, later to be celebrated in Egypt as *yawm al-jihad*, the Egyptian delegation—*al-wafd al-misri*—was established by Zaghloul. Britain's refusal to permit the delegation to travel, and the Wafd's subsequent campaign of *tawqilat*—mass collection of signatures of endorsement—further generalized demands for independence and brought large numbers of Egyptians into new forms of public politics.

---

21. Beinin and Lockman, *Workers on the Nile*, 83.
22. Point Five proposed: "A free, open-minded, and absolutely impartial adjustment of all colonial claims based upon a strict observance of the principle that in determining all such questions of sovereignty the interests of the populations concerned must have equal weight with the equitable government whose title is to be determined." See: National Archives [United States], *President Woodrow Wilson's 14 Points (1918)*, https://www.ourdocuments.gov/doc.php?flash=false&doc=62, accessed January 7, 2019.

"Spontaneous and Massive"

Marius Deeb observes that the success of the *tawqilat* campaign, welcomed by hundreds of thousands who signed the Wafd's statement, "was unwittingly a silent rehearsal for the 1919 popular uprising."[23] When Zaghloul and his colleagues were arrested on March 8, 1919, the country was swept by demonstrations that soon embraced strike action in the cities and uprisings throughout the countryside, launching Egypt's first mass movement since the 'Urābī Uprising almost forty years earlier.

Protests by students in Cairo were followed by a large demonstration in the city center and clashes with the occupation forces, resulting in deaths among demonstrators and among British and Australian troops. Police Commander Russell was reluctant to mobilize the Egyptian army as many units of the force openly supported the Wafd.[24] When he attempted to intervene with protesters he encountered "a howling mob of the most horrible roughs I have ever seen."[25] His contemporaneous account of the incident testifies to the attitude of British officials, little changed since the era of Milner and Cromer:

> The whole mob was shrieking and yelling and waving their weapons in the air. If you can imagine a drawing by Hogarth of a scene made up by Dante's Inferno and the French Revolution, add to that mad Oriental fanaticism—and you have something like this mob.[26]

Significantly the "mob" represented a cross-section of Cairo society: student deputations from al-Azhar and from the city's schools, and groups of professionals and tramway workers whose strike in support of the Wafd had paralyzed the city. Demonstrations were soon underway nationwide on a scale, notes Nathan Brown, that was "a complete surprise to everyone involved."[27] Neither nationalist leaders nor the British expected serious disturbances after the arrest of Saad Zaghloul and his colleagues on March 8, 1919, Brown observes. The British were wholly unprepared for the ensuing nationwide uprising and quickly concluded that "outside orchestration" was to blame.[28]

British officials variously blamed Bolshevik, German, or Young Turk agents as clandestine elements who had initiated the events. Zaghloul and his colleagues—who had been placed in Qasr al-Nil Prison before being transported to Port Said and exiled to Malta—are said to have greeted news of the demonstrations with

---

23. Deeb, *Party Politics in Egypt*, 42.
24. Seth, *Russell Pasha*, 143.
25. Ibid., 144.
26. Ibid.
27. Nathan Brown, *Peasant Politics in Modern Egypt* (New Haven: Yale University Press, 1990), 203.
28. Ibid., 203.

disbelief, concluding that the British had fabricated accounts in order to justify their own detention and deportation.[29] The movement was in fact "spontaneous and massive"[30] and soon increased in numbers and in scope as support for the Wafd was combined with economic demands raised by workers and, in the countryside and provincial towns, attempts to cut communications, to seize food, and—in some areas—to establish independent local governments.

Workers and Unions

Labor activity had been on the rise before *yawm al-jihad*: the events of March 1919 now offered more favorable conditions for collective action to support both political and economic change. Tramway workers in Cairo backed the exiled Wafdists and set out their own demands including a large wage increase, an eight-hour day, and paid rest days.[31] Taxi drivers and bus drivers also stopped work. Commander Russell wrote: "They have been very successful and things are completely disorganized to the point of discomfort for everyone including the Egyptians."[32] When British officials attempted to run tramway cars under armed guard a popular boycott ensured that they remained empty.[33]

The tramway strike was eventually settled—largely on the workers' terms. Railway workers in Cairo had meanwhile also stopped work and had cut railway lines near Imbaba—a form of sabotage already underway in rural Egypt and which continued despite an edict from the colonial authorities that any such act would be viewed as a capital offense. In March there were further strikes, including in government workshops and depots, the Alexandria tramway, the Cairo electric company, the Hawamdiyya sugar refinery, the postal service, and port and customs agencies. These focused on demands including the eight-hour day, compensation for illness and dismissal, and guarantees against abuse and ill-treatment by supervisors, management, and owners, notably those in foreign-owned utilities.[34]

When the pace of industrial action eased in late April, Russell wrote that "things have quieted down," suggesting "it really looks now as though we were

---

29. Ibid., 204.
30. Beinin and Lockman, *Workers on the Nile*, 90.
31. Other demands included better treatment from supervisors, changes to disciplinary procedures, severance pay, and free uniforms: Beinin and Lockman, *Workers on the Nile*, 91.
32. Seth, *Russell Pasha*, 146.
33. Russell gave testimony as to the effectiveness of the strikes and boycotts: "The post office is only just working, the street cleaning and watering has ceased, which is a great menace to health, trams have stopped and the railways can only run a few trains with British military drivers." Seth, *Russell Pasha*, 146.
34. Beinin and Lockman provide a lengthy list of industries and services affected: Beinin and Lockman, *Workers on the Nile*, 98–9.

[sic] round the corner."³⁵ Mass strikes resumed in the summer, however, affecting tram, bus, and railway workers, and closing sugar refineries, quarries, tobacco factories, banks, bakeries, shops, and restaurants. Some were prolonged—in the case of Cairo's tramway workers, for fifty-six days—an unprecedented stoppage that concluded in October with arrangements largely favorable to the workers.

These disputes were associated with the mushrooming of trade unions, established across transport, manufacturing, the press and printing, finance and the retail sector. In August the daily newspaper *La Bourse Égyptienne* headlined: "*Il pleut des syndicats!*"³⁶ British officials reported that by 1921 there were thirty-eight labor unions/syndicates in Cairo, among which the principal bodies had been established during the 1919 events.³⁷

Peasants and "Soviets"

The countryside had been seriously affected by militarization measures imposed by Britain. Peasants were mobilized intensively in the Labour Corps, the Camel Corps and in specialist units in transport, construction, and provisioning of British and Imperial troops. The policy of "administrative pressure" was intensified toward the end of the conflict, as local officials across the country—even down to the village level—were required to provide specific numbers of recruits, seriously affecting the rural economy, especially as maintenance of agricultural productivity required intensive inputs of labor to irrigation systems across the Nile Delta and in much of the South. British officials set prices for crops and controlled supplies of fertilizer. They also directed the key export crop, cotton, solely to Britain, India, France, and Russia—in effect to the Allied states—while regulating prices paid in Egypt, where cultivators received a fraction of the world price. Goldberg concludes that the measures brought intense pressure on food supplies, leading to extreme hunger in some areas and to the spread of disease, notably typhus and influenza.³⁸ In 1918, he notes, deaths exceeded births for the first time since the 1880s.³⁹

Increasingly, access to food was determined by social status and economic resources: Goldberg observes that "the army had enough; the rich—whether Egyptian or not—could always buy it."⁴⁰ He adds:

---

35. Seth, *Russell Pasha*, 147.
36. Beinin and Lockman, *Workers on the Nile*, 111.
37. Deeb, *Party Politics in Egypt*, 66. Beinin and Lockman also cite Egyptian sources suggesting that by the end of 1919 there were twenty-one unions operating in Cairo, seventeen in Alexandria, and others in the Suez Canal cities, the Delta towns, and elsewhere; Beinin and Lockman, *Workers on the Nile*, 119.
38. Goldberg, "Peasants in Revolt," 266.
39. Ibid., 267.
40. Ibid.

In the end it was the poor and politically defenseless who found themselves in the Labor Corps, just as it was the poor and politically defenceless who suffered most from the requisition of commodities and animals. Thus agrarian differences rapidly assumed the character of class grievances and the tensions ignited by the war appeared as class tensions.[41]

It was in these circumstances that rural communities responded to arrest of the Wafdists and pursued their own agendas for survival. Demonstrations took place nationwide: Brown comments that "No area in Egypt remained unaffected."[42] Protests included sabotage of railway and telegraph lines, destruction of roads, burning of railway stations, and attacks on government offices and British troops. Colonial officials reported rioting by "riff-raff":[43] the "docile" Egyptians described by Milner now threatened anarchy. Thousands of troops were deployed while the Royal Air Force (RAF) attacked demonstrators from the air and bombed villages close to railways tracks affected by the protests—Britain's most aggressive intervention in Egypt for almost forty years. Within days of the first protests the RAF used scores of airplanes to assault a defenseless population—an initiative that preceded bombardments in Somaliland and Iraq often seen as the first use of air power against civilians.[44] On March 17, 1919, the RAF commanding officer in Egypt told officials in London:

> During the last two days aeroplanes have machine-gunned with excellent effect crowds engaged in damaging railways and are now ordered to use bombs when targets offer. Have formed five squadrons from training squadrons and over 100 machines are now occupied. General situation is such as to necessitate considerable military measures being taken, and the acting Commander-in-Chief has come to Egypt to direct operations.[45]

The British had expected their assaults to pacify protesters: instead, demonstrations spread across the country, including to Upper Egypt. On April 7, Britain abruptly changed strategy, releasing Zaghloul and his colleagues. Egyptians celebrated and, drawing confidence from the impact of the protests, strikes and rural insurgencies continued. Now, notes Burns, "a campaign of reprisals was begun and carried out

---

41. Ibid., 271.
42. Brown, *Peasant Politics in Modern Egypt*, 204.
43. Fahmy, *Ordinary Egyptians*, 138.
44. Both Somaliland and Iraq were bombed in 1920. Officials made efforts to conceal the earlier attacks in Egypt, fearing interrogation by British politicians. They advised that "any communiqués from Egypt dealing with the burning of villages etc should be carefully censored from before publication, otherwise questions in Parliament are almost certain to arise" (message from Sir Ronald Graham, Commander of the Royal Air Force in Egypt, to the Foreign Office: Fahmy, *Ordinary Egyptians*, 139, 211n25).
45. Fahmy, *Ordinary Egyptians*, 138–9.

with terrible severity."⁴⁶ In May the British government admitted that over 1,000 Egyptians had been killed and some villages entirely destroyed.⁴⁷

Local actions undertaken by rural Egyptians aimed to disrupt communication and transport, including the movement of conscripts, crops, and animals; to secure food from government stores; to release recruits to the Labour Corps detained by the authorities; and to confront British troops who inhibited the protests.⁴⁸ Significantly, there were no reports of damage to pumps, irrigation systems, or canals—key resources for continuing cultivation. The common element was an effort to defend local communities against further depredation. In some areas there were land occupations and attempts to establish independent local control of social order and administration. This, British politicians proposed, was evidence that rural insurgents aimed to create local "soviets," that a "Bolshevik tendency" was at work and that social revolution was in the making.⁴⁹ As with the workers' movement, however, the scenario imagined in the British Residency was false: evidence from Soviet archives confirms that events in Egypt were not a matter of immediate interest for Bolshevik strategists.⁵⁰ The 1919 Revolution was a homegrown movement, without the engagement of Russia or other external influences. It was also more extensive, energetic, and innovative than even its nationalist leaders thought possible.

"Utter Surprise"

In his detailed analysis of the emergence of the Wafd, Marius Deeb suggests: "the 1919 popular uprising was not an organized and premeditated movement which was engineered by the Wafd or any other group."⁵¹ In Cairo, leading participants came from among students, notably at al-Azhar, soon joined by professionals and workers. Protests "radiated from Cairo northwards, that is to the Delta, gradually spreading

---

46. Eleanor Burns, *British Imperialism in India* (London: Labour Research Department, 1928, 29).

47. Ibid., 29. This conservative estimate, offered by a senior British official in debates in the British Parliament, contrasts with the 3,000 deaths suggested by Egyptian historian 'Abd al-Rahman al-Rifi'i: Brown, *Peasant Politics*, 205, 251n60.

48. Exchanges of messages between British officials indicate that stores of grain collected for the army were the target of "pillage" by groups of rural demonstrators. Brown, *Peasant Politics*, 205, 251n62.

49. George Lloyd, *Egypt since Cromer* (London: Macmillan, 1933), 300, 353.

50. Masha Kirasirova, "An Egyptian Communist Family Romance: Revolution and Gender in the Transnational Life of Charlotte Rosenthal," in *The Global Impacts of Russia's Great War and Revolution* [Book 2, *The Wider Arc of Revolution*], ed. Choi Chatterjee, Steve G. Marks, Mary Neuberger and Steven Sabol (Bloomington: Slavica Publishers, 2019), 309–36.

51. Deeb, *Party Politics in Egypt*, 45.

to the South."⁵² There was no formal organization at the national or provincial levels: initially local leadership came from among the *effendiya* and from rural notables, groups whose members often overlapped and who soon found their expectations of change greatly exceeded by those of the mass of participants whose grievances and aspirations, Deeb suggests, "represented uniform and genuine class interests."⁵³

The leadership of the Wafd was upper class and, in the context of Egyptian society, essentially conservative. Key figures reflected the concerns of landed interests and of liberal capitalists frustrated by the British occupation and European control of the economy (significantly, Talat Harb—later to be the architect of an independent economic strategy for Egypt—provided active support). Control of the Egyptian state, they believed, should lie with the country's indigenous elite—people like themselves, whom they viewed as appropriately qualified for government. They expressed strong reservations about mass public action. 'Abd al-'Aziz Fahmi, one of the early Wafdist leaders, told student activists who met at *bayt al-umma* (Zahglul's residence) to organize the initial protests: "Do not play with fire ... Let us work in calm and do not add oil to the flames."⁵⁴ The leadership was alarmed by popular violence, fearing threats to property and social order. On March 24 it issued a statement that highlighted the British authorities' warning of military measures against those involved in attacks on transport or public property. Wafdist leaders declared:

> It is obvious to everyone that attacks on persons or on property are forbidden by divine law and by positive law, and that sabotage of the means of transport clearly harms the people of our country.... Therefore the undersigned see it as their sacred national duty to refrain from any attack and ask that no one violate the law, so as not to obstruct the path of all those who serve the nation by legal means.⁵⁵

Wafdist leaders both encouraged mobilizations in their support and were increasingly anxious about the radical tone of protest and emerging self-organization. They warned that attempts to cut transport links not only would affect the movement of crops but would also "hamper commercial transactions."⁵⁶ Deeb comments that this was consistent with leading Wafdists' economic interests: their appeal to conform to the law, he suggests, revealed "utter surprise and inability to predict the course of events, let alone to organize it."⁵⁷

---

52. Ibid., 45.
53. Ibid.
54. Verbatim account of eyewitness Zuhair Sabri, student activist in 1919 and later a key figure in the Wafd, in Zaheer Qureishi, *Liberal Nationalism in Egypt: Rise and Fall of the Wafd Party* (Allahabad: Kitab Mahal, 1967), 51.
55. Beinin and Lockman, *Workers on the Nile*, 93.
56. Deeb, *Party Politics in Egypt*, 44.
57. Ibid.

New Politics

The protests of 1919—and critically, the response of the colonial regime—initiated a long period of mass struggles in which the accumulated frustrations of millions of people were expressed in new forms of public politics. General disinterest among historians has understated these developments. Qureishi, for example, suggests that "the period of strikes lasted only a couple of weeks" and that "lawyers alone held out."[58] But the new mood was infectious, encouraging rallies, marches, lobbies, sustained strikes, boycotts, land occupations, and other demonstrative actions. At the same time activists undertook a host of less visible initiatives, circulating countless leaflets and pamphlets, and establishing newspapers and magazines, cultural circles and literary groups, as well as labor unions, provincial councils, and rural "republics."

What features of this movement gave it the character of a revolution—and what were the implications? Although there is no evidence of intervention from ideologues or activists outside Egypt, it is Leon Trotsky, one of the leaders of the insurgency in Russia in 1917, whose experiences provide an important insight into the Egyptian movement. Writing in 1934 of radical mass movements that had challenged the established order, he observed: "The most indubitable fact of a revolution is the direct interference of the masses in historic events."[59] Under most circumstances, he wrote, history was made by those associated with the state: kings, ministers, bureaucrats, parliamentarians, and journalists. However,

> [A]t those crucial moments when the old order becomes no longer endurable to the masses, they break over the barriers excluding them from the political arena, sweep aside their traditional representatives, and create by their own interference the initial groundwork for a new regime.... The history of a revolution is for us first of all a history of the forcible entry of the masses into the realm of rulership over their own destiny.[60]

The Egyptian movement "broke barriers," most importantly, it moved public politics into what, with reference to Egypt, Sami Zubaida calls "the modern political field."[61] The Wafd encouraged popular expectations of full independence and Egyptian control over the state and the economy, including national institutions and government agencies. It also generalized ideas about parliamentary representation and democratic participation. The mass of people enthusiastically supported the Wafdist agenda; at the same time they aspired to more radical change: to greater control over their own lives, notably by means of collective organization. This was

---

58. Qureishi, *Liberal Nationalism in Egypt*, 54.

59. Leon Trotsky, Leon (1934) *The History of the Russian Revolution* (London: Victor Gollanz, 1934), 17.

60. Ibid., 17.

61. Sami Zubaida, *Islam, the People and the State* (London: Routledge, 1989), 50.

a "forcible entry" into political and social affairs—one that challenged dominant values and practices, including in the areas of religion and gender relations.

For some years the Copts had been a focus of hostility from nationalist leaders and from supporters of Hizb al-Watani, which before the First World War dominated the nationalist arena.[62] One outcome was a hardening of communal identities and the development of partisan initiatives including conferences and congresses called on the basis of religious allegiance. When the Wafd was formed in 1918, however, its leadership group combined Muslims and Christians, among whom most were wealthy landowners. The movement that emerged the following year quickly rendered marginal issues of communal difference. During months of marches, strikes, and rural insurgencies, national unity became a key principle, asserted demonstratively by the Wafdist flag, bearing a cross within a crescent.

Mosques and churches became organizing centers for the movement, with Muslim prayer-leaders and Coptic priests jointly addressing people of all social statuses and religious groups. In demonstrations of solidarity and mutual respect, Muslims and Christians celebrated feasts and holy days of both religious traditions: during Ramadan of May 1919, a large deputation of Coptic notables visited al-Azhar to convey "the good wishes of the Coptic community."[63] In a demonstration in Cairo an Azhari sheikh carrying a picture of the Coptic Patriarch together with a flag of the Cross and crescent led chants of "Long live our holy union."[64] This collective confidence and solidarity embraced the Jewish community, as reported by a British official in Cairo in April 2019:

> A noticeable feature of this afternoon's procession which I myself saw was two carriages full of Jews, amongst whom, was one of the Chief Rabbis. They were carrying the Jewish Flag [i.e. with the Star of David] attached to the Egyptian flag and the Rabbi made several speeches which were loudly cheered.[65]

Beinin and Lockman comment on the absence of any evidence during the 1919 events of sectarian strife—a significant feature of the revolution in the context of earlier hostilities.[66] They note in particular the solidarity expressed in large industrial and transport enterprises in which Muslims and Copts worked

---

62. Tensions rose in the pre-war period when Butros Ghali, one of the leading figures in the Coptic community, was assassinated by a supporter of the Nationalist Party. Inter-communal tensions intensified, leading to rival conferences of Muslims and Christians demanding specific rights from the colonial authorities. See Donald Reid, "Political Assassination in Egypt, 1910–1954," *The International Journal of African Historical Studies* 15, no. 4 (1982): 625–51.
63. Fahmy, *Ordinary Egyptians*, 149.
64. Ibid., 141.
65. Ibid.
66. Beinin and Lockman, *Workers on the Nile*, 102.

side by side and undertook strike action "with apparently total unanimity."[67] Such solidarities were also evident in relation to "foreign" workers, the *mutamassirun*—members of Egypt's European communities, notably Italians, Greeks, and immigrants from the Levant—who dominated skilled trades and higher-paid jobs in industry and services. The strike wave of summer 1919 saw collective actions that embraced workers of all ethnic/communal identities, despite efforts by the British to target key organizers of non-Egyptian origin.[68]

Women to the Fore

The historiography of the 1919 Revolution demonstrates, above all, "the need to incorporate non-elites into the historical narrative."[69] Gender relations among the middle class and elite had been in a process of change since the mid-nineteenth century, with female participation a notable feature of emerging nationalist currents. Beth Baron observes that when the Revolution of 1919 began, "Decades of organizing [had] prepared women for public action."[70] On the arrest of Saad Zaghloul, his wife Safiyya addressed women who flocked to *bayt al-'umma* to demonstrate support, becoming *umm al-misriyyin*—a key symbol of the aspiration for independence. Muslim and Christian women participated together in several carefully planned marches in central Cairo: this was widely reported and subsequently noted in histories of the period. All were of the elite and the middle class but as demonstrations spread across Egypt, working-class and peasant women became active participants. Their presence was seldom recorded. Nawal El-Saadawi observes:

> [L]ittle has been said about the masses of poor women who rushed into the national struggle without counting the cost, and who lost their lives, whereas the lesser contributions of aristocratic women leaders have been noisily acclaimed and brought to the forefront.[71]

Women were particularly prominent during meetings in churches and mosques in popular areas, persistently making radical contributions, so that in May 1919 a British intelligence report alleged that "Egyptian ladies" were "induced to go to

---

67. Ibid.

68. The British and the pro-occupation press attacked Italian activists they saw as dangerous radicals, prompting solidarity action from print workers: Beinin and Lockman, *Workers on the Nile*, 112S.

69. Fahmy, *Ordinary Egyptians*, xii.

70. Beth Baron, *The Women's Awakening in Egypt: Culture, Society, and the Press* (New Haven: Yale University Press, 1994), 186.

71. Nawal El-Saadawi, *The Hidden Face of Eve: Women in the Arab World* (London: Zed, 1980), 176.

the mosques to make seditious speeches."⁷² Eyewitness accounts by the American journalist William T. Ellis attest to the scale of engagement of women of the working class and urban poor, especially on April 7, 1919, when huge crowds celebrated the release of Zaghul and the delegation. "Egypt was never before as democratic as on this day of days," wrote Ellis: "the fiesta was a cross-section of the nation's life."⁷³

The breadth and depth of the mass movement, and its demonstrative public actions, lead Fahmy to reference the work of the Russian philosopher/literary theorist Mikhail Bakhtin and his idea of the carnivalesque. For some months in 1919, streets, public squares, cafes, bars, mosques, and churches became places in which the voices of people hitherto silenced were heard repeatedly. Here, speeches, chants, songs, readings, and recitations delivered and received by people marginalized in everyday life were evidence that earlier structures of authority had been breached. For a brief time, says Fahmy, the colonial regime was ineffective and "alternative centers of power" were created.⁷⁴

The Wafd and the Left

The British gradually suppressed the most energetic elements of the movement. It continued nonetheless as a process of contestation of British rule and an attempt by Egyptians to extend control over economic and political affairs. Most significant was the impact of the national movement on the working class: Beinin and Lockman comment that the events of 1919 "opened the floodgates of labor organization and militant action," embedding trades unions in workplaces across the country and stimulating the growth of radical currents highly critical of the Wafd and mainstream nationalist parties.⁷⁵

The British were again convinced that "Bolshevists" were intervening in Egyptian politics; they also suspected German and even Islamist influence.⁷⁶ When a radical current emerged, however, it was stimulated by Egyptian activists without intervention from abroad. By 1920 intellectuals and working-class militants had determined to form a communist party. The radical mood provided a large audience, especially in Cairo and in Alexandria, where British officials

---

72. Fahmy, *Ordinary Egyptians*, 148.
73. Ibid., 140.
74. Ibid., 165. Bakhtin's ideas were mobilized similarly to address developments during the Egyptian uprising of 2011: see Samia Mehrez, *Translating Egypt's Revolution: The Language of Tahrir* (Cairo: American University in Cairo Press, 2012).
75. Beinin and Lockman, *Workers on the Nile*, 119.
76. See reports to the Foreign Office sent in February 1920: Beinin and Lockman, *Workers on the Nile*, 140.

said that "the Red Flag was seen flying in the streets."[77] The British focused special attention on Joseph Rosenthal, long active in the labor movement in the city. Communism in Egypt, they said, was a "one-manshow . . . and that one man is Rosenthal."[78] There were in fact many groups, clubs, and literary figures claiming to act in the name of Egyptian socialism. Their various, widely differing views inhibited collaboration and it was not until August 1921 that an Egyptian Socialist Party (ESP) emerged, immediately facing harassment from the British authorities. In 1922, after internal disputes, it affiliated to the Comintern—the international communist movement centered in Moscow—declaring itself the Communist Party of Egypt (CPE). The ESP/CPE was a small organization which, although active in numerous labor struggles, remained at the margin of Egyptian politics: its significance in the history of the 1919 Revolution is as a marker of continuing radicalization among the intelligentsia and militant workers.

The Wafd viewed the left as a fundamental threat. As early as July 1919 Saad Zaghloul had urged the party's leadership to recognize that calls for radical change "benefit our enemies."[79] When a Wafdist government was eventually established in 1924, labor struggles intensified and Zaghloul—then prime minister—moved against all forms of extra-parliamentary opposition and in particular against worker activists and the radical left. During an intensive campaign launched by central government, communists were described as foreign troublemakers responsible for "deceptions and lies."[80] Communist leaders were jailed and activists without Egyptian citizenship were deported. The British noted with satisfaction the role of "prominent Zaghlulist politicians" in targeting "communist strikers."[81] By 1925 the CPE had been suppressed and the Wafd had asserted control of the workers' movement, declaring that further economic change must be delayed until Egypt achieved full independence.[82]

Throughout the 1920s relations between the British, the monarchy, the Wafd, and rival nationalist currents were complex and sometimes contradictory. Relations between the Wafd and the mass of people were more straightforward, however. Although the party continued to enjoy widespread support it was

---

77. Suliman Bashear, *Communism in the Arab East, 1918–1928* (London: Ithaca, 1980), 27. Rosenthal had moved to Alexandria from Beirut, becoming active in labor struggles during the late 1890s. See Tareq Israel and Rifaat El-Sai'd, *The Communist Movement in Egypt 1920–1988* (Syracuse: Syracuse University Press, 1990), 14; also Kirasirova, "An Egyptian Communist Family Romance," 310.

78. Hanna Batatu, *The Old Social Classes and the Revolutionary Movements of Iraq: A Study of Iraq's Old Landed and Commercial Classes and of Its Communists, Ba'athists, and Free Officers*, (Princeton: Princeton University Press, 1978), 374.

79. Ismael and El-Sa'id, *The Communist Movement in Egypt 1920–1988*, 22.

80. Beinin and Lockman, *Workers on the Nile*, 150.

81. Bashear, *Communism in the Arab East, 1918–1928*, 94.

82. Bashear comments that the CPE had become "a persecuted group fighting its very right to political existence": Bashear, *Communism in the Arab East, 1918–1928*, 94.

increasingly elitist and intolerant of initiatives it did not control. In common with many mainstream nationalist movements of the twentieth century it was shaped by the aspirations of the elite, and in particular the latter's wish to exercise full control of the state. The party saw itself as an expression of the nation, unifying people of varying social statuses and ethno-religious identities. Deeb observes that Wafdist leaders viewed opponents as "dissenters" who worked against the nation's interests.[83] In particular they viewed independent collective action with alarm: when in 1924 trades unions organized to secure improved wages, conditions, and rights at work, Wafdist leaders warned: "The unions cannot lead the workers unless the government leads them [the unions] morally and helps them to protect the workers' rights and achieve their just demands."[84] Paternalism swiftly became repression, as the short-lived Wafdist government jailed activists, launching a sustained attack on the most radical elements. The long-term impact was significant, removing the radical wing of the popular movement and opening space for other currents that advocated societal change.

From Nationalism to Islamism

By suppressing the popular movement the Wafd presented opportunities for more conservative nationalists to secure influence. When the Liberal Constitutionalist Party agreed to form a government under royal decree its cabinet became known as *al-qabda al-hadidiya*—the government of the "iron grip." The party restricted voting rights to owners of property: Prime Minister Ismail Sidqi asserted that "suffrage . . . is not a right to be exercised by the whole population."[85] The Wafd did not benefit, failing to increase mass support: the party soon experienced a series of splits and retreated in the face of new forces in Egyptian politics—Young Egypt, and the Muslim Brotherhood.

The success of the new currents, most importantly the Muslim Brotherhood, was associated with their refusal, observes Maghraoui, "to play according to the rules of the liberal constitutional regime."[86] The Brotherhood had begun as a modest group—what Carrie Rosefsky Wickham calls a classic "anti-system" group situated—outside—and against—the established political order.[87] Its founder Hassan al-Banna lamented the disunity and factionalism evidenced by nationalist parties and the inability of Egypt's elites, who dominated parliament, to meet the

---

83. Deeb, *Party Politics in Egypt*, 135.

84. Speech in June 1924 by the leading Wafdist 'Abd al-Rahman Fahmi, who also warned workers that unions must work to seek the sympathy and approval of the government or face the consequences: Beinin and Lockman, *Workers on the Nile*, 164.

85. Maghraoui, *Liberalism without Democracy*, 132.

86. Ibid., 132.

87. Carrie Wickham, *The Muslim Brotherhood: Evolution of an Islamist Movement* (Princeton: Princeton University Press, 2013), 22.

needs of the mass of people. Founded in 1928, the Brotherhood grew rapidly: by the mid-1930s it had established branches across Egypt, playing an increasingly prominent role in anti-colonial activities and in effect displacing the Wafd as the leading advocate of self-determination. The organization set its purposes within Islamic traditions; at the same time, in a novel development, it operated as a modern political party focused upon the nation-state. Like the Wafd, it pursued self-determination; unlike the Wafd and its nationalist rivals it aimed to transform the nation-state into an Islamic state.

This modernist politics in Islamic idiom reflected the experiences of Banna and his early supporters. Richard Mitchell notes that as a student Banna participated in the demonstrations of 1919 and recalled "with special bitterness" the presence of British soldiers in his home town of Mahmudiyya.[88] Khalil El-Enani comments that these early experiences "fostered al-Banna's nationalist sentiment against foreign powers and bec[a]me a feature of the MB's identity."[89] Unlike most of his childhood contemporaries Banna completed his education in modern rather than traditional Islamic institutions. Though influenced strongly by Sufism he also focused upon contemporary political debates, especially when in 1923 he moved to Cairo—a city in cultural and political ferment and still profoundly affected by the upheaval of 1919. According to his own account, Banna and his friends were preoccupied by the circumstances of Egypt under occupation—"the state of the nation . . . the sickness . . . and the remedies."[90] Unlike earlier Islamist ideologues, notably Jamal al-Din al-Afghani—a man he was later to describe as "the spiritual father"[91]—Banna was an activist and organizer, and established a series of groups that aimed to counsel and assist young Muslims he believed to be disoriented by the impacts of colonialism and of European culture in general. Significantly, the Brotherhood's first recruits were among workers at the British labor camp in Ismailiyya, a garrison town on the Suez Canal.

Initially the new organization did not engage directly with public politics. As it grew, however, establishing branches in cities along the Canal, in the Eastern Delta and eventually in Cairo, Banna paid close attention to enhancing public visibility and what Gudrun Krämer calls "corporate identity."[92] Now Banna developed strategies similar to those earlier pursued by the Wafd, establishing newspapers and journals, producing leaflets and pamphlets, and focusing on "grassroots

---

88. Richard Mitchell, *The Society of the Muslim Brothers* (Oxford: Oxford University Press, 1969) 3.

89. Khalil, Al-Enani, "The Power of the Jama'A: The Role of Hasan Al-Banna in Constructing the Muslim Brotherhood's Collective Identity," *Sociology of Islam* 1 (2013): 41–63, 43.

90. Mitchell, *The Society of the Muslim Brothers*, 5.

91. Ibid., 321.

92. Gudrun Krämer, *Hasan al-Banna*, (London: Oneworld Publications, 2009) 32.

mobilization."⁹³ The Brotherhood took on the key features of a modern political party, with members, local units, a general conference, centralized leadership (the General Guidance Office), systematic organization and recruitment, and—by the early 1930s—a political program that, observes Sami Zubaida, was "imbued with the assumptions of the modern national political field."⁹⁴

Most accounts of the Brotherhood's activity during this period emphasize its concern with personal conduct based on Quranic principles. There has been less interest in its program of economic and social reform, and the organization's success in constructing a complex network of educational and welfare bodies. Ziad Munson observes that the Brotherhood was rooted in specific religious traditions *and* in attempts to address major societal problems—to meet the needs of Egyptians whose expectations had been first raised, then frustrated by the advance and retreat of the national movement.⁹⁵ Using the concept of political opportunity structure in the context of Social Movement Theory, Munson suggests that the retreat of the Wafd "left Egyptian politics in disarray and opened a door of opportunity for new challengers."⁹⁶ In the absence of a popularly legitimated leader or party, Munson argues, large numbers of Egyptians were attracted by the Brotherhood's efforts to construct a novel social infrastructure that included mosques, schools, clinics, and youth projects.⁹⁷ A strategy of "public works" brought millions of people into contact with the organization and its ideas, including its demands on government for expansion of hospitals, improved working conditions for agricultural and industrial workers, a minimum wage, and government intervention to minimize unemployment. Munson compares this favorably with the efforts of Egypt's communists who, by the late 1920s, had been marginalized by the government and the colonial authorities.

In the mid-1930s the Brotherhood re-emphasized its anti-colonial policies, backing the Palestinian uprising against British occupation and Zionist settlement—a campaign that raised its profile at home and abroad. Banna now formally recognized a dual agenda—the organization's work "in [both] the external and internal political struggle."⁹⁸ By 1936 it claimed 150 branches and a presence across Egypt.⁹⁹ Most members came from among the *effendiya*, although the Brotherhood was also active in working-class areas, drawing in activists

---

93. John Calvert, *Sayyid Qutb and the Origins of Radical Islamism* (London: Hurst, 2010), 84.

94. Zubaida, *Islam, the People and the State*, 155.

95. Ziad Munson, "Islamic Mobilization: Social Movement Theory and the Egyptian Muslim Brotherhood," *Sociological Quarterly* 42, no. 4 (2001): 487–510.

96. Ibid., 490.

97. Ibid., 501.

98. Mitchell, *The Society of the Muslim Brothers*, 16.

99. Krämer, *Hasan al-Banna*, 45–6.

including some prominent industrial militants.[100] Here there were again parallels with the Wafd but whereas the latter had grown as part of the 1919 uprising, the Brotherhood emerged during a period of decline in popular politics. Beinin and Lockman observe that it was "a symptom of political disillusionment . . . the obvious failure of Egyptian liberalism to achieve full political independence or improve the standard of living of the people."[101]

Mitchell identifies an "ethical duality" at the heart of the Brotherhood project. Its leaders argued for wholesale reform of Egypt's political, economic, and social life facilitated by "the people from below";[102] at the same time, they intensified communal tensions by arguing against "Christian imperialism."[103] They championed individual rights while limiting women's entitlements: "true female progress," they argued, should be measured in terms of roles in the home and within the family.[104] The transgressive initiatives of 1919, including cross-communal activities, women in leadership and "carnival square," were unthinkable.

Revolutionary Process

Maghraoui warns against assessments of the Brotherhood "simply as a negative reaction against failed politics or social and economic depression," arguing for the importance of "modern, legitimate politics within Islamic discursive traditions."[105] This is an important corrective to analyses in which Islamic traditions are viewed as static and incompatible with modernist agendas. The Brothers were nonetheless activists who emerged during the retreat of a mass movement. Their founders had witnessed a "forcible entry of the masses" into the political arena *and* the latter's subsequent exclusion by the nationalist leadership, undertaking a withdrawal toward specifically Islamic visions of change in which Muslims rather than the mass of people were key actors. The Brotherhood bore the mark of the revolutionary process: its anti-colonial impulse, widespread ambition for societal change, and contestation of the state. At the same time, it reflected a decline in popular politics that was also part of the dynamic of the mass movement. Here it is the long view of the 1919 Revolution that assists in understanding the challenge to colonialism, the rise and fall of the Wafd and the emergence of a novel form of Islamic activism.

---

100. Beinin and Lockman trace the political trajectory of Taha Sa'd 'Uthman, a member of the Brotherhood who became a leading trade union activist and eventually joined the radical left: *Workers on the Nile*, 282–3.
101. Beinin and Lockman, *Workers on the Nile*, 363.
102. Mitchell, *The Society of the Muslim Brothers*, 223.
103. Ibid., 222, 230, 260.
104. Ibid., 257.
105. Maghraoui, *Liberalism without Democracy*, 144.

Chapter 5

BRITISH RESPONSES TO THE 1919 REVOLUTION

James Whidden

Introduction

The 1919 Revolution was one of several shattering events that forced the British to reconsider their relations with the colonial world after the Great War of 1914–18. At one end of the spectrum of future possibilities was the belief that a British "legal geography" precluded the possibility of exporting a British-type constitutional system to Africa or Asia, with the exception of the settler colonies (where the indigenous were excluded from rights and liberties).[1] On the other end there were the Wilsonian principles of self-determination for all nations.[2] The 1919 Revolution provoked intense debates on this issue among British officials in London and Cairo. Liberal imperialists or reformist British policy-makers could imagine Egypt following a path already laid out in colonial locations like Australia, Canada, New Zealand, and South Africa, where self-governing autonomy had been attained. But that path suggested that even British liberals could only envisage Egypt's future as fitting into a British constitutional framework—empire, dominion status, commonwealth, or a constitutional monarchy in the image of Britain's.[3] That vision

---

1. The idea that the British believed that English law could not be applied (or necessarily even followed by British subjects) in colonial locations is one of the central observations of proponents of the analytical device, "legal geography." See Eliga H. Gould, "Zones of Law, Zones of Violence: The Legal Geography of the British Atlantic, c. 1772," *William and Mary Quarterly* 60, no. 2 (2003): 471–510.

2. Erez Manela, *The Wilsonian Moment: Self-Determination and the International Origins of Anti-colonialism* (Oxford: Oxford University Press, 2006).

3. The desire to contain Egypt within an imperial framework was asserted by Winston Churchill, among others. See Richard Toye, *Churchill's Empire: The World that Made Him and the World He Made* (London: Pan Books, 2011), 119 and 149. See also Churchill's comments in FO371/6301 8245/260/16, "Imperial Conference" and FO371/10889 143/32/16, where he argued that Egypt should be either a dominion or a crown colony. For more generalized assessments of the British commitment to colonies following a path within an imperial framework, see John Darwin, "Britain's Empire," in *The British Empire: Themes and Perspectives*, ed. Sarah Stockwell (Oxford: Blackwell, 2008), 1–16; Andrew Thompson,

fell short of full autonomy, or as the Egyptians said, "complete independence" (*istiqlal tamm*).[4] Nevertheless, from a British perspective, the idea of including Egypt in the constitutional framework of empire as in the settler colonies was a positive reading of the extension of British liberties. Liberal theory had hitherto been applied only in the negative sense that concessions to nationalists would not lead to liberty, but to tyranny. This interpretation of "liberty" was a typical colonial device: nationalism in Egypt, India, or Ireland (the hotspots in 1919) would be nothing less than a religious ascendency, in Egypt a Muslim one, in India a Hindu, and in Ireland a Catholic.[5] Thus, in colonial liberal theory religious freedom was reserved for minorities, and denied for majorities on the principle of safeguarding religious liberty. Commentary on the Egyptian situation in 1919 indicates that the dominant view in 1919 was that Egyptian nationalism was ethnic or religious extremism, incapable of sustaining a pluralistic or representative form of government.

Yet, as the stages of the 1919 Revolution played out, a "liberal constitution" was written. It was premised on the idea that Western constitutional law could be exported to non-Western locations.[6] Constitutional reform suggests that liberals in Britain and Egypt won the debate. Certain constitutional arrangements limited the franchise and empowered the monarch, but not unlike the unwritten British constitution of the nineteenth century. As a result of these constitutional revisions, in 1923 the Liberal-Constitutional Party and the Wafd (Delegation) Party competed in open elections. The British countenanced the coming to power of the Wafd in 1924, a nationalist movement that had been suppressed in 1919. All this suggests the inauguration of a liberal era; however, in the final stage of the revolution, which could be described as a counter-revolution, the Wafd government was brought down after only ten months in power; in its place came a palace administration. Liberal nationalism suffered a major setback with the reentry of the ruling dynasty into politics. The fall of the Wafd, followed by

Imperial Britain: The Empire in British Politics: c. 1880–1932 (Harlow: Longman, 2000), 164; John Darwin, "The Dominion Idea in Imperial Politics," in *The Oxford History of the British Empire, Vol. IV: The Twentieth Century*, ed. Wm. Roger Louis (Oxford: Oxford University Press, 1999); "An Undeclared Empire: The British in the Middle East, 1918–1939," in *The Statecraft of British Imperialism: Essays in Honour of Wm. Roger Louis*, ed. Robert O. King and Robin Kilson (London: Frank Cass, 1999).

4. Saad Zaghlul, *Mudhakkirat Sa'd Zaghlul*, ed. 'Abd al-'Azim Ramadan (Cairo: Al-Hay'a al-'Misriyya al-'Amma lil-Kitab, 1987–1998), vol. 7, October 14, 1918.

5. Emily Jones, *Edmund Burke and the Invention of Modern Conservatism, 1830–1914: An Intellectual History* (New York: Oxford: Oxford University Press, 2017). As the author shows, modern conservatism had to bow to the cultural hegemony of liberalism, and therefore adopted its language on rights to create a modern conservative political language.

6. Marcel Colombe, *L'Évolution de l'Égypte* (Paris: G.P. Maisonneuve, 1951), 5, noting that the Egyptian constitution was based on the Belgian. The Belgian was modeled on the British.

royalist interventions and various coalition governments, meant that nationalist demands for "complete independence" were delayed until the revolution of 1952, and, perhaps more importantly, liberal institutions were atrophied.

What was the British part in these events? Was British policy designed to limit Egyptian independence and re-establish authoritarian, colonial power? Was the creation of a Liberal-Constitutional Party a divide-and-rule strategy in the absence of the sort of ethnic and communal divisions exploited in Iraq and Palestine? The conventional answer to these questions was, yes, there was a pact worked out between British colonial agents in the Foreign Office and the old regime in Egypt, evident in the creation of a monarchy by British decree in February 1922 with the consent of collaborating Egyptian ministers.[7] Subsequently, the constitution was a document that represented the ideological identification of Egyptian elites with their British sponsors, not a pact between the Egyptian government and its people.[8] It was only superficially a "liberal constitution," camouflaging the powers of the old regime.[9] As some observers then and subsequently noted, however, there was no evidence of a plot involving British agents and the king.[10] But there were ideological differences between revolutionary, liberal, and monarchist parties, comparable to developments in Europe. While revolutionaries and liberals imagined a simple transference of Western constitutional precepts to colonial locations, conservative thinkers tended to assume that the location, the "Oriental" society, would shape constitutional practice, even if a British-like system were adopted. Geography impacted on constitutional principles.[11] It was this belief,

---

7. Elie Kedourie, *Chatham House Version and Other Middle Eastern Studies* (London: Weidenfeld and Nicholson, 1970), is one example of the point of view that the liberal opposition to the Wafd was of British invention. British reports of the era noted that Wafd nationalists interpreted the liberal party and their constitutional bid as a manifestation of British power and therefore was described as divide-and-rule strategy: FO371/8973 4591/351/16, Allenby to Curzon, January 28 to February 5, 1923. This perspective was replicated in numerous histories of the era; however, more recent academic accounts suggest that the liberal-constitutional party in Egypt was motivated by ideological principle, as well as the colonial pact with elites: Selma Botman, "The Liberal Age," in *The Cambridge History of Egypt, vol. 2, Modern Egypt*, ed. M.W. Daly (Cambridge, Cambridge University Press, 1998), 289.

8. Abdeslam Maghraoui, *Liberalism without Democracy* (Durham: Duke University Press, 2006).

9. Ibrahim White, *La Nouvelle Constitution de l'Égypte* (Paris: Librairie de Jurisprudence Ancienne et Moderne, 1926).

10. Colombe, *L'Évolution de l'Égypte*, 22, notes that there was no evidence of an accord between Allenby and King Fu'ad in November 1924.

11. An example of this was the way the Paris postwar settlement assumed an arena of civic political culture in Western Europe, but only a zone of ethnic conflict in Eastern Europe and the Middle East.

shared by Egyptian monarchists and conservative imperialists, that fueled the counter-revolution.[12]

Egyptian Nationalism by 1919

A cartoon from a 1924 issue of the satirical journal *Kashkul* depicted the leader of the Wafd Party, Saad Zaghloul, as an effendi schoolteacher, dressed in suit and fez, instructing a class of turban-wearing rural shaykhs dressed in the traditional outfit of the fellahin, the *jallabiyya*.[13] Nationalism was an ideology associated with a bourgeois or "effendi," cultural leadership. Liberty from British colonialism was only one facet of the national project, others included uniting the leadership and its urban "class," the *effendiyya*, with the majority population, the *fellahin*, mostly rural agriculturalists.[14] The nationalists wanted to homogenize Egyptian culture, give it a national brand, and calibrate its temporal trajectory to bourgeois culture in Europe.[15] The culture of the nationalists was therefore premised on the reform of fellahin society through its transformation, including reforming social structures, such as the family, as represented by the seclusion of women and polygamy. The norm among the bourgeoisie or *effendiyya* was, by the early twentieth century,

---

12. It was significant that old regime elements were transformed in consequence of revolutionary events, adopting party organization and ideological positions, which, together with revolutionary and liberal position, suggests that Egypt was on the brink of a democratic transition by 1924. On the role of conservatives in revolutionary, democratic transformation, see Ellis Goldberg, "Arab Transitions and the Old Elite," in *The Arab Thermidor: The Resurgence of the Security State* (London: Middle East Centre, 2015), https://pomeps.org/wp-content/uploads/2015/03/POMEPS_Studies_11_Thermidor_Web.pdf, accessed November 4, 2019. Goldberg argues that democratic transition requires the participation, not the exclusion, of elements of the old regime in the new post-revolutionary institutions. A similar argument has recently been applied in a comparative analysis of democratic transition in Europe, noting that conservative party participation was essential in democratic state-building, Daniel Zimblatt, *Conservative Parties and the Birth of Democracy* (New York: Cambridge University Press, 2017).

13. Memorandum, Allenby to MacDonald, April 12, 1924, FO371/10020 3532/22/16, where *Kashkul* was described as the most popular journal in Egypt because it appealed to "illiterates." The journal has been described variously as Islamic and royalist in academic discussions. That the cartoons were all found in FO files, suggests that British officials were aware of the significance of these cultural divisions. Reproductions can be seen in James Whidden, M*onarchy and Modernity: Politics, Islam, and Neo-Colonialism between the Wars* (London: I.B. Tauris, 2013).

14. Michael Gasper, *The Power of Representation: Publics, Peasants, and Islam in Egypt* (Stanford: Stanford University Press, 2009).

15. Wilson Chacko Jacob, *Working Out Egypt: Effendi Masculinity and Subject Formation in Colonial Modernity, 1870–1940* (Durham: Duke University Press, 2011).

monogamy, single-family dwelling, and educational services for boys and girls. Effendi technicians lectured in journals on how to manage the home scientifically, proper hygiene, and exercise. Indeed, education had the meaning of educating and nurturing (*tarbiyya*) the nation into maturity.[16] Consumerism in effendi literature extolled the value of wearing the proper attire, certain lifestyles at work, and leisure, designed mostly for urban classes.[17] Also, the nationalist project involved transforming techniques of production in the agricultural and industrial sectors. Much of the groundbreaking research on Egyptian modern history has been on these themes, with effendi nationalism developing in a modernist dialog with the colonial powers, particularly Britain and France. Therefore, research has involved analysis of governmental or professional discourses that mirrored colonial theories, such as the division of the world between the civilized and uncivilized, productive societies and the stagnant. Effendi nationalists, many of them working alongside Europeans in the administration, professions, or business, were intent to demonstrate to the Europeans, particularly the British as the occupying power, that Egypt had come of age. Sovereignty and independence were understood in this sense of national arrival at modernity, including political rights, the rule of law, protections for minorities, and representative government.[18]

Educational reform was central to this national project, its ideological and organizational coherence, in the state school system, private schools administered by Europeans, or private Egyptian schools, as well as civil and political societies (*ijtima'iyyas*) devoted to various social and civic services or political programs. Mustafa Kamil, as the exemplary effendi nationalist, had been active in educational services and press campaigns that transformed the cultural orientation of Egyptians, particularly youths, instilling a subjective sense of devotion and service to the nation through its modernization, as well as commitment to a uniform national march toward independence.[19] The student strikes in 1906 were an

---

16. Timothy Mitchell, *Colonising Egypt* (Cambridge: Cambridge University Press, 1988), 97–100.

17. Mona Russell, *Creating the New Egyptian Woman: Consumerism, Education, and the National Identity* (New York: Palgrave, 2004).

18. Lisa Pollard argues that by 1919 effendi nationalism had reached maturity, something recognized by the British, *Nurturing the Nation: The Family Politics of Modernizing, Colonizing and Liberating Egypt, 1805–1923* (Berkeley: University of California Press, 2005), 211.

19. "Abd al-Rahman al-Rafi'i, *Mustafa Kamil ba'ith al-haraka al-qaumiyya: ta'rikh Misr qaumi min sana 1892–1908* (Cairo: Maktabat al-Nahda al-Misriyya, [1939] 1950). Rafi'i argued that Kamil embodied the spirit (*ruh*) of his generation (*jil*), identifying the nation with youth, vigor, and ideological commitment. Kamil was involved in educational renewal and its part in the reformation of cultural attitudes, particularly the formation of a uniform national identity, superseding the religious, ethnic, and class divisions that had characterized pre-national Egypt. His project was typical of the *effendiyya*, as defined in academic discourses on the subject. Kamil published articles on these themes in his journal

example of this activism, underlining the fact that by 1919 the Egyptians had well-established nationalist organizations, including societies, fraternities, journals devoted to disseminating nationalist ideas, not only resistance to British military occupation, but building the sorts of social structures and civic associations that sustained a national community. In Mustafa Kamil's thought a homogenous society needed to be constructed from the existing materials, the diverse classes, sects, regions, and nationalities within Egypt. Kamil was a non-state actor, but nationalists in the administration regarded their work also as transformative, often viewing fellahin society through the same lens as the European colonizers: that is to say, the nationalist perception was that their leadership constituted a civilizing encounter with an uncivilized society. This negative perception of the fellahin justified reformist projects designed to transform society, yet by the early twentieth century this paternalistic colonizing posture had also discovered in the fellahin a reservoir of authentic Egyptian identity. The *effendiyya* regarded itself as the moral guardian of Egyptian identity. In sum, the effendi had a complex relationship with the majority society, its nationalist ideology premised on the essential unity of Egyptian society, regarding Egyptianness as essentially homogenous, Nile Valley-centered, Cairo-centered, and state-centered. The dominant language of nationalism, expressed in Arabic in opposition to the often Turkish-speaking or at least Ottoman-Egyptian culture of the ruling dynasty and elite, as well as the various vernaculars of regional communities across "Egyptian" territory, was largely founded on Cairene culture, reformulated by the nationalists for mass consumption.[20]

The cultural dominance of the *effendiyya* can be disputed.[21] Alongside a coherent ideology, liberal, nationalist, and modernist, it was composed of individuals from the middle stratum of landholders (*a'yan*), monopolizing much of the wealth, and therefore with access to the schools that opened career opportunities in the professions and state administration. Attainment of these led to the new status of effendi. Education and wealth gave this "class" immense influence. Yet, the very success of the *effendiyya* in mobilizing popular support for the national cause introduced elements into political society from its rural base, as well as marginal groups and the urban lower classes. Egypt remained a heterogeneous society, with the obvious cultural distinction being the division between the elite and the fellahin majority. This divide was represented popularly in the press. For instance, common tropes in the press from the late nineteenth century portrayed the effendi as the wearer of fez and suit against the rural fellahin or urban *baladi* (popular

---

Majalla al-Madrasa from 1893 and in *al-Liwa'* before forming the Watani Party in 1907 (Ibid., 96, 104–8, 195).

20. Ziad Fahmy, *Ordinary Egyptians: Creating the Modern Nation through Popular Culture* (Palo Alto: Stanford University Press, 2011).

21. Marilyn Booth, "Wayward Subjects and Negotiated Disciplines: Body Politics and the Boundaries of Egyptian Nationhood," *International Journal of Middle East Studies* 45, no. 2 (2013): 353–74.

classes), dressed in turban and *jallabiyya*. Often the effendi was lampooned as self-interested, slavenly devoted to European modernity. It is not surprising therefore that many Egyptians' subjective sense of their cultural values deviated from intellectual, effendi articulations of Egyptianness, and while these might not have openly been in conflict with effendi nationalism before 1919, the move toward full sovereignty and its attendant effendi dominance after 1919 led to the emergence of political and cultural currents in opposition to the dominant discourse of nationalism. Egyptian culture was diverse and dynamic and would not easily fit into the mold created by the effendi cultural leadership. These divisions were of course already apparent in politics. Shaykh Shawish's religious or cultural nationalism contrasts with Lutfi al-Sayyid's liberal nationalism; and each were distinct to Mustafa Kamil's territorial patriotic nationalism. But these distinctions hardly captured the diversity of subjective positions, sometimes founded on not only religious but also regional and class position. While some in the cultural leadership might have chosen a proto-Islamist message, just as significant were the various constituencies that might respond to different appeals, such as the Sa'idi or Upper Egyptian, the Christian and Jewish Egyptians, the *baladi* Egyptians, the fellahin, the migrant workers, the *Shami* (Syrian), all of these groups indicated social and cultural cleavages in the nation as imagined by the effendi nationalists. But even within effendi national culture, among that bourgeois formation that defined the *effendiyya*, the dominant nationalist characterization was critiqued, indicating an underlining questioning of national culture that challenged bourgeois ideals. This suggests also that there were diverse constituencies that the cultural leadership appealed to.[22]

It has been observed: "Nationalism often borrowed, built upon, or incorporated religious practices and symbols, giving rise to religious-nationalist fusions."[23] This aspect of effendi nationalism has been ignored in much of the historiography because of effendi theorizing on nationalism as a secular phenomenon, where "civil religion, secular rituals, and territorial ties" were regarded as having replaced older loyalties.[24] It was also ignored by the nationalists, who represented their movement as mature and cohesive and therefore unwilling to countenance the diversity of political orientations in 1919 and afterwards. The use of old symbols of community in nationalist ideology might have been designed as purely functional, a means of mobilization and fusion of the community. But they carried a paradox also. The 1919 slogan "Patriotism is our religion" was later turned back on the effendi cultural leadership in 1923 to underline the unrepresentative character of the effendi leadership in its relationship with the majority population, or the failure of effendi culture to embrace the "authentic" culture of the fellahin, rooted in religious faith. This was a major line of political fissure capitalized on by the

---

22. Ibid., 361–2.

23. Beth Baron, *Egypt as a Woman: Nationalism, Gender, and Politics* (Berkeley: University of California Press, 2005), 189.

24. Ibid.

opposition to the Liberal-Constitutional Party in 1923 and the Wafd Party in 1924. The British were close observers of these fissures, evident in the British reaction to the 1919 Revolution.

The Reaction

The initial response from March 1919 was to dismiss the revolution as an anarchic expression of religious or racial intolerance manipulated by an irresponsible nationalist leadership. Why irresponsible? Because the nationalists, according to official British reports, were unrepresentative. This was an old colonial doctrine readily available to deny the extension of liberal reform to Egypt. Typical of the writings of Lord Cromer (consul-general 1883–1907), the doctrine was based on the theory of an imperial duty to the majority population, the "fellaheen," the rural population of farmers, a population that the British had always imagined as segmented into regional, village, tribal, or religious communities, exploited by a rapacious oligarchy.[25] Cromer applied the language of the French Revolution to the situation, describing the nationalists as a "Jacobin" faction within a political society formerly "Girondist." The radicals exploited the xenophobia of the base population to the peril of the hierarchy, Ottoman-Egyptian and colonial, the guardians of civil institutions. These ideas were typical of British political theory in the late nineteenth century and characteristic of British responses to nationalists in Ireland and their supporters in England.[26] In Cromer's reading of Egyptian events, moderate opinion, associated with the rural "gentry" was superseded by

---

25. Earl of Cromer, *Modern Egypt*, vol. 2 (London: Macmillan, 1908), 148 and 186–99, where Cromer is quite explicit on the predatory character of the Egyptian elites, "Pasha" and "Sheikh." Colonial doctrine, as formulated by him, identified with the fellahin and distrusted the educated Egyptians, or as Cromer said, "Europeanised Egyptians" (the *effendiyya*). That the doctrine continued to be influential can be seen in analysis of the revolution, where the causes were found in those "fellah," that is to say those not from the "Turkish" class of pashas, that had risen in status through education at the European schools, of whom Zaghlul was exemplary as the "first fellah." Younger members of this educated "fellah" category were marked by their anti-British political radicalism. These types were described by advisers to the Egyptian government, Reginald Patterson and Maurice Amos, as a new "middle class" and thus fit the designation *effendiyya*, as commonly used in academic discourse. Amos stated that the use of the term "fellah" in colonial doctrine was ideological, representing a school of colonial domination that denied the legitimacy of the nationalists, Sir Maurice Amos, "The Constitutional History of Egypt for the Last Forty Years," *The Grotius Society* 14 (1929): 153.

26. On the importance of the French Revolution in defining British conservative political thought, particularly the binary of parliamentary constitutionalism against utopia-driven revolutionary radicalism, see Jones, *Edmund Burke and the Invention of Modern Conservatism, 1830–1914*.

revolutionary nationalism in the hands of those educated in European political theories, particularly revolutionary French, normally associated with the pre-war Watani Party led by Kamil.[27]

As Lord Curzon reported to the House of Lords on March 24, 1919, peasant revolts targeted communications "with a system and method that seem to indicate a carefully planned organisation." Tenants had risen against landlords. The Bedouin, a "lawless element," plundered. But these acts followed a plan that showed the hand of a nationalist organization.[28] Curzon condemned the revolutionary "movement" for its disorder and violence. Western-educated Egyptians (or those exposed to such ideas), in this analysis, were viewed as the origin or inspiration of political activism, described in pejorative terms as misguided "revolutionaries."[29] Such reports decoded the revolutionary political language in 1919 as evidence of the "extremist" character of ethnic nationalism, its rejection of political compromise, pluralism, religious freedom, and freedom of expression.[30]

Yet, the sustained and popular character of the 1919 revolt forced the British government to offer concessions, including the freeing of the exiled and imprisoned leadership of the Wafd. Thus, Lord Milner led a "Mission" that was delegated from late 1919 to assess the cause of the revolt. Eventually, it advised concessions designed to appeal to "moderate" nationalists.[31] Signaling an end to

27. On the Girondists, see Cromer, *Modern Egypt*, vol. 2, 177–80 and 235–41. Cromer compared the revolutionaries in 1882 to the "French Jacobins," *Modern Egypt*, vol. 1, 289 and 325. A similar discourse on the dangers of French culture and the "doctrinaires" can be found in his Annual Reports, *Parliamentary Papers*, Accounts and Papers, 106/54, Egypt No. 1 (1907). For the post-1919 period, the British attribution of revolutionary terror to the Wafd, as a justification for intervening in Egyptian parliamentary democracy, is followed by Colombe, *L'Évolution de l'Égypte*, 29–37.

28. Lord Curzon, *Parliamentary Papers* (Lords) 33 (1919), March 24, 1919: 878–80. Curzon identified the revolution with a technically sophisticated leadership. See also FO141/744/8916, "General Army Headquarters. Cairo," March 26, 1919, and a file in the same series, dated April 21 referring to the "effendi" leadership. The effendis dominated the Wafd executive, but the majority membership of the Wafd were rural "notables," a group sometimes described as the rich fellahin in British accounts. An Egyptian assessment of the membership of the Wafd is given in the Egyptian National Archives (ENA), Abdin Files, Box 216, "Political Parties, 1919–1947," showing that the Wafd in 1919 consisted of rural notables (*a'yan*), many carrying the status of village mayor (*'umda*), members of provincial councils (*majlis al-mudiriyya*), district inspector (*nazir*), or tribal deputy (*wakil qabila*).

29. FO141/744/8916, "General Army Headquarters, Cairo," March 26, 1919.

30. FO141/744/8916 and a file in the same series, dated April 21, referring to the "effendi" leadership.

31. FO371/4978 5168/6/16, "Report of the Special Mission to Egypt." The mission was initially designed to frame a new constitution enabling self-governing institutions under the protectorate, but the report eventually called for the abolition of the protectorate and a treaty that secured Britain's special interests in Egypt, known as the "Reserved Points."

the protectorate and support for Egyptian self-government, Milner's proposals marked a shift in imperial thinking. Churchill responded by describing Milner's proposals as "revolutionary" and objected to any "parleying with rebels."[32] He first sounded warning bells with the leaking of the Milner Report in September 1920.[33] At the same time, Egyptian "moderates" split away from the Wafd, voicing criticism of Zaghloul and his national leadership during the negotiations in London in 1920 and again in 1921. Zaghloul distanced himself from the negotiations by claiming that British proposals fell short of "complete independence" (*istiqlql tamm*), the central platform of the Wafd from its inception in late 1918. Adli Yakan, who formed a government in March 1921, attempted to lead negotiations with the British in May 1921. The Wafd responded with massive protests accompanied by violent confrontations, particularly in Alexandria.

Colonial analysis from the spring of 1919 pointed to the "extremist" political language of the Wafd, identifying phrases such as "sacred union" (*ittihad muqaddas*) or "Patriotism is our religion" (*al-wataniyya hiya dinna*). The first slogan repeated a French nationalist motto that imagined the nation as organically whole, to the exclusion of aliens, and signified a nation at war against its enemies, foreign and domestic. The latter slogan was first used in Egypt in 1919 and might have inspired the assassination attempt on the prime minister, Yusuf Wahba, who had enabled the reception of the Milner Mission to Egypt in late 1919 (boycotted by the Wafd).[34] Also, so-called "Orientalist" interpretations appeared alongside these descriptions of the radical, revolutionary threat to liberty. In an official inquiry into the causes of violence during demonstrations in 1921 it was shown by British officials that nationalist ideology appealed to religious feeling, the "sacred" qualities of the cause. For instance, Wafd pamphlets and manifestos described the "moderate" nationalists as "dissidents" (*munshaqqin*) or "infidels" (*murtaddin*).[35]

32. J. A. Spender, *The Changing East* (London: Cassell, 1926), 74–5.

33. As Colonial Secretary, Churchill also voiced his opposition to Milner's policy at the Imperial Conference of 1921: FO371/6301 8245/260/16.

34. On the idea of a sacred union, see Zaghlul's response to the report of the Milner Commission, in Abd al-Rahman al-Rafi'i, *Thawra sana 1919: Tarikh misr qaumi sana 1919 ila sana 1921* (Cairo: Maktaba al-nahda al-misriyya, 1946), 166. See also, FO371/6295 6037/260/16. Commentary on this sort of political language can be found in Louis Joseph Cantori, *The Organizational Basis of an Elite Political Party: The Egyptian Wafd* (Chicago: University of Chicago, PhD, 1966), 247. On the use of the slogan "patriotism is our religion" by the Wafd leadership in 1919, see Mounir Fakhry Abdel Nour, "Reflections on the 1919 Independence Movement: Copts in the 1919 Revolution," Conference Paper, *The Egyptian Revolution of 1919: Birth of the Nation*, University of London, March 2019. For context, see Dina Ezzat, "The Coptic Contingent," *Al-Ahram Weekly* (March 7, 2019), Issue 1433, http://english.ahram.org.eg/NewsContent/1/1199/327758/Egypt/-Revolution/-A-peoples-revolution-The-Coptic-contingent-------.aspx, accessed December 9, 2019.

35. *Parliamentary Papers*, 42/24, Egypt no. 3 (1921), "Military Inquiry into the Alexandria Riots, May 1921," 240. Cantori, *The Organizational Basis of an Elite Political Party*, 319.

5. British Responses to the 1919 Revolution 103

The conclusion to be drawn by reactionaries was that radical nationalists, the revolutionaries, did not represent political principle or political community, only the intolerance of a religious collective. The revolution was inspired by tales of heroes and martyrs from Islamic history, where the motives for political action were honor and shame.[36] This analysis demonstrated, for some British observers, that the revolutionaries could not play by constitutional rules, and therefore proved that the revolution was a millenarian movement typical of "Oriental" societies, capitalized on by the "effendi," those educated in modern theories of national politics but not fully removed from "Islamic" or "Oriental" cultures.[37]

Egyptian "moderates" and monarchists also adopted this critique of Zaghloul. Thus, the slogan "Patriotism is our religion" appeared again in a cartoon from a 1923 issue of the journal *Kashkul*, where an effendi politician is depicted leading a fellah subject to the polling station. The caption had the effendi claim that he had not written a single word of that political slogan.[38] In other words, the

---

36. This was the point underlined in the inquiry, cited earlier, but these attributes of the revolution have been followed in Rheinhard Schulze, *Die Rebellion ägyptischen Fallahin 1919* (Berlin: Baalbek Verlag, 1981) and Cantori, *The Organizational Basis of an Elite Political Party*, who said that Zaghlul had acquired the symbolic authority of the shaykh in each community, which, when replicated across the entirety of society, created the conditions for his universal leadership (Ibid., 420). This type of content in nationalist ideology is supported by Naguib Mahfouz, *Fountain and Tomb* (Boulder: Three Continents Press, 1988) 28, where Zaghlul was also described as a "shaykh."

37. This line of analysis can be found in FO371/4978 4369/6/16, "Report of the council of Cairo Non-official British Community." For similar treatments, FO371/4978 5168/6/16, "Report of the Special Mission to Egypt," where Milner reported that nationalism was pursued by the "educated and semi-educated classes, who constitute less than 10% of the 14 million inhabitants" and was "meaningless to 92% of illiterates and fellahin who make up 2/3s of the populace."

38. FO371/8963 10383/10/16, "Zaghloul Pasha's Electoral Campaign." By 1919 the effendi was a generic type in Egyptian culture. The question might be asked if the British had a similar understanding of this type. That this cartoon was collected by British analysts suggests it was. That the term "effendi" was commonly used by British in this period, see for instance Middle East Centre Archives, GB 165-0184, John De Vere Loder, Memoirs, December 23 1917. See FO371/4978 4369, where Egyptian society is divided between the "millions of fellaheen" and the "effendis," defined as "gov't employees and students aspiring to these posts." Difficult to determine when the modern idea of the effendi was first used by the British in the sense of a cultural designation but Butrus Ghali's assassin, Ibrahim al-Wardani, was described in this way, *Times*, February 22, 1910: 1. Commentary from British colonial sources in the pre-war period resembles subsequent academic analysis of the *effendiyya*. The *Times*, November 23, 1924: 1, used the term "effendi" to describe the assailants that assassinated Sir Lee Stack. Finally, to underline the importance of the concept of "effendi" in colonial political analysis, the police investigation into the assassination of

Wafd exploited religious feeling to build a political constituency among the rural population. The diagram satirized the artificial character of the political activist, the effendi, suggesting that the language of nationalism was meaningless to the common Egyptian, the fellahin, a group, as it suggests, unfamiliar or hostile to the idioms of modernist political language.[39] That the cartoon was recorded in Foreign Office files suggests that the British identified the significance of these political divisions in the nationalist camp. From the "dissentient" nationalists (the "moderates") would emerge the Liberal-Constitutional Party, representing those that accepted the colonial conditions or "reservations" written into the British government's unilateral declaration of Egyptian independence in 1922. The Wafd rejected the reservations as an affront to the principle of "complete independence."[40]

Imperial Reform

A relief from the Zaghloul monument in Alexandria, an iconic piece of nationalist art produced after the 1919 Revolution, depicts the High Commissioner Reginald Wingate receiving Zaghloul at British headquarters, November 13, 1918. The nationalist imagery has Wingate as imperial proconsul on his throne, backed by a line of British soldiers. While the image suggests that Zaghloul's demands for "complete independence" were rejected, in fact, Wingate was willing to entertain the demands of the nationalists. That he did so gave those demands legitimacy. Wingate returned to Europe in early 1919 promising the Egyptian nationalist leaders, Zaghloul and his associates, that he would deliver their demands to the British cabinet.[41] That he failed to win them a hearing at the Peace Conference led

---

Stack established that a political group led by "effendis" was responsible, Thomas Russell, *Egyptian Service* (London: John Murray, 1949), 214.

39. On the application of the term "effendi" to the Wafd of this period, see Marius Deeb, *The Wafd and its Rivals* (London: Ithaca Press, 1979), 272 and 320, who speaks of the centrality of the *effendiyya* in the Wafd, including the educated but unemployed effendi. Deeb describes the *effendiyya* as those who molded opinion, set up the nation's "ideals and stamped it with its particular character" (Ibid., 12). See Michael Eppel, "Note about the Term Effendiyya in the History of the Middle East," *International Journal of Middle East Studies* 41, no. 3 (2009): 535–9 and Lucie Ryzova, *The Age of the Effendiyya* (Oxford: Oxford University Press, 2015), offering an extended analysis of this cultural type in the period after 1919.

40. The reservations were British protection of minorities, imperial communications, the status of the Sudan as a separate administrative unit, and the right of the British to defend Egypt from foreign aggression.

41. Zaghlul, *Mudhakkirat Sa'd Zaghlul*, vol. 7, February 3, 1919, records that Wingate departed Cairo for Paris on January 20 with the promise that he would insist that the Wafd or Delegation should travel to Paris and that he would arrange for Zaghlul to address the conference.

to the resignation of the Egyptian ministry on the first of March, an important step in the revolution; it also led the British cabinet to dismiss Wingate from his post as high commissioner.

The cabinet rejected the legitimacy of the Wafd. Wingate was more liberal, appreciating the substance of nationalist demands for national self-government, if not "self-determination."[42] Wingate was not alone in his assessment. In anticipation of the Milner Report in May 1920, Valentine Chirol, writing for the *Times*, asked if it was the intention of the British government to repeat the "fatal blunder" of the veiled protectorate when Eldon Gorst and Herbert Kitchener chose to placate the ex-Khedive at the cost of the support of the "best elements of the Nationalist Party."[43] After the Milner Report was leaked in September 1920 conservative imperialists, like Churchill, rallied to block it; but reformists, like Chirol, defended the Milner Proposals as an "offer of partnership." His arguments were not that different from Curzon's, as he said, Egypt was unready for national self-determination because the population was largely illiterate. Also, he said that the "Independence Party" did not represent the majority, and that its methods and ideology threatened a resurgence of the "reactionary forces of the Islamic world." But he clearly felt the need to conciliate nationalist opinion in Egypt by adopting the reformist path of self-government within a British constitutional geography.[44]

Such attitudes distinguished liberal imperialists from the "die-hards," a term that from 1922 would be applied to conservative imperialists. The former represented the Milner Report as a restoration of Egypt's constitutional autonomy and a measured extension of the principles of British liberty against the powers of an "Oriental" despot, a principle shared with liberal nationalists in Egypt. This argument was strongly advanced by British advisers at the various Egyptian ministries, very much against the preferences of the British cabinet. One of these advisers, Maurice Amos, a legal expert at the Egyptian Ministry of Justice, submitted a series of memoranda in support of the policy associated with the Milner Report. Amos rejected the colonial doctrine of a society divided between rural majority (he refused to employ the term "*fellahin*" because he regarded it as ideologically loaded) and educated minority by arguing that Egypt was divided only by opinion: first, there was the moderate party of the "educated and older members of the professions"; secondly, the revolutionary party consisting of students at religious and state schools, and the younger professionals emanating from each. It is significant that he regarded national opinion as shared by these two social sectors, religious and state schools, against the colonial doctrine that

---

42. Valentine Chirol, *The Egyptian Problem* (London: Macmillan, 1921), 142–3, where Chirol credits the nationalists with "perspicacity" for their "close study" of the constitutional implications of the war aims declared by Wilson and Lloyd George.

43. FO371/4984 4069/93/16, May 1, 1920, Allenby to Curzon, V. Chirol in the *Times*, "The Sultan's Position in the Protectorate."

44. "Home Rule in Egypt," *The New York Times*, September 9, 1920: 1. See also Chirol, *Egyptian Problem*, 299–301.

Egyptian society was divided between mass and elite, "traditional" and "modern," (fellahin and effendi), with little cultural correspondence between the two.⁴⁵

As Amos argued, the educated classes had various means to shape public opinion and even if influenced by European languages and cultures, translated these ideas into local idioms through the mediums that represented the old and new types of political practice: religious and political party ideology. Rather than isolated communities of village, quarter, clan, and sect, Amos suggested that networks of press and telegraph, mosque and café, enabled the building of informed political constituencies. Nationalism was not a foreign intrusion, indecipherable to the average person, but rather was current and posed a real threat to those groups in Egypt or Britain unable to respond and speak that language. By asserting the legitimacy of the nationalist leadership and its constitutional demands, Amos thus enveloped Egyptian nationalism within the constitutional frontiers of empire. That the revolutionaries were representative of Egyptian national opinion demanded constitutional reform in Egypt comparable to imperial reform in the settler colonies. By highlighting politics (contesting groups or parties) rather than social or cultural essentials (effendi, shaykh, fellahin, Bedouin) his analysis marked a major break with the old colonial doctrine. A liberal imperialist policy had, however, to be forced upon a reluctant cabinet. After much persuasion from Amos, backed up by High Commissioner Edmund Allenby, a reluctant British cabinet made the unilateral declaration of Egyptian independence, February 28, 1922.

By 1922 it seemed the revolution had inaugurated a liberal era. Indeed, one result of the 1919 Revolution was to strengthen the hand of the Egyptian liberals against the ruling dynasty. The liberals in Egypt made a bid to change the balance of political forces in Egypt through constitutional reform. The Egyptian monarch responded by blocking any concessions to liberal demands, either elections or a constitutional regime that established ministerial responsibility to a parliament, rather than the ruler, as had previously been the case. Egyptian liberals campaigned against the monarchists in the press, alerting public opinion to this threat to liberty. The British officials on the ground, observing the work of the constitutional commission, threw their support behind the liberals.⁴⁶

To undermine the liberal experiment and restore royal autocracy, the monarchy turned against the Liberal-Constitutional Party in 1922, the year of its formation, by purchasing political journals that maligned the Liberal-Constitutionals as colonial

---

45. Maurice Amos, Memorandum, FO371/6295 4919/260/16, April 16, 1921, "Alternative Proposals for the Future Government of Egypt" and Amos, Memo, FO371/8961 3397/10/16, Allenby to Curzon, March 24, 1922, "Note of Sir Maurice Amos," and Amos, "The Constitutional History of Egypt," 153.

46. FO371/8961 4589/10/16, Allenby to Curzon, 24 Mar. 1922, "Egyptian Constitution," with the correspondence indicating that the monarchists limited the scope of liberal reform through the constitutional commission, but the restoration of full autocracy was blocked by the Liberal-Constitutionals with British support.

agents and enemies of the nation.⁴⁷ Meanwhile the Wafd directed its propaganda campaign at the Liberal-Constitutionals also, not the king. This amounted to a political alliance between the monarchists and the Wafd against the liberals. It was cemented in May 1923 when Hasan Nash'at, previously a member of the Wafd, began to act as liaison between Zaghloul and the king. The king's strategy involved, firstly, turning to destroy the Liberal-Constitutionals, and secondly, separating a "conservative" faction from the Wafd Party.⁴⁸ That this campaign was led by a former member of the Wafd Party, Nash'at, indicated that the struggle was not between social sectors, traditional and modern, but between differing political positions within the cultural leadership.

The Liberal-Constitutional government—challenged from the right and the left, monarchist and revolutionary—fell in late 1922, and replaced, eventually, by a royalist cabinet. Coming shortly after Zaghloul's second exile from Egypt, the Wafd refused to recognize the 1922 declaration and its colonial reservations. As a result, the Wafd also refused to participate in the constitutional commission, which then became a battleground between Liberal-Constitutionals and monarchists. Indicating that the British government sought a reformed administration, colonial agents helped the liberals on the commission check the monarchists and establish the sovereignty of parliament in the constitution.⁴⁹ The constitution was not simply a pact between Egyptian old regime elements and the British government.⁵⁰ That formula does not capture the complexity of colonial politics. The monarchy's ability to shape the document was limited by British support for the liberal position; however, in its final version, written during the stewardship of a monarchist appointee to the ministry, the constitution enshrined the king's powers of patronage, or as the prominent liberal 'Abd al-Khaliq Tharwat observed, secured the "traditional" rights of the Islamic prince.⁵¹ Colonial observers noted that these powers marked the beginning of the formation of a king's party. However, the evidence does not indicate that the British officials endorsed the formation of a monarchist autocracy; that development had to wait for the coming to power of a Conservative government in London in late 1924.

In effect, the constitution was a compromise between liberal and conservative nationalists, with the intention of excluding the more revolutionary Wafd Party.⁵²

47. ENA, "Majlis al-Wuzara," Box 1/3/B, *La Liberté*, July 29, 1922, where the monarchist publicist insisted that the king was ignorant of the machinations of the Liberal-Constitutionals.

48. ENA, Abdin, Box 218, "Review of Parties," Hizb al-Ittihad, letter dated January 1925 and FO371/10887 1257/29/16.

49. FO371/8961, Allenby to Curzon, April 23, 1922, "Egyptian Constitution."

50. The classic statement of this position was Kedourie, "Sa'd Zaghlul and the British," *Chatham House*.

51. FO371/8963 85/85/16. See also Kedourie, "Sa'd Zaghlul and the British," 175.

52. FO371/8973 4591/351/16, Allenby to Curzon, Situation Report, April 28 to May 7, 1923, "The Constitution," where journals reviewed showed that there was not any conflict

Ironically for the liberal architects, strengthening the liberal position with the support of liberal imperialists in Britain meant that the monarchists would work parallel to the Wafd Party to destroy the Liberal-Constitutional Party in the electoral campaigns of 1923, resulting in a parliament dominated by the Wafd Party.

Reaction Again

The collusion of Wafd Party and monarchy began during the electoral campaign. As it turned out this tactic had serious ramifications for future developments, opening a pathway for the monarchy's coming to power.

From February 1922, the Liberal-Constitutional government used its powers of state patronage to pack the administration with its clients, who in turn would lean on constituents in electoral campaigns. But when that government fell, succeeded by a ministry more amenable to the monarchists, the king's supporters applied similar pressure in the department of the Ministry of Interior to appoint electoral officials and redraw electoral boundaries. Zaki Bey Ibrashi, a client of the king, and Mahmud Fahmi Nuqrashi, a confident of Zaghloul, together drew up the constituencies to the advantage of Wafd candidates.[53] A department set up in 1923 to organize the agricultural cooperatives was controlled by members of the Wafd. These were then transformed into vehicles to corral voters.[54] It was these stratagems that were lampooned in the 1923 cartoon that depicted effendi and fellahin arm-in-arm.[55] While liberal critics derided the Wafd in this way for abandoning principles, these tactics ensured the Wafd's victory in the elections.

This was a surprising result for British officials that had envisioned a Liberal-Constitutional government and now confronted a revolutionary government. Rather than take an obstructionist position toward the Wafd, however, the British let the political and ideological divisions in Egypt play themselves out. The monarchist campaign to topple the Wafd government began at the opening of parliament, without any evidence of collusion with the British authorities. To start, the king forced Zaghloul to read the speech from the throne that recognized the autonomy of Sudan. This led to heated disputes in parliament where more radical deputies challenged Zaghloul, accusing him of surrendering the territory.[56] The king also provoked the Wafd government by rejecting civilian oversight of

between the "throne" and the "people."

53. FO371/10022 9303/22/16, *Egyptian Gazette*, January 8 and 12, 1924.
54. FO371/8961 2512/10/16.
55. FO371/8963 10383/10/16.
56. Jayne Gifford, *Britain in Egypt: Egyptian Nationalism and Imperial Strategy, 1919–1931* (London: I.B. Tauris, 2019). This work argues that the status of the Sudan was a key consideration for British policy-makers in Egypt, with the Wafd perceived as the primary obstacle to that policy.

royal prerogatives, like appointments to ministries and religious institutions. After another round of failed negotiations with the British government in the summer of 1924 (partly a result of monarchist obstructions), the complexion of the government changed with the appointment of more revolutionary members of the Wafd to ministerial positions. All of these events had an impact on conservative opinion.[57] The wealthiest landholders appear to have made the decision to strike at the Wafd while they still had some measure of control over their local constituencies, as testified by Muhammad Badrawi Ashur, the largest landowner in Lower Egypt.[58] Loyalty to the ruling family as guardian of the integrity of the Egyptian state was another factor.[59] Zaghloul's rhetoric (veiled republicanism as it was described in British reports) posed a direct threat to the century-long monarchical tradition.[60] After the assassination of Sir Lee Stack on November 19, 1924, British intelligence reports cited Wafd speeches from September 1924 (after the failed treaty negotiations) as incitement to revolutionary violence.[61] A series of reports documented the incendiary language of the Wafd leadership in the run-up to the assassination (the assassins were described as "effendis").[62] All of this supported conservative imperialist opinion that imperial reform from 1920 had only led to revolutionary "Terror."[63] The Wafd government fell in late 1924, succeeded by a cabinet containing royalists and a few of the less prominent Liberal-Constitutionals (most liberals refused to participate).[64] British conservative imperialists also seized the opportunity to stall the revolutionary bid for complete independence and, as it turned out, limit the scope of liberal reform.

57. Press Reports, FO371/10022 9971/22/16.

58. On Badrawi, as well as other prominent defectors from the Wafd, see FO371/10887 1257/29/16.

59. Zaki Fahmi, *Safwat al-'Asr* (Cairo: Mataba'at al-I'timad, 1926), a royalist tract, includes an extended essay on this principle in the introduction and underlines it in each biographical entry; similar arguments were made in the monarchist press throughout 1924 and 1925.

60. FO371/10044 10208/368/16.

61. FO371/10020 1727/22/16 and FO371/10887 2237/29/16. British intelligence reports on Wafd extremism and the assassination of Stack.

62. *Times*, November 23, 1924: 1 and Russell, *Egyptian Service*, 214 and FO371/10022 9971/22/16.

63. FO371/10887 2337/29/16 includes a report two years after the assassination. See also FO371/11582 637/25/16. The son of the British adviser to the Egyptian Ministry of Interior, Henry Keown-Boyd, refers to this in his memoir, *Lion and Sphinx, The Rise and Fall of the British in Egypt, 1882–1956* (Durham: Memoir Cub, 2002).

64. FO371/11582 637/25/16, 1926 and FO141 787/27, 1928, "Political Murders in Egypt." A report made by an independent panel of inquiry into the murder of Sir Lee Stack showed that Shafiq Mansur, the lead political assassin in the case, claimed that Nash'at, the king's political agent, had inspired the assassination. Nash'at had been involved in the Wafd's "secret apparatus" or militant wing before joining the monarchists.

The case to include Egypt within the orbit of a reformed empire, as initiated in the settler colonies, was maligned according to the old doctrine that Egyptian self-rule amounted to misrule.⁶⁵ The authoritarian elements in Egyptian political society lined up behind the king and conservative imperialists in Britain. But colonial officials in Cairo or London did not determine this outcome. The formation of a conservative monarchist party was not a consequence of British power, but rather was political, indicating the ability of the monarchists to build a body of support in the parliament, and, eventually, in the constituencies. The monarchists appealed not only to elites, the great pashas, but also to the middle stratum elements that had formerly flocked to the Wafd.⁶⁶

The building of a conservative party to counter liberals and radicals is an essential part in the building of a stable democracy; however, the process needs to be attended by a respect for civil, democratic institutions. Confounding democratic processes, the monarchists in Egypt found in the tragic events of November 1924 a pathway to dismantle the liberal institutions of 1923. To do so, they exploited the specter of revolutionary "Terror" (even if invented by themselves). The British reacted in such a way as to throw support behind the monarchy. Indeed, British anxieties—the fear of revolutionary violence—led to the fall of the Wafd government.⁶⁷ Afterwards, British agents and their clients in Egypt did not adhere to the liberal precepts of the constitution, as might have been envisaged by liberal imperialists and their Egyptian allies in 1923. Rather than work within the liberal-constitutional system created in that year, the king and his advisers (including

---

65. Lord Lloyd, *Egypt since Cromer* (London: Macmillan, 1933), a conservative imperialist critique of Egyptian nationalism and liberal imperialists as told by the high commissioner. Lord Lloyd ensured that the Wafd stayed out of power between 1925 and 1929.

66. ENA, Abdin Palace Files, Box 218, "*Dossier al-Ḥukuma al-Malakiyya al-Miṣriyya*" (Report of the royal government of Egypt), n.d. This dossier includes a telegraph from Damanhur, Beheira, addressed to the "Master of Ceremonies," listing the Ittihad Party membership. The list indicates that the social composition of the monarchist party was similar to the Wafd's, containing pasha, beys, effendis, shaykhs, and *a'yan* (rural notables), yet the percentages indicate a greater number of shaykhs (mostly legal experts with certificates from al-Azhar) in the monarchist ranks. ENA, Abdin Files, Box 218, Telegram addressed to Nash'at Pasha, "ra'is al-diwan al-malaki" (July 12, 1925), contained a declaration of loyalty to the king signed by individuals from the Wafd's general membership, as well as former members of the Wafd Central Committee. Memorandum, "Egyptian Press," February 2, 1925. FO371/10887 335/29/16 shows that Stack's assassination in 1924 cost the Wafd Party the confidence not only of the British government but of a significant sector of Egyptian political society.

67. Of 214 seats in the 1925 parliament, the Wafd took 113 (53 percent) and the coalition of Ittihad, Liberal-Constitutional, and independents, 95. This was a loss of sixty-eight seats for the Wafd and thus created the check on Wafd domination that the British and Egyptian liberals had sought to design in the 1922 constitution and 1923 electoral law.

British diplomatic staff) attempted to restore full autocracy, evident in the king's proroguing of the parliament and the rewriting of the electoral law in 1925. These policies were countenanced by the Conservative government that came to power in London in late 1924 and the new appointee as high commissioner, Lord Lloyd, in 1925.

Conclusion

After the Revolution of 1919, an attempt was made on the part of the British, at least among liberal imperialists, to create a self-governing Egypt (not full sovereignty or "complete independence"), as previously instituted in the settler colonies. This was a major shift in imperial policy and designed to synchronize with the Wilsonian moment. The post-1919 arrangement in Egypt is unique in that it involved a straightforward transference of British constitutional law to Egypt, as if geography did not matter, unlike the mandates. This put the British in Egypt in a unique position, evident in the election of a Wafd government in 1924, defying all predictions that it was unrepresentative of the Egyptian population. That unexpected outcome, followed by the Wafd's insistence on "complete independence," led to a counter-revolution under the purview of a Conservative government.

According to nationalist narratives the revolution was a natural stage in the nation's evolution; but critical studies have shown that the characterization of the nation as a unit, indivisible, a family, occluded fissures in the nation along class, cultural, regional, and religious lines. The project to build an indivisible nation was beset with obstacles, exploited by old regime elements and conservative imperialists. The full spectrum of Egyptian political society might have found a place in representative institutions; however, neither the monarchist party formed in late 1924 nor the Conservative government that came to power in Britain in the same year had confidence that these institutions could be exported to Egypt. As a result, the venture to include Egypt within a British legal geography faced entrenched opposition in Cairo and London, resulting in the restoration of something like the old regime by 1925.

Is it fair to say that counter-revolution was inevitable? Given the events between 2011 and 2013, it might be tempting to come to such conclusions. If so, what are the dynamics that led to these similar results? In short, the example of 1919 suggests that it took more than British calculations. The British were not united in their objectives. A liberal empire is a contradiction in terms and British officials were susceptible to these contradictions. Some seemed willing to enable a liberal experiment in Egypt, others held to the old belief that Western institutions were not exportable. If negotiations with Zaghloul would necessarily mean abandoning the military bases in Egypt, policy-makers met resistance at cabinet level and the War Office. Likewise, US policy in Egypt from January 2011 wavered, holding out support for democratic reform without abandoning clients in the Egyptian administration, even if that meant countenancing brutal suppression of democracy advocates of various ideological persuasions. But in each case, the counter-revolution would not have followed its seemingly predictable path without institutional and popular support for the restoration. Old regime elements exploited revolutionary miscalculations, like the Islamist constitutional reforms in 2012 and Zaghloul's contest with the monarchists in 1924. In each case, the liberal imperialists could watch while Egyptian conservatives, with nudging from conservative imperialists, brought the country back to something like the old status quo.

Chapter 6

LORD ALLENBY AND THE 1919 REVOLUTION

AN AMBIVALENT COLONIZER

Zeinab Abul-Magd

In the Egyptian popular culture, there is a stereotypical image for the British colonizer that often appears in movies and TV shows. The British high commissioner is always portrayed as a red-faced, rigid, furious man who speaks in firm, short orders. This image might accurately apply to many high commissioners sent from London to control Egypt over seven decades of British occupation of the country, but it is far from matching with Lord Allenby's persona. Serving in this position from 1919 to 1925, Lord Allenby was a peculiarly ambivalent colonizer in Egypt and other Arab lands around it. After leading the "Egyptian Expeditionary Force" during the First World War to victoriously take over Jerusalem and the rest of Greater Syria from the Ottomans, Field Marshal Edmund Allenby was handsomely rewarded by the important position of the high commissioner of Egypt. His appointment came less than three weeks after massive uprisings erupted across the country, the 1919 Revolution, against the continuity of the British protectorate over Egypt after the end of the war. Thus, Lord Allenby witnessed all the events of the revolution and played an important role in its outcomes, including him decisively declaring Egypt's conditioned independence in 1922. He developed a complex relation with the leaders of the revolution, especially Saad Zaghloul Pasha.

For many years of residing in controlling Egypt, Allenby was an ambiguous figure as he maintained a complicated relation between the colonizer and the colonized in Egypt and other neighboring Arab areas. He is the celebrated and decorated war hero who conquered Jerusalem for the British army in 1917, and did the same thing in Damascus in 1918 and seized the entirety of Greater Syria. However, when he assumed authority as the military administrator of Palestine, he adamantly defended the rights of the Palestinians against the rapid Zionist expansion. He similarly backed the demands of the Syrians against their future French mandate. Allenby assumed his duties in Egypt while the Paris Peace Conference was taking place in 1919, where his country denied the Egyptians a seat at the negotiating table to decide on their own affairs. Allenby arrived in Egypt with the same army that he commanded to conquer Palestine and Syria, and used it to brutally crush the ongoing Egyptian uprisings. However, he challenged London's policy when he brought back Saad Zaghloul Pasha from his first exile, supported the Egyptian delegate's trip to the Paris Peace Conference, and eventually stubbornly pressured the British cabinet to declare the country's independence in February of 1922.

In short, Allenby was the unconventional colonizer who evidently did not believe in colonialism after all. He is the military conqueror whose troops defeated Arab lands and ruled over Egypt, while he simultaneously and stubbornly defended the rights of the Egyptians and other Arabs to self-determination. Prominent Egyptian historian Afaf Lutfi Al-Sayyid Marsot, the daughter of one of Cairo's famous nationalist leaders against the British, wrote that Lord Allenby "forced the British government into making some concessions" to accommodate many of Saad Zaghloul's persistent demands toward Egypt's independence.[1] Another prominent Arab historian, Majid Khadduri, wrote that the 1919 Revolution was fortunate to have Allenby as Egypt's high commissioner to negotiate with. Khadduri asserted that:

> Lord Allenby—a soldier who possessed all the wisdom of the statesman—could foresee that only a conciliatory settlement would turn Egypt into a friend of Britain. He pressed upon the British Cabinet . . . the necessity of an immediate proclamation of independence; hence the Declaration of February 28, 1922, which abolished the protectorate and martial law and conferred upon Egypt independence.[2]

Brian Guardian, a British historian, affirmed that Allenby forced the British cabinet to recognize and approve his proposal for Egypt's independence.[3] Who was Allenby? What type of relation he had with the Egyptians before he arrived in the country as its colonial ruler amid a boiling revolution against his imperial crown? What was his relation to the most popular leader of this revolution, Zaghloul Pasha, and other Cairene aristocrats who headed the uprisings? Why did he insist on granting Egypt its independence? How did his urgent trip to London to negotiate with his own cabinet for Egypt's independence take place? What exactly happened in London in those meetings between Allenby and the British cabinet ministers in the crucial days leading up to his declaration of the country's independence in 1922? Finally, what misfortunate events he encountered in post-independence Egypt until he had to quit his post and leave

---

1. Afaf Lutfi al-Sayyid Marsot, *A History of Egypt: From the Arab Conquest to the Present* (Cambridge: Cambridge University Press, 2007), 95–6.
2. Majid Khadduri, "The Anglo Egyptian Controversy," *Proceedings of the Academy of Political Science*, (January 1952), 85.
3. Brian Gardner, *Allenby of Arabia: Lawrence's General* (New York: Coward-McCann, Inc, 1966), 277.

the country? After all, Allenby did not eventually leave his post and depart for good from Egypt on a happy note.

Through closely tracing the relation between Allenby and the colonized Egyptians before, during, and after the events of the 1919 Revolution, this chapter attempts to answer all the abovementioned questions. Allenby was appointed as the high commissioner of Egypt at the beginning of March 1919, until he left the country in May 1925. This chapter relies on a large base of archival records driven from the British National Archives in order to reconstruct his story, including Allenby's official telegrams sent from Cairo to London and addressing the prime minister and the Foreign Office as the events escalated between 1919 and 1922. It also includes minutes of his meetings with cabinet officials in London and his heated discussions with them to stubbornly argue for Egypt's independence. The chapter also relies on personal letters that Allenby sent to his mother and wife, which were collected and published by his biographers. Besides, it utilizes secondary analysis presented by war historians about this period, and taps into Arabic sources. This chapter argues that Allenby's experience with the Egyptian revolutionaries was far from reflecting the stereotypical image of the relation between the European colonizer and his coercively colonized subjects.

Before arriving in Egypt as its administrator, Field Marshal Allenby was the commander of the "Egyptian Expeditionary Force" (EEF), which the British army recruited to combat the Ottoman Empire at the Eastern Front. Although this force had its headquarters in Cairo, it recruited non-Egyptian officers, from England, Australia, New Zealand, and colonized India. Egyptians served in the EEF mainly as workers in the Labor Corps, as they undertook non-combatant duties such as construction and transportation for the British troops in Sinai, Palestine, Syria, and so on. Allenby had his first encounter with and relation to Egyptians through these low-class laborers at the frontlines, before he later met the country's aristocratic pashas and large landowners who led the 1919 events in Cairo.

This chapter will begin with Allenby's story from those frontlines, where he commanded the EEF's laborers and had a prolonged relation with low-class Egyptians, before moving to his arrival in Cairo and examining his peculiar relation with the country's nationalistic elite. It will examine his complicated relation with the principal leader of the 1919 Revolution, Saad Pasha, and his decisive role in its outcomes. The most important part in this role was his persistent and tireless requests from London's politicians to grant Egypt its independence. After three years from the onset of the revolution, Allenby succeeded in bringing the country its independence with the February 28 declaration in 1922, the same declaration that allowed Saad Pasha's party to sweep parliamentary elections and form the first cabinet of a partially independent Egyptian kingdom. Allenby might have assumed that he would have the best relation with the country's revolutionaries after his achievements on their behalf and in politically empowering Saad Pasha, but he was wrong. Unfortunately, his career in Egypt had a tragic end, intertwined with a fatally disgraced fall from power for Saad Pasha himself too.

Allenby Meets the Egyptians: A Labor Corps at the Frontlines

Before taking command of the EEF in 1917, Allenby spent many years of his life as a military leader of average or even humble skills. Since his time as a cadet at the military college of Sandhurst, Allenby had not been known as a particularly clever army student or a combat hero. His level was always below that of his peers. However, his career suddenly shifted and he turned into a victorious hero after coming to the Middle East during the Great War—he met his biggest luck on Arab lands. He finally accomplished military success when he was assigned to lead the EEF, which included tens of thousands of Egyptian laborers recruited from the poor villages of the country.

Allenby was born in 1861 to an upper-class, propertied English family. As a young boy, he had a huge body but a reserved personality. He was not a particularly sharp student during schooling years and didn't enjoy any special talents, even in sports despite his big build. His father died when he was only seventeen years old, and after that he decided to sit for the civil service exam to work in the colonial administration in India. This was the best job that a young man from his social class hoped for at the time, but he failed the exam twice. His next best option was to become an army officer, so he joined Sandhurst and graduated from it in 1881.[4] He was known to be a disciplined and obedient young officer who responded to orders rigidly without any attempt at innovation or taking risk in operations. When the Great War erupted in 1914, he was sent first to the Western Front, namely France, to command a cavalry division. He utterly failed in this mission and lost control over his troops most of the time. While leading the Third Army in an offensive in the French city of Arras, he was defeated by the Germans in April 1917, and his reputation was irreparably damaged at the Western Front. He was known then as the "bull" because he was able to blindly charge but wasn't able to retreat at the right time. As a result, he was transferred to the Eastern Front to lead the EEF against the Ottomans.[5]

Allenby arrived in Egypt for the first time to take charge of the EEF on June 28, 1917, and he left behind his nineteen-year-old son, his only child, fighting as a soldier in France. The EEF then suffered from lack of organization and discipline under its previous commander, and repeatedly failed in advancing into Gaza. Allenby spent his days reorganizing and training its officers before launching a new campaign from Sinai to Gaza. After about a month of intense preparations, he received a telegraph from his wife carrying the dreadful news that their only son was killed in action. Allenby didn't waste much time in mourning, as he started a Gaza campaign shortly afterwards. He astoundingly succeeded in invading Gaza by the end of October of the same year. At this point, the British prime minister,

---

4. General Sir. Archibald Wavell, *Allenby: A Study of Greatness. The Biography of Filed-Marshal Viscount Allenby of Megiddo and Felxtowe* (New York: Oxford University Press, 1941), 23–110.

5. Ibid., 127–8; 171–85.

Lloyd George, asked him to present the holy city of Jerusalem as a Charismas present to the British people by the end of the year. Surprisingly, Allenby succeeded in conquering Jerusalem on December 9, 1917. He famously entered the city on foot on December 11, humbly leaving his horse outside the city's gate, in order to seek a non-hostile relation with the Arab inhabitants. Less than a year later, he conquered Damascus in October 1918.[6]

After concluding the campaigns in Greater Syria, Allenby published an official, comprehensive report covering the operations and logistical work undertaken by the EEF between 1917 and 1918. In this report, he unexpectedly praised the role that the Egyptian laborers played to logistically facilitate the operations and aid the troops. Tens of thousands of Egyptian workers were deployed and sent to the EEF, especially from Upper Egypt, to carry out different duties. Allenby asserted the Egyptian authorities responded quickly to his routine requests to recruit and deliver them to his camps. Allenby listed in this report the exact numbers of the workers who served in the "Camel Transport Corps" and "Egyptian Labor Corps," besides other Egyptian military units. He asserted that they all presented valuable hard work to the troops.[7] Observing their industrious effort, Allenby commented,

> During the operations in the hills of Judea, and of Moab, the troops often depended for their supplies on the Camel Transports Corps. The drivers displayed steadiness under the fire and devotion to duty in the face of cold and rain, which they had never experienced previously. The Egyptian Labour Corps shared these hardships. The construction and maintenance of roads was a task of considerable importance and difficulty during the rainy season, an threw a great strain on the Egyptian Labour Corps. Its successful accomplishment reflects credit on the Corps.[8]

The Egyptian laborers at Allenby's force were from various types of skilled, semi-skilled, or unskilled workers. Their number annually was 270,000 men hired under six-month contracts. Allenby's report mentioned that the workers were regularly replaced by the end of the contract's period or due to death. They were distributed among the labor, camel, donkey, horse, and other corps. They served in the construction and maintenance of railways, paving roads, extending pipe lines, mining building bricks, building water tanks, uploading and offloading ships, stocking arms and ammunition storages, carpentry, and more. Allenby's report asserted that they were primarily recruited from south Egypt on a regular basis, but the need for them increased by the end of 1916. As a result, a permanent recruitment unit was established in Upper Egypt toward a steadier supply of the

---

6. Ibid.

7. General Sir Edmond Allenby, *A Brief Record of the Advance of the Egyptian Expeditionary Force, July 197 to December 1918*, 2nd ed. (London: His Majesty Stationery Office, 1919), 24.

8. Ibid.

army with camel drivers and other laborers, and recruitment then started to take place in the Delta for the first time too. In the early days of the war in 1915–16, they were sent to the "Mediterranean Expeditionary Force" to serve in places such as France, Salonica, and Mesopotamia, until they were more pressingly needed at the EEF.[9]

Allenby's report explained that the Egyptian government's Directory of Labor (*Mudiriyyat al-Ashghal*) and its "Inspectorate of Recruitment" established twenty-six offices across the country from Alexandria to Aswan to provide and distribute workers to the EEF. Allenby described the associated rigorous process as follows:

> A strict system of medical inspection and examination was enforced and an advance of L.E. 3 made to the all recruits accepted to enable to provide for their dependents. . . . Recruiting camps for the reception of Egyptians were opened in Sohag, Assiut, and Roda Island. Cairo, whence special trains, conveying 2,000 recruits at a time were run to the respective Base Depots on the Suez Canal (Kantara) where the men were disinfected, clothed, equipped, and organized into companies or detachments.[10]

Allenby pointed out the problem of lacking enough British officers who could speak Arabic to supervise such large numbers of workers in the EEF. However, in the same vein he praised the ability of the Egyptian laborers to work with little supervision under only a few officers to observe them.[11] Allenby admiringly described the hard duties they undertook and how they were always cheerful while doing them. He wrote,

> [T]hose who have seen many thousands of Egyptian Labour Corps labourers in task work, either driving a cutting with pick and fasse through Palestine clay, or in their thousands carrying baskets of earth to pile up some railway embankment, will long remember such examples of intensive labour. No less striking was it to watch the lone of laden boats leaving the steamships off the coast and making their way through the surf to the beach, there to be hauled high up by teams of cheerful Egyptians working to whistle signals under their own officers.[12]

It is worth mentioning here that Egyptian historian Latifa Muhammad Salim gives a contradictory account for the conditions of these laborers in the British army. In her book on Egypt in the First World War, she relies on contemporary newspapers' coverage to argue that these workers suffered from oppressive conditions, starting from stations of recruitment to working sites in camps. In addition, she insists that sending Egyptian villagers to the frontlines of the Allies

9. Ibid., 107.
10. Ibid., 108.
11. Ibid., 108–9.
12. Ibid., 109.

and their wretched conditions there were among the main causes for the eruption of the 1919 Revolution. She indicates that these poor workers joined voluntarily at the beginning because of good payments and other perks included in the contracts, such as free food rations and housing and guarantees to go back to their villages after their contracts expired. But when battles fiercely escalated in Sinai and Palestine and the British military authorities demanded thousands more workers, they turned into a policy of forced conscription using oppressive methods to gather them. Salim asserts that contemporary observers largely attribute the 1919 uprisings to the brutal conscription practices in Egyptian villages. Despite the great services these laborers presented to the Allies, they immensely suffered in their camps as the British imperial forces treated them with cruelty—Salim adds.[13]

The Great War ended with the armistice of November 1918. The Egyptian laborers in Allenby's EEF returned home to their villages in the south and the north of the country afterwards. However, they were not alone in going back to Egypt. They were accompanied by thousands of Allenby's foreign officers who were sent to camp in Egypt and wait to be discharged and eventually go home to their respective countries. When the 1919 events erupted only five months later, in March, these were the same officers who would be redeployed to crush the uprisings and who notoriously used extensive violence against the revolutionaries in Egypt's cities and villages.

Allenby's Force and the 1919 Revolution

When the 1919 Revolution broke out, Allenby was not in Egypt yet. But the officers of his EEF were already there, and they were redeployed across the country. The British authorities found their combat skills and large numbers suitable to depend on to suppress the uprisings. In fact, the EEF's officers did not enjoy a good reputation during the war in Egypt when they came to Cairo for their brief breaks. Whenever the Australian, New Zealander, and Indian officers of Allenby came to Egypt, they indulged in corrupt behavior and caused social chaos—in the eyes of the conservative population of the country. As historian Mario Ruiz asserts, they frequented brothels and night clubs and often walked in the neighborhoods of the city while heavily drunk. When the revolution erupted, their reputation got even worse that they now engaged in violent campaigns to crush the rebels.[14]

The EEF was created in 1916 with a headquarters in Cairo, and its first battle was in Sinai in order to drive the Ottomans out of the Suez Canal area. Although the British troops had already camped in Egypt since its occupation in 1882, whether in the Suez Canal or other areas, the Great War complicated their presence

---

13. Latifa Muhammad Salim, *Misr fi al-Harb al-'Alamiyya al-'Ula* (Cairo: Dar al-Shuruk, 2009), 313–24.

14. Mario M. Ruiz, "Manly Spectacles and Imperial Soldiers in Wartime Egypt, 1914–1919," *Middle Eastern Studies* 45, no. 3 (May 2009): 351–3.

inside the country. As soon as the war erupted, London declared Egypt a British protectorate and imposed martial laws in 1914. Ruiz indicates that the war led to intensifying undesired interaction between British officers and soldiers and the civilian inhabitants of Egypt, amid dire economic conditions that the war inflicted on societies at all fronts.[15]

During the war, regardless of class, race, and religious differences, British troopers mixed up for the first time with Egyptian civilians. While doing so, they often violated their military orders and disturbed the Egyptians' urban spaces and daily life by their immoral behavior.[16] Ruiz describes how Egyptian cities were inundated by imperial soldiers during the long years of the war, and thousands of them filled bars and night clubs. Their high commanders thought that their behavior harmed the reputation of the empire and discredited its army. As result of visiting brothels, many of the troopers caught contagious diseases, and the British authorities reacted by imposing strict hygiene regulations on the local sex workers in these establishments and raided some of them to close them down. Drunken troopers attacked civilian passersby on city streets, and many of them fled their barracks or deserted military service altogether.[17]

As soon as the events of the Egyptian revolution started in March 1919, these very officers and soldiers of the EEF launched their last offensive before going home, where for several weeks they committed the notorious British massacres against the protesters. Allenby was not with them in Cairo yet at this point. Ruiz indicates that when protesters' attacks on foreign buildings increased, the British officials issued their orders to the different army units to occupy towns and villages. Peasants in the countryside initially avoided clashing with them, but the troopers' brutal treatment pushed them to fight back. For example, about fifty-five Australian soldiers opened random fire at around 3,000 peasants who carried only knives, small axes, or stones to resist them. Those villagers were accused of trying to ambush Allenby at a train station en route to Cairo. Egyptian snipers targeted the Australian soldiers as their patrols inspected villages or provinces, and two soldiers were killed in one incident. All the inhabitants of the village the two soldiers were sniped were flogged as a form of collective punishment, and many of them died out of their severe wounds. This cruel penalty succeeded in stopping sniping activities carried out by the protesters. However, the EEF continued to use flogging to punish those who incited protests. In the fierce clashes that went on between the soldiers and a group of inhabitants between March 15 and 31, the British army set numerous villages on fire and murdered between 1,000 and 3,000 civilian Egyptians. This was followed by setting up military tribunals to issue collective sentences.[18]

15. Ibid.
16. Ibid.
17. Ibid., 358–60.
18. Ibid., 364–5.

British historian James Kitchen asserts that for full six weeks, from mid-March to the end of April, the empire used the EEF to apply the highest degree of violence to terminate the revolution. The troopers of the EEF accomplished the mission brutally, the revolution quickly lost its momentum and vigor, and the colonial government restored public order. Although previous British historians claimed that the empire used minimum force to stop the protests and that the EEF mostly applied self-restraint in confrontations with the masses, Kitchen unearths many archival records to reveal the opposite. He followed the violent actions documented particularly in the logs of two infantry battalions, and showed that the central authorities left the small military units to decide on their own responses toward resistance against them in rural and urban areas. Thus, they mostly used excessively violent tactics.[19]

In order to highlight the atrocities committed by the EEF during the revolution, Kitchen recorded the number of causalities on both sides in spring 1919. The number of Europeans who were killed during the events was relatively low within the context of a violent insurgency. Only thirty-one Europeans were killed, including four British, and thirty-five were injured. Causalities among military personnel were significantly low, as only three British officers were killed, along with seventeen British from various ranks and nine Indians. The numbers of the wounded were seventy-eight British and thirty-six Indians troopers. On the other side, 748 Egyptians were killed and 1,015 injured during the few weeks in which the events peaked in March and April. By the summer of 1919, the British authorities' official estimates confirmed that 800 Egyptians were killed and 1,500 injured. At the same time that the empire was tackling the Egyptian revolution, it had to deal with other revolts in its colonies in India, and many historians described the treatment of protesters in Punjab in particular as the archetype of British brutalities and colonial tyranny. However, Kitchen affirms that what happened in Egypt in 1919 was evidently much "bloodier." The British authorities killed 463 protesters in Punjab, which is almost half of the murdered Egyptians.[20]

It might be hard to blame Allenby for the crimes committed by his EEF in Egypt during these weeks, because he was not commanding the force then and had not arrived in Egypt yet to assume his duties as the new high commissioner. The leader of the EEF at the time was Lieutenant General Edward Bulfin. In fact, Allenby during this period was preoccupied with and involved in the events of the Paris Peace Conference, in his persistent attempt to defend the rights of the Palestinians against the Zionist expanding settlements and the rights of the Syrians for self-rule under an Arab king rather than French mandate.

---

19. James E. Kitchen, "Violence in Defence of Empire: The British Army and the 1919 Egyptian Revolution," *Journal of Modern European History* 13, no. 2 (2015): 249–51.
20. Ibid., 252–5.

Allenby Supports the Arabs?

Before and during the 1919 Revolution, Egypt was not in isolation from the regional events in Palestine and Greater Syria, in which Allenby played more than a pivotal role. Ironically, Field Marshal Allenby is the military leader who conquered Palestine and Syria only to be the same official who later supported the Arab inhabitants of these two countries toward their independence from their British and the French colonizers. He did so as the temporary military governor of these lands for about two and a half years, and continued his effort after moving to Egypt and while dealing with the 1919 Revolution.

Before colonizing Palestine and Syria, the British Empire had infamously concluded a secret agreement with Sharif Hussein, the Ottoman-appointed ruler of Mecca during the war, and his sons, especially Emir Faisal. Allenby was eventually brought for the execution of this agreement at the Eastern Front. In hidden correspondence between Sharif Hussein and Sir Henri McMahon, the British high Commissioner of Egypt, in 1915–16, he pledged to help the British take down the Ottoman Empire by combating its garrisons in Arabia, Greater Syria, and Iraq. In return, the British promised Hussein and his sons to back them in establishing a new Arab kingdom and hopefully their own Islamic caliphate that should include these territories of the collapsed Ottomans. Subsequently, Emir Faisal formed the "Arab Revolt" army that fought next to Allenby's EEF in Palestine and Syria. Whereas Sharif Hussein fulfilled his pledges in the agreement, the British did not. Interestingly, Allenby took the side of the Arabs in the dispute that erupted between his government and Faisal after the end of the war.

Faisal's army closely collaborated with Allenby's EEF to invade one area after the other in Palestine and the rest of Greater Syria, and advanced north until he finally took over Damascus well before the British entered it. The British spy and officer T. E. Lawrence (Lawrence of Arabia) had served at Cairo's central command before Allenby sent him to support Faisal's army. Throughout the war, Allenby expressed his admiration and great appreciation of Faisal's efforts and markedly believed in the importance of the Arab Army's operative role as auxiliary troops on the ground. In the meantime, the British concluded other secret agreements with the French, such as the infamous Sykes-Picot of 1916, to promise France colonial control over the same areas that Faisal was enthusiastically seizing in Syria. Moreover, in the following year, the British issued the Balfour Declaration that promised areas in Palestine to the Zionists in 1917.

At the end of the military campaigns in Palestine and Syria, Allenby had to deal with a difficult situation that he was not prepared to deal with, especially that he had no previous political or diplomatic skills to deploy, in order to deliver the bad news to Faisal that McMahan's promises to his father were not to be delivered. After Faisal victoriously entered Damascus in a large parade and was recognized as Syria's new Arab ruler by its elite inhabitants, Allenby summoned him to a troubling meeting at a local hotel to officially inform him that Husain's family would have no control over Syria and Palestine. However, in the following years, Allenby strongly supported Faisal's political claims over the region and his demand to be appointed the king of Syria, and he backed the emir's trip to Paris to attend the peace conference and negotiate for Arab independence in 1919.[21]

In Palestine, after seizing Jerusalem and most other surrounding cities, Allenby was appointed as transitional military governor of the region for thirty months. Allenby entered Jerusalem in December of 1917, on foot leaving his horse outside the city's gate in order to show humbleness and avoid triggering old historical memories of the crusades or local hostilities. He continued to rule over Palestine as its military administrator until June of 1920, while also occupying the post of the high commissioner in Egypt. Allenby seized Jerusalem only one month after his cabinet granted the Balfour Declaration to the Zionist organization, vowing to enable the creation of a homeland for European Jewish settlers in Palestine. Thus, Allenby's duties as ruler included facilitating the immigration and settlement of European Jews coming to the area. However, Allenby publicly resented the project and applied policies that discouraged the process. His policies also attempted to keep the rights of the local Palestinian inhabitants, especially the peasants by aiding them in managing their lands. Allenby's decisions displeased the leaders of the Zionist organization in London and Palestine, and they accused him of being biased for the Arabs against Jews. When London appointed a British Zionist, Viscount Herbert Samuel, as the first civilian high commissioner of Palestine to succeed Allenby, he opposed this appointment. Allenby predicted that Samuel's arrival would trigger widespread violence.[22]

In Syria, Faisal had formed an alliance with the secret societies of Arab nationalists that had rejected the Ottoman rule before the war. With a coalition of Arab officers and intellectuals, Faisal succeeded in seizing Damascus before Allenby's army in 1918. However, Britain already gave Syria to France in secret agreements concluded during the war. Allenby had to inform Faisal about submitting himself to French control in Syria, which he refused and countered with armed resistance. Allenby supported Faisal against the French claims and backed him in his negotiations at the Paris conference, and so did his former officer Lawrence. In his correspondence with the British cabinet during the conference, Allenby strongly rejected imposing a French mandate system over Syria and argued for Faisal's right to independently rule the country. When the US president, Woodrow Wilson, sent a commission to survey the political demands of the local inhabitants of Greater Syria, Allenby supported the work of its members.[23] As the military administrator of Syria and Palestine, he allowed the populations of both areas to submit petitions demanding the right to self-determination to this commission in the summer of 1919. When the Egyptian protests erupted, Allenby attempted to alarm London that Faisal might lead similar events along with Arab nationalists in Syria, urging the cabinet to consider responding to Arab demands.

---

21. See: Gardner, *Allenby of Arabia*.

22. See: John J. McTague Jr, "The British Military Administration in Palestine, 1917–1920," *Journal of Palestine Studies* 7, no. 3 (Spring, 1978): 55–76.

23. See the archival recodes of King-Crane Commission, Oberlin College.

Even after France succeeded in imposing a mandate system over Syria, Allenby resented abandoning Faisal and forcing him to submit to French rule.[24]

Eventually, Allenby's effort to support Arab rights in both Palestine and Syria failed, and he witnessed this failure from his post as Egypt's high commissioner in Cairo. British troops fully were withdrawn from Syria by the end of 1919, and the French army defeated Faisal's Arab resistance army. In Palestine, the British mandate was declared in 1920, and this was followed by large waves of Zionist immigration and settlements. In the meantime, the Egyptian revolution was simmering next door.

Lord Allenby and Saad Pasha: A Complicated Relation

Less than two weeks after Allenby's arrival in Egypt to take office in March 1919, he issued an order to end Saad Zaghloul Pasha's exile and allow his return to the country. When the Paris Peace Conference started in January of the same year, Saad Pasha and other leaders of the Wafd Party had demanded to attend the conference in order to negotiate for Egypt's independence from the British protectorate. Despite Egypt's considerable contributions to the war efforts, supporting the British army by tens of thousands of laborers besides immense food and other logistical provisions, the colonial administration had denied its nationalist leaders the right to travel to France and join the talks. The Egyptians were particularly furious to see that Emir Faisal was allowed to attend the conference and they were not. Confrontations with the colonial administration had escalated, and on March 8 Sir Reginald Wingate, the British high commissioner at the time, ordered the arrest of Saad Pasha and his fellow leaders and sent them to exile in Malta. Sir Wingate soon left his position and Allenby arrived to replace him on March 25. The new high commissioner quickly proceeded to pacify unrest, as he issued an order on April 7 to end Saad's exiling sentence and allowed him to travel to Paris along with other leaders of the Wafd Party. This was supposed to initiate good working ties between Allenby and Saad. However, revolutionary events rapidly escalated anew to generate a very complicated relation between Allenby and Saad in the following five years.

Allenby's tangled relation with Saad Pasha included many stages, from its start in 1919 till it tragically ended in 1924. It had a positive start when Allenby allowed Saad to leave his exile and travel to France in April 1919, then allowed his return to Cairo after two years of unsuccessful negotiations in March 1921. The relation took a negative turn when Allenby sent Saad to his second exile in December 1921. Shortly afterwards, Allenby announced Egypt's conditioned independence on February 28, in 1922, and allowed Saad to return to the country in September

---

24. See: Matthew Hughes, "General Allenby and the Campaign of the Egyptian Expeditionary Force, June 1916–November 1919," PhD Dissertation, War Studies Department at King's College, University of London, 1995, ch. 7.

of 1923 in order to run in the first parliamentary elections after the country's partial independence and the promulgation of a new constitution. Saad's Wafd Party swept the elections, and he formed the cabinet and headed it in February 1924—under Allenby's colonial administration. The relation between the two men improved for a few months, before it relapsed again when Egyptian anti-colonial insurgents suddenly assassinated the sirdar of the British army in Egypt and the governor of the Sudan.

In his book about Allenby's years in Egypt, published in 1944, Field Marshall Viscount Wavell recounted what happened when Allenby arrived in Cairo on March 25. The revolution was still at its heated peak, but the iron hand of the EEF's troopers was steadily crushing it. Allenby immediately talked to his advisers, and invited the country's elite to meet with him at the same night he arrived. He delivered the following speech to them:

> I have been appointed High Commissioner for Egypt by His Majesty the King, and it is my desire and duty to assist in bringing to the country peace, quiet, and contentment. My intentions are: First, to bring the present disturbances to an end. Secondly, to make careful inquiry into al matters which have caused discontent in the country. Thirdly, to redress such grievances as appear justifiable.[25]

Before completing his first week in office, on March 31, Allenby phoned London to request releasing Saad Pasha from exile. This was an unexpected call for the cabinet, because it assumed it had sent a rigid military man who would put matters under strict control. It was surprised to hear him, on the contrary, responding to the protesters' main demand, which they had repeatedly declined, to allow Saad to go to Paris. The Foreign Office consulted with Sir Wingate, the previous high commissioner who had issued the order to exile Saad, but he strongly objected to Allenby's desire and insisted that such substantial concession might signal British weakness.[26]

Eventually, Allenby succeeded in convincing his cabinet of the value of releasing Saad, and the decision was issued on April 7. Sooner afterwards, on April 18, Saad arrived in Paris. Nonetheless, on the following day, President Woodrow Wilson declared his support for the continuity of the British protectorate in Egypt. This was a catastrophic announcement for Saad and the members of the delegation from the Wafd Party who accompanied him to the conference. Internal disputes erupted among them, and rift led many party members to defect.

Allenby took another important step to support the Egyptians' demands. He backed inviting an investigation commission led by Lord Alfred Milner, to examine the situation and make recommendations to the cabinet. However, Allenby and Saad had differences over the work of this commission. Milner and

---

25. Quoted in Field-Marshall Viscount Wavell, *Allenby in Egypt. Being Volume II of Allenby: A Study of Greatness* (New York: Oxford University Press, 1944), 38–9.

26. Ibid., 39.

other members of his commission arrived in the country on December 7, 1919, in order to hold meetings with Egyptian leaders, but the Wafd Party insisted that they should talk only to Saad Pasha as the popularly selected representative and leader of the nation. Saad was still in Paris at the time, so most of the other Egyptian nationalist leaders boycotted Milner's meetings, and he eventually had to leave the country empty-handed three months later in March 1920. Despite the failure of his talks, Milner recommended the cabinet to end the British protectorate over Egypt upon his return to London. Allenby strongly supported this recommendation and traveled to London himself in the autumn of the same year to persuade his government to adopt it, but the cabinet ignored him along with Milner's report. British historian Brian Gardner asserts that Allenby didn't agree to all the terms in the settlement document proposed by Milner, but he supported its main article regarding fully abolishing the British protectorate and endorsing a comprehensive Anglo-Egyptian treaty granting the country its independence while protecting the British interests in the Suez Canal and the Sudan. Allenby pressed that the British should recognize Egypt's independence first before discussing any other terms in the agreement later. He insisted that the protectorate system was not necessary because the naval forces stationed in the region and the existence of a military base in the Suez Canal area were enough to protect British interests, display the imperial power, and guarantee Egypt's adherence to the terms of a signed agreement. Once more, London did not expect Allenby, next to Milner, to propose recommendations backing the revolution and found them shocking. One camp in the cabinet entirely rejected them, and it included young Winston Churchill who worked diligently to halt Allenby's efforts either in London or during a trip he took to Cairo. One of Churchill's controversial visits to Egypt disturbed the nationalists and infuriated Allenby for transgressing his authority as the high commissioner.[27]

After Saad Pasha instructed his followers in Cairo to boycott the commission, he traveled from Paris to London along with other Wafd members to meet with Milner, from June to August of 1920. The two sides settled on an agreement draft in which Milner tried to respond to most of the Egyptians' demands regarding independence, but with a condition to preserve British interests in the country in order to motivate his cabinet to approve it. Allenby came from Cairo to London in August and pressingly advised his cabinet to adopt this draft. Milner published the document in the same month and called it the "Milner-Zaghloul Agreement" and asserted that it was mainly general outlines toward a detailed settlement to be negotiated later.[28] However, Saad eventually backed off and announced that he did not accept this agreement, probably fearing public backlash and losing his popularity in Egypt as he always campaigned for complete, not conditional, independence. Saad declared that the Egyptian people should accept this draft

---

27. Gardner, *Allenby of Arabia*, 232–3.

28. See Lord Alfred Milner's report, "Report of the Special Committee to Egypt," December 9, 1920, The British National Archives, CAB 24/117/49. Also see: "Report of the British Special Mission to Egypt. B. The Memorandum of August 18, 1920," 903–4.

first before his endorsement of it, and he sent letters to Cairo to investigate the reaction of different nationalist forces to it. Allenby was not pleased with Saad's maneuvering and bargaining tactics and thought that this would waste a good opportunity. The negotiations did eventually break down and the chance was lost for both sides.[29] As a matter of fact, the terms of independence stated in Milner's draft are the same that Allenby's declaration of independence would include three years later in February 1922 and, more important, that Saad Pasha would willingly accept then.

After his inability to persuade the British government to adopt Milner's recommendations, Allenby returned from London to Egypt. Saad also returned to the country in the following year, in March 1921, after fruitless negotiations toward full independence in both Paris and London. Allenby came to realize the degree of popularity that Saad enjoyed, and followed a policy of appeasement with him and his followers. In a letter that he sent to his mother when Saad came back to, Allenby wrote "Saad Zaghloul arrived in Cairo yesterday. I kept all officers and soldiers out of the streets and left the whole management to the Egyptians. There was a gigantic and enthusiastic but quite orderly crowd, and not a single mishap occurred."[30] In another letter that he sent after a month of Saad's arrival and facing some unrest, he wrote: "I bide my time, as I want the Egyptians to settle their policies for themselves, and I don't want to interfere with my troops unless the life, limb, or interests of Europeans are in danger."[31]

In the same year, Adly Yakan Pasha formed the cabinet, and its ministers were tasked with negotiating with the British about Milner commission's recommendations and reaching a full agreement regarding their conditions for independence. Saad Pasha fiercely opposed these negotiations, and revolutionary violence erupted again across the country in order to stop them. As chaos returned to Cairo, Adly Pasha's government resigned in December 1921. Saad Pasha encouraged his supporters to mobilize for more protests and escalate unrest, and incited other pashas to refuse to join the new cabinet of Adly. After months of a power vacuum with no possible government in sight, Allenby decided to punish Saad Pasha by sending him to exile outside the country again.

Despite getting rid of Saad, the country remained in a state of chaos and political stalemate without a cabinet for weeks—until early 1922. Allenby asked Abdel Khalek Sarwat Pasha to form the government in order to resolve the crisis. Sarwat Pasha was not a close supporter of Saad or his Wafd Party, and thus did not mind collaboration with Allenby. But as political turmoil continued to escalate, Sarwat Pasha couldn't achieve this difficult mission without asking the British government to lift the protectorate system first. Thus, Allenby found his administration at a dead end, even after sending Saad away. His only way out was obtaining the country's independence from his government at any expense.

29. Wavell, *Allenby in Egypt*, 61–2.
30. Ibid., 49.
31. Ibid., 50.

Thus, he decided to travel to London in early February 1922, and after fierce discussions with his government, he came back at the end of the same month with the declaration of Egypt's independence.

What Happened on the Eve of February 28?

After Allenby exiled Saad Pasha in December 1921, his administration lost the ability to govern the country and his only way out was to grant it independence. He sent a countless number of telegrams and confidential letters to Prime Minister Lloyd George, to request so, but his proposal was repeatedly rejected—as Foreign Office records at the British Archives show. Thus, Allenby decided to travel to London himself in early February 1922 to stubbornly demand his plan in person. He threatened his cabinet to resign if they didn't respond positively. The British government eventually gave in and endorsed his proposal, and Allenby traveled back to Cairo by the end of the month to announce the news. He arrived on February 28 to immediately read his declaration of ending the British protectorate and turning Egypt into a constitutional monarchy.

What exactly happened during Allenby's few crucial days in London? What type of conversations took place in the long meetings and heated debates between him and the cabinet members? The British Archives keep numerous documents with the recorded minutes of every meeting Allenby had with the government officials in February 1922. These are the meetings that would have the most decisive impact on the outcomes of the 1919 Revolution.

Allenby departed from Egypt on February 3, and arrived in London a week later on February 11. The following week, between February 15 and 21, was full of furious and stressing arguments in stretched meetings with the prime minister, the Foreign Office, and other cabinet ministers.

Three weeks before making his decision to travel to London, specifically on January 12, Allenby sent an urgent telegram to the cabinet informing them about the crisis of not forming a government and the need to reach an ultimate solution. Elite figures were reluctant to join Sarwat Pasha's proposed cabinet for fear of public stigmatization as betrayers of Saad. Allenby attached to this telegram a letter that he drafted in which he recognized the independence of the country, and proposed to submit to Sultan Fuad—the monarch of Egypt then. He believed that such move should help encourage politicians to accept posts in Sarwat Pasha's cabinet and resolve the governmental stalemate. Allenby asked his government to approve the letter in order to enable Sarwat Pasha to move ahead. In this letter, Allenby addressed the sultan with a reconciliatory tone, indicating that the intentions of the British government had been misinterpreted. He asserted that "Great Britain . . . sincerely desires to see an Egypt enjoying national prerogatives and international position of a sovereign state. . . . As to any desire to interfere in internal administration of Egypt, His Majesty's Government have sufficiently stated and repeated that their most ardent is to place in Egyptians hands . . . their own affairs."[32] Allenby detailed the terms of independence to Fuad in this letter as follows:

> 10. With this object in view I am happy to be able to announce to your Highness that his Majesty's Government are prepared to recommend to British parliament, without waiting for conclusion of a treaty, abolition of the protectorate and recognition of Egypt as an independent sovereign state . . . 11. As regards to internal administration of Egypt His Majesty's Government will view with favour creation of a parliament with right to control the policy and administration of a constitutionally responsible government. 12. I propose to abolish regime of martial law . . . 13. As soon as this state of affairs has been established His Majesty's Government will examine . . . in most friendly spirit the conclusion of an agreement on following points which will remain for settlement: A. Security of communication of British Empire. B. Defence of Egypt against foreign aggression or interference, direct or indirect. C. Protecting foreign interests in Egypt.[33]

In order to urge his government to respond swiftly and approve submitting the letter to Fuad, Allenby sent another telegram on the same day marked "*Most Urgent. Private and Personal*" to the Foreign Office to further bring his proposal to the minster's attention. Allenby asserted in this second telegram that this was the last opportunity that Britain had for settling the conflict. He stated, "I count on you to see that my proposals are accepted. . . . If they are rejected I consider that finest opportunity we have ever had will have been missed. I don't think that such opportunity will ever occur again."[34] Nevertheless, Allenby faced rejection and frustration this time. The Foreign Office's response, that came six days later, informed him that the cabinet was not convinced with his proposal. They argued that it did not indicate that the Egyptians shared his views and there were no guarantees that they would meet British requests if the protectorate was abolished.[35]

On January 15, Allenby sent another telegram to the cabinet to inform them encore about the ongoing crisis with forming a government. Sarwat Pasha's efforts yielded no results. He indicated that he met with prominent members of the Wafd who confided in him their intention to secede from the party and their willingness to contribute to resolving the crisis. According to him, they accepted the conditions of independence stated in his letter to the sultan, and agreed that all Egyptian territories were necessary to defend the British Empire's communications. They also expressed their anti-Saad Pasha's stance stating that "under no circumstances should Saad Zaghloul be allowed to return to Egypt. This is general feeling in all

---

32. The British National Archives, CAB 24/132/14, 72–3.
33. The British National Archives, CAB 24/132/14, 74–75.
34. The British National Archives, F.O 800/153, 134.
35. The British National Archives, F.O 800/153, 135.

circles desirous of carrying through a settlement."[36] Once more on January 17, Allenby sent a "*Most Urgent*" telegram to the cabinet indicating that the expected secessions in the Wafd did not happen. He added that the Wafd members he spoke to were still willing to support Sarwat Pasha in forming a government, but not openly. The only thing they could do to help at this point was to be "benevolently neutral and endeavour to help unobtrusively."[37]

The cabinet's negative responses to Allenby's urgent telegrams continued to be frustrating to him. On January 24, he received a telegram insisting that the cabinet excreted all needed effort in order to reconcile with the demands of the Egyptians and Allenby's requests, and that the ministers were "disappointed" with Allenby's inability to persuade the Egyptians to accept London's proposals. The cabinet stated that the general principles of the government's policy regarding Egypt had been made clear to Allenby since the previous month and the "limits to which we were prepared to go. These limits have been stretched to the utmost in our anxiety to arrive at a settlement."[38]

In reaction, Allenby decided to travel to London to submit his proposal in person, insist on its acceptance, and threaten to resign if it wouldn't. He departed from Cairo on February 3, and the trip took him a week. In the morning of February 15, at 11:00 a.m., he had a long meeting with the prime minister, Lloyd George, the minister of foreign affairs, Lord Curzon, and other state officials. At this meeting, Allenby explicitly threatened to resign from his post in Egypt if his proposal for the country's independence was turned down encore. He asserted that the cabinet was mistaken to assume that it was possible to resolve the ongoing crisis and for a government to take form in Egypt before granting the country its independence. No Egyptian government would agree to negotiate or sign a settlement treaty with Britain without guarantees of independence, he affirmed. He added that he reassured Sarwat Pasha that the protectorate would be lifted, to enable him to form a government, but he should wait for a discussion on other articles of the settlement to take place later. Allenby reiterated his request of the cabinet's approval of his letter to Sultan Fuad. In turn, Lloyd George argued that Egypt was not an independent state when the war erupted and the British made it a protectorate; it was under Istanbul's Ottoman sultanate. Thus, for him Egypt was not entitled to demand a political status that had not existed before the war. He added that the Egyptians would consider abolishing the protectorate an end of the British military occupation of the country, and the empire did not have any intentions to evacuate its troops from the region. At this juncture, Allenby fiercely stated that this went against his policy as the high commissioner of Egypt and he would not be able to return to the country to resume his duties. As the debate grew more tense, Allenby offered his resignation and asked the prime minister to accept

36. The British National Archives, CAB 24/132/14, 67.
37. The British National Archives, CAB 24/132/14, 144.
38. The British National Archives, CAB 24/132/73, 411.

it. On this day, the first meeting between Allenby and the cabinet was concluded without any results.³⁹

In the evening of the same day, at 6:00 p.m., Allenby had another long meeting with the same cabinet members whom he had met in the morning, including the prime minister and the minister of foreign affairs. This time, he stubbornly insisted on resigning if his proposal was to be rejected. He demanded again the cabinet's approval of his letter to the sultan—the same draft of the letter that he had sent to London in a telegram on January 12. As the meeting minutes reflect, the politicians in the room attempted to pressure Allenby to reconcile and relax his demands. Lloyd George tried very hard to persuade him to change his mind and abandon the idea of giving Egypt its independence, but the latter responded with abrupt sentences of refusal. The prime minister indicated to Allenby that there were government politicians who strongly opposed his plan, and namely mentioned Churchill, but Allenby still stood his grounds. He repeatedly asserted that the situation in Egypt was irresolvable without the letter and that his proposal was non-negotiable, and again asked the cabinet to either take it or accept his resignation. Showing signs of retreat, Lloyd George then told Allenby that he had waited for five weeks, since he first sent the letter in January, and it would not hurt to be patient for only five more minutes. The meeting ended with the cabinet approving Allenby's letter to Sultan Fuad, or a shortened version of it, that abolished the protectorate but with references to some points of reservation.⁴⁰

The breakthrough finally took place in the meeting of February 20. After a full week of anxiously waiting, and at 12 a.m. of that day, Allenby met for the last time with Lloyd George and his minister of foreign affairs. Members of the parliament and other government officials were present in the room during this critical meeting, and it was a brief conversation this time. Allenby received the news of the approval of a shortened version of his letter to Fuad and was authorized to announce it to the public immediately upon his return to Cairo. He was asked to seek a confirmation from Sarwat Pasha to form a cabinet immediately afterwards. The British parliament committed to abolishing the protectorate the next day, after Sarwat's certain move to form a government. Lloyd George added that his government limited Egypt's independence with a number of conditions, which included keeping British troops in the country, British protection of the interests of foreigners, and discussing British authority over the Sudan.⁴¹

The mission was accomplished, and Allenby departed back to Cairo right away. His return trip took a week, and he arrived in the country on February 28, 1922. On the same day, he read to the public the declaration of Egypt's independence— the British recognized the country as a sovereign state and abolished martial laws. The British Empire maintained the right to protect its communication in Egypt, militarily defend the country against any foreign attacks, protect foreign interests

---

39. The British National Archives, CAB 23/35/42, 382–95.
40. The British National Archives, CAB 23/36/1, 5–13.
41. The British National Archives, CAB 23/36/4, 40–4.

and minorities, and control the Sudan. Allenby's read proclamation was very brief, but it was to be followed by negotiations for a comprehensive treaty. Based on it, Egypt was turned into a constitutional monarchy with Fuad as its first king, and Sarwat Pasha's newly formed cabinet drafted the country's first post-independence constitution and it was promulgated a year later, in April 1923. Parliamentary elections were held in the following year, 1924.

The February 28 declaration of Egyptian independence was an ultimate point of success for the 1919 Revolution. After three years of violent protests demanding autonomy, the revolution finally reached its goal. However, many observers questioned the value of this conditioned independence, as the British military occupation did not withdraw from the country and Egypt lost authority over the Sudan. As for the popular leader of the revolution, Saad Pasha, he accepted Allenby's declaration as it was regardless of its flaws. As mentioned earlier, Allenby's declaration included the same proposals of Milner's report, which Saad rejected two years earlier. Saad Pasha was allowed to come back from his second exile, and participated in the first parliamentary elections under the new constitution. Saad and his Wafd Party swept those elections and formed a new cabinet in February 1924.

Allenby and Saad: A Tragic End

Less than two years after Allenby's declaration and less than nine months after Saad's heading the cabinet for his first time under a new constitution, the revolutionaries assassinated the commander of the British army in Egypt. This incident deeply embarrassed Allenby in front of London and placed him in a very difficult situation. He felt that all the risks that he took went in vain. His frustration led him to react brutally by applying oppressive policies that he previously carefully avoided during his time in Egypt. The same crisis forced Saad Pasha to resign, and Allenby himself resigned shortly afterwards.

The political conditions in Egypt were expected to calm down and stabilize after Saad reached power, with halting the assassination operations of British officers and officials. It was also anticipated that the two countries would reach a comprehensive treaty, resolving their dispute over the presence of British troops in Egypt and the Sudan question. However, the sudden assassination of Major General Sir Lee Stack, the sirdar of the British army in Egypt and governor of the Anglo-Egyptian Sudan, in November 1924 led to sharp deterioration in the situation. Allenby reacted furiously, as he forced the Egyptian government to pay a horrendous fine of half a million sterling pounds, and took measures to separate the Sudan from Egypt by evacuating the Egyptian army units from there. After the failure of his cabinet to restore security in the country with such a major assassination case, Saad Pasha had no choice but to resign. Allenby similarly resigned by the end of the year, but London forced him to stay on his post in order to humiliate and punish him for misjudging the abilities of Saad Pasha to control the boiling streets and contain violence. His resignation was finally accepted many months later and he departed from Egypt for the last time in May 1925.

Saad Pasha did not live long after these events. He died in Cairo in August 1927. Allenby lived for almost another decade until he died in May 1936. A few months after Allenby's death, Egypt and Britain finally signed the treaty that he struggled but failed to accomplish amid revolutionary unrest during his time in the country. This was the 1936 Anglo-Egyptian treaty that delivered most of the 1919 Revolution's demands—including partial military evacuation but not full independence yet.

Thus, it took seventeen years for the 1919 Revolution to reach its goals, at least partially in the 1936 evacuation treaty. Hundreds of Egyptians were killed by British forces during these years, and thousands of others were injured, jailed, or exiled outside the country. Egypt wouldn't reach its demand of full evacuation of the British troops until 1956. During seven decades of British occupation of Egypt, Lord Edmund Allenby was perhaps the only colonizer who peculiarly supported the independence rights of his colonized subjects.

Chapter 7

CROSSING THE GLOBAL COLOR LINE

1919 AND COLONIAL RACISM

Kyle J. Anderson

> Whereas England wants to treat Egyptians like African savages (*li-'nn kanit ankiltara turid an taftarad al-misriyyin wahush ifriqiyya*) and insult the fortunes of our women, just as they have oppressed the fortunes of our men, shame on you! . . . we protest to your Excellency over what has happened so far.

Petition to the French Embassy, March 20, 1919[1]

Figure 7.1 is a petition from an anonymous lawyer in Egypt who called himself Abu Shadi, sent to the French embassy on March 20, 1919. The immediate cause for his protest was a massacre at Nazlat al-Shubak where, as Katherine Halls' research has documented, British soldiers assaulted and gang-raped at least a dozen women during the 1919 Revolution.[2] Abu Shadi goes on to discuss the horrors of that tragic event, but it is this line at the beginning of his petition—seemingly an afterthought and not explained fully—that I want to interrogate closely in this chapter. What was he referring to when he accused the British of treating Egyptians like "African savages"? What are the connotations of such an accusation? And how did it generate mobilizing force in revolutionary Egypt?

The key to answering these questions, I believe, involves paying attention to globally circulating ideas about the racial identity of Egyptians and how these changed before, during, and after the First World War (1914–18). The war clarified Egypt's previously ambiguous position within the British Empire in at

---

1. Archives Diplomatiques, Minsitère des Affairs Étrangères, La Courneuve (MAE) K/56/1/12: "Africa, Consular" (April 21, 1919).

2. Katharine Halls, "'Not Worthy of Belief': Testimonies of Rape in Egypt, 1919," presented at *Interwar Revolutions in the Middle East/North Africa* (London: King's College, 2019).

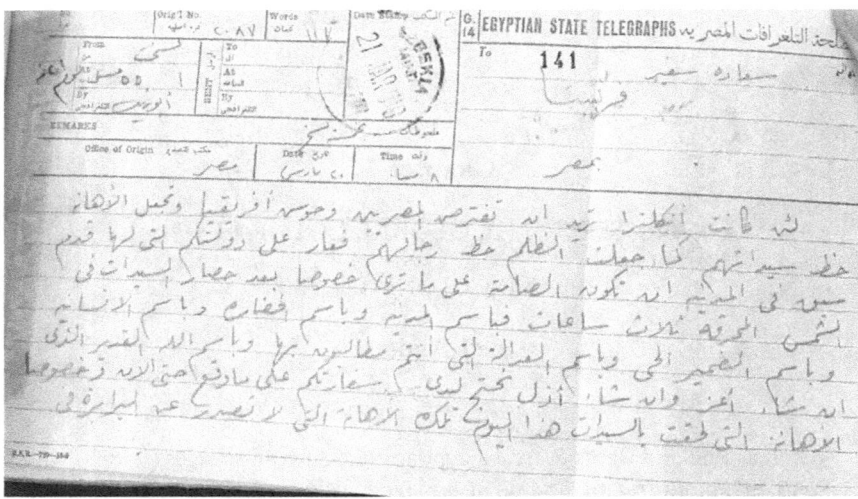

Figure 7.1 Petition from Abu Shadi. *Source*: Archives Diplomatiques, Ministère des Affaires Étrangers, La Courneuve, K/56/1/12.

least three ways: the country became an official protectorate, there was a massive influx of white troops in cities and military outposts, and hundreds of thousands of Egyptians were recruited from the countryside—many by force—to work as migrant laborers for the British army. I have argued elsewhere that the war was the clearest example for nationalist intellectuals and activists in Egypt to see what African Americans had recognized for at least a generation as the "color line."[3] The color line was transformative because it implied a simple, binary divide between white and nonwhite races, which represented a major shift in conceptualizing race globally from approximately the end of the Franco-Prussian War (1870) until the era of the two world wars (1914–45).

The binary global color line took shape against the backdrop of complex racial taxonomies that resulted from efforts to apply the developing scientific method to human history in the generations before 1870.[4] Entire categorical schemata of races developed, with writers and scientists in Egypt and across the world also

---

3. Frederick Douglass, "The Color Line," *North American Review* 132, no. 295 (June 1881): 567–77. Gretchen Murphy, *Shadowing the White Man's Burden: U.S. Imperialism and the Problem of the Color Line* (New York: New York University Press, 2010), 13. For the first use of the term "global color line" in print, see W. E. B. Du Bois, "The Souls of Black Folk," in *Du Bois Writings*, ed. Nathan Higgins (New York: Library of America, 1986 [1903]), 359. For more, see Kyle Anderson, *The Egyptian Labor Corps: Race, Space, and Place in the First World War* (Austin: University of Texas Press, 2021).

4. Ivan Hannaford, *Race: The History of an Idea in the West* (Baltimore: Johns Hopkins University Press, 1996).

taking part in their construction.⁵ As Cemil Aydin has shown, the dominant racial taxonomy during the thirty or so years that the British army occupied Egypt, from 1882 until the First World War, racialized Egyptians alongside Muslims as "Mohammedans," and defined the latter especially in opposition to Black Africans.⁶ But this taxonomy suddenly melted away during the war, as Egyptians were formally placed under British protectorate and drafted by the hundreds of thousands into the so-called Coloured Labour Corps alongside others from China, India, South Africa, Fiji, and so on.

The 1919 Revolution, I argue, was partly motivated by a reaction to this perceived mis-racialization of Egyptians during the war. In response to being treated like "people of colour," nationalists articulated a sense of Egyptian racial distinctiveness. The Egyptian response to colonial racism shared some of the key intellectual assumptions of the late imperial imaginary; namely, the notion that humans are organized into biologically distinct, hierarchically ordered communities. Nationalist activists and intellectuals were represented as "real Egyptians" who were biological heirs to an ancient "civilization," superior to Black Africans, and not deserving of political subordination to white supremacy. However, the importance of the race concept in Egyptian nationalist thought has gone underexplored. The following sections of this chapter attempt to sketch an outline of the changing approaches to Egyptian race adopted by British administrators and Egyptian nationalists before, during, and after the First World War, culminating in the 1919 Revolution.

---

5. Omnia El Shakry, *The Great Social Laboratory: Subjects of Knowledge in Colonial and Postcolonial Egypt* (Stanford: Stanford University Press, 2007); Marwa Elshakry, *Reading Darwin in Arabic, 1860–1950* (Chicago: University of Chicago Press, 2013).

6. Consul-General Herbert Kitchener expressed this tendency in British thought when he said of attempts to institute liberal political reforms in Egypt: "We are bound to consider carefully whether . . . the endowment of a Mahommedan country with a political system copied from Europe might not to incalculable harm. . . . Party spirit is to them like strong drink to uncivilized African natives." See the British National Archives (TNA), Foreign Office Files (FO) 371/1635 No. 395: Kitchener to Balfour (December 29, 1912). In Kitchener's mind—perhaps no less than in the minds of Egyptian Islamic modernists like Muhammad 'Abduh—there appears to exist a unique form of "Islamic Civilization," which places Muslims above the status of Black Africans lacking the qualities of civilization. Where Kitchener and 'Abduh would have quarreled is over the question of whether Muslims as a group were strangers to the finer points of democratic governance, but the status of Africans could be overlooked or ignored in such a hypothetical debate, see Eve Troutt-Powell, *A Different Shade of Colonialism: Egypt, Great Britain, and the Mastery of the Sudan* (Berkeley: University of California Press, 2003).

Instituting a Racial Caste System in Egypt

In the New World Empire of Spain in the sixteenth and seventeenth centuries, a complicated social structure based on race, known as the *casta* system, developed. Spaniards who could trace their lineage back to the Iberian Peninsula, especially the original *conquistadores,* constituted the upper crust of this system, while their mixed-race descendants born to indigenous mothers formed a middle class of *mestizos.* This middle class, in turn, had more privileges than either the indigenous majority of the population, or the enslaved Africans who were later imported to the continent.[7]

In colonial Egypt, state policy effectively developed in such a way that a vaguely similar racial caste system took shape. In its simplest form, it put white Europeans. This colonial elite existed in relationship with Ottoman-descended state elites in Egypt that began with a sense of intra-imperial cooperation, and those who could claim foreign status at one of the European consular offices could benefit from an extended penumbra of colonial power. It was the British military alliance with the Ottomans that brought Egypt back into the Ottoman fold with the Treaty of London in 1841, and this alliance continued during the Crimean War (1853-56). But the Anglo-Ottoman relationship became increasingly tense just as Muslims were becoming racialized in late-nineteenth-century thought. The racialization of Muslims described by Aydin affected British views of indigenous Egyptians, who had traditionally been shut out of the upper echelons of Ottoman state institutions, but now became in some senses elided with their Ottoman contemporaries. Meanwhile, it ignored or accorded a different, more liminal status to religious minorities like Christians and Jews.

Ottoman-Egyptians and Egyptians-as-Muslims thus came to occupy a kind of middle strata under the British occupation prior to the First World War. Meanwhile, Black Africans, who were imported via Sudan by the tens of thousands each year in a burgeoning Trans-Saharan slave trade, were largely viewed as constituting the bottom of the social hierarchy. Even though Islamic law regarding who was eligible for enslavement was traditionally understood to ignore racial distinctions, recent research has shown how, in practice, and especially in nineteenth-century Egypt, there was a link between the condition of enslavement and Blackness.[8]

---

7. Peggy K. Liss, *Mexico under Spain, 1521–1556: Society and the Origins of Nationality* (Chicago: University of Chicago Press, 1975); Colin A. Palmer, *Slaves of the White God: Blacks in Mexico, 1570–1650* (Cambridge, MA: Harvard University Press, 1976).

8. ʿImad Ahmad Hilal, *Al-Raqiq fi Misr fi-l-Qarn al-Tasiʿ ʿAshar* (Cairo: al-ʿArabi li-l-Nashr wa-l-Tuwziʿ, 1999); Kenneth Cuno and Terrance Walz, *Race and Slavery in the Middle East: Histories of Trans-Saharan Africans in Nineteenth-Century Egypt, Sudan, and the Ottoman Mediterranean* (Cairo: American University in Cairo Press, 2010). For more on the role of slavery and Blackness in Islamic law, including appeals to Egypt's al-Azhar mosque to seek approval for the mass enslavement of Black Africans in seventeenth-century Morocco, see Chouki El Hamel, *Black Morocco: A History of Race, Slavery and Islam*

Ehud Toledano has uncovered multiple stories of free or freed Black people in Egypt who found themselves at risk of being captured by slavers and sold.[9] This is why, for example, manumission papers became an important item for Africans in Egypt during the Tanzimat period.[10]

Paradoxically, efforts on the part of British imperial officials to suppress the African slave trade—which they saw as a unique scourge of "Mohammedan" countries, especially after the wave of abolitionism that culminated in the American Civil War—played an important part in the institution of white supremacy in Egypt.[11] The 1860s saw the beginnings of what was, at first, mainly a diplomatic effort by the British to use abolition as an occasion for expansion of influence in Egypt.[12] In this initial wave of abolitionism, European consular agents used their extraterritorial legal rights to free slaves who presented themselves to the consulate.[13] But this practice was seen as an infringement on the prerogatives of the Egyptian government, and was soon ended. In the 1870s, Khedive Isma'il signaled a willingness to suppress the slave trade by appointing Europeans, mainly Englishmen, as provincial governors and leaders of abolitionist expeditions. For example, Samuel Baker was sent on an expedition to equatorial Sudan sponsored by the Khedive, partly with the goal of extinguishing the slave trade, but also aiming to expand Egypt's African empire from its base in Khartoum further up the Nile.[14] After Baker, Isma'il appointed the famed general Charles Gordon as governor of the equatorial province, and soon after, Governor-General of Sudan. He was given a mandate to suppress the slave trade. Gabriel Baer mentions at least seven other Europeans employed by the Egyptian government in influential

---

(Cambridge: Cambridge University Press, 2013). Toledano notes in Egypt the "conviction that all Africans were slaves, regardless of what they do," see Ehud Toledano, *As If Silent and Absent: Bonds of Enslavement in the Islamic Middle East* (New Haven: Yale University Press, 2007), 117.

9. Toledano follows the story of Haci Mehmet, a freedman who brought a legal case to court in order to protest his attempted re-enslavement in Alexandria. This attempt was only possible because "an 18-year old African man in Alexandria could have been safely assumed to be either a slave or a freed person," see Toledano, *As If Silent and Absent*, 89. Another young man, Bilal, a manumitted slave from Cairo, was captured and re-sold in Jidda before making an appeal to the British consulate there for freedom, see Toledano, *As If Silent and Absent*, 117.

10. Toledano, *As If Silent and Absent*, 114, 118. Toledano also traces the persistence of African cultural influences in Egypt, which he attributes to the slave trade, through the practices of *zar* rituals in Egyptian Sufism, see Toledano, *As If Silent and Absent*, 211.

11. Troutt-Powell, *A Different Shade of Colonialism*.

12. Gabriel Baer, "Slavery and its Abolition," in *Studies in the Social History of Modern Egypt*, ed. Gabriel Baer (Chicago: University of Chicago Press, 1969), 177.

13. Ibid.

14. "Sir Samuel Baker's Expedition," *The New York Times* (July 19, 1873): 4.

posts for abolitionist purposes before the British military occupation of Egypt began in 1882.[15]

The abolition of slavery in Egypt was, in essence, tied up with the importation of a class of white governmental employees from Europe into the country. These officials depended on Egyptian middlemen, and often maintained an attitude of disdain for Black people despite their official abolitionary pretenses. For example, in a letter to the Foreign Secretary from 1880 in which he asked to be appointed a Slave Commissioner in the Red Sea, the British adventurer Richard F. Burton derided an official of the Egyptian government born to a Nubian father and Ethiopian mother for being "almost a black" and therefore incapable of doing his job. Later in the text, he complains of Isma'il's "anti-European and pro-Mohammedan policy."[16] Many more Europeans came to work as employees in the Egyptian Ministries of Education, Finance, and Public Works during the occupation. By 1906, there were 1,252 British officials working in the Egyptian government.[17] These men self-identified as "Anglo-Egyptians," and they left behind a substantial body of primary source literature for historians.[18]

After their military victory at Tal al-Kabīr in 1882, white British officers took command of what remained of the defeated Egyptian army. These men reported to the top British diplomat on the ground, the Consul-General, rather than answering to the still-intact Egyptian military hierarchy. Joint Anglo-Egyptian garrisons, housing approximately 6,000 British troops in total, were set up under the Consul-General's direction in Cairo, Alexandria, on the Suez Canal, and along the Nile River.[19] This new Anglicized Egyptian army was deployed as a fighting force in 1885 to relieve Gordon in Khartoum during a siege undertaken by the forces of Muhammad Ahmad, also known as the *mahdi*.[20] Attempts to re-take Sudan from the *mahdi*'s troops would dominate British military efforts in Egypt for the next

15. Baer, "Slavery and its Abolition," 178–80.

16. Isabel Burton, *The Life of Captain Sir Richard F. Burton* (London: Chapman & Hall, 1893), 195.

17. Lanver Mak, "More than Officers and Officials: Britons in Occupied Egypt, 1882–1922," *The Journal of Imperial and Commonwealth History* 39, no. 1 (February 2011): 23.

18. In addition to sources cited elsewhere in this chapter, see Bimbashi McPherson and Barry Carman, *A Life in Egypt* (London: BBC, 1983); Clara Boyle, *A Servant of the Empire: A Memoir of Harry Boyle* (London: Methuen and Co., 1938); Edward Cecil, *The Leisure of an Egyptian Official* (London: Hodder and Stoughton, 1921); James Rennell Rodd, *Social and Diplomatic Memoirs, 1894–1901* (London: Edward Arnold and Co., 1923); Douglas Sladen, *Egypt and the English* (London: Hurst and Blackett, 1908); and *Oriental Cairo: The City of the 'Arabic Nights'* (London: Hurst and Blackett, 1911); William Wilcocks, *Sixty Years in the East* (London: Blackwood & Sons, 1935).

19. Claire Cookson-Hills, "Historical Perspectives on Whole-of-Government Approaches: The 1882 British Occupation of Egypt," *Canadian Army Journal* 15, no. 1 (2013): 66.

20. Ibid. Troutt-Powell, *A Different Shade of Colonialism*.

fifteen years. In 1898, the Anglo-Egyptian army succeeded in defeating the *mahdi*'s successor and re-establishing government of Sudan from Cairo.

The Anglo-Egyptian army that was built during these so-called Mahdist Wars (1885–98) was arranged according to a racial hierarchy. It included white officers at the top, Ottoman-descended middling officers below them, Egyptian infantry troops, and *fallahin* combined with imported Indigenous Americans doing logistical labor behind the front lines, all fighting against Black Sudanese.[21] In the course of these battles, a new position was created for Commander-in-Chief of the Anglo-Egyptian army, who also functioned as Governor-General of Sudan after its reconquest. Known as the *sirdar*, he was a white Englishman with a special residence in Cairo in the posh neighborhood of *al-Gazira* (Gezirah).

Ideas about race also influenced the reconstitution of the Egyptian government under British occupation. After the 'Urābī revolt, all but one of the ministers from 'Urābī's government stayed on, with most of the punitive attention focused on 'Urābī himself. But the Consul-General functioned as the de facto leader of the country, and Evelyn Baring (Lord Cromer) was appointed to this position in 1883. He exercised his influence through his own appointments to the various ministries, which initially all came from the significant population of Europeans already resident in Egypt. Over the course of twenty-four years, Baring assigned "advisers" to the various ministries, and their "advice" soon became policy without technically unseating the Ottoman-Egyptian government. These advisers were all white, Christian men from British or Anglo-Indian backgrounds.

One of them was Thomas Russell, and his published memoirs show how ideas about race influenced Anglo-Egyptian officials in the years before the war. Born to a minor aristocratic lineage, he graduated from Cambridge and was recruited to Egypt in 1901 by his cousin, a veteran of the Sudan campaigns and adviser to the Minister of Interior.[22] Part of Russell's training once he got to Egypt involved tours of duty in the Anglo-Egyptian military. He was placed as the second officer in command of a squad of fifty Sudanese infantry recruits.[23] One illustrative story culminated when "a humorous black in the front rank exploded with a laugh like a tyre bursting and was led out by the ear in front of the parade to receive a couple of resounding slaps on his rubber face from the enraged [Egyptian] instructor with a telling-off for 'insulting his English officer.'"[24] This incident clearly illustrates the racial caste system I am talking about; with the white trainee Russell on top, the Egyptian officer acting as an intermediary below him, and a Black African soldier

---

21. Ibid.
22. Thomas Russell, *Egyptian Service, 1902–1946* (London: John Murray, 1949), 11.
23. Russell not only notes the "friendly black hands" of the men but also writes, "no amount of kindness . . . could shut my nose when downwind of my dusky companions as they sweated at physical drill," see Russell, *Egyptian Service, 1902–1946*, 16.
24. Russell, *Egyptian Service, 1902–1946*, 16.

on the receiving end of the kind of violent punishment that had been outlawed for white British soldiers in the nineteenth century.[25]

Exclusive spaces were created for white Anglo-Egyptians like Russell to socialize with one another. Percy F. Martin's *Egypt: Old and New* (1923) lists an itinerary that would have catered to these elite whites:

> The Gezirah Sporting Club . . . is reached in about ten minutes by carriage from either the Continental or Shepheard's Hotel in Cairo. Whilst its hospitable doors have always been opened to visitors non-resident in the capital . . . exception has been taken not without some reason to the policy which tends to bring about the exclusion of Egyptians from any active participation in the management of the sports; neither have they been encouraged to become members of the Club, except in certain cases.[26]

Similarly, in Ronald Storrs' memoir *Orientations* (1937), he recalls how the nearby Turf Club "was the fenced city of refuge of the higher British community, many of whom spent anything between one and five hours daily within its walls." He also noted how "it was difficult for foreigners [i.e. anyone not British or Egyptian] to be elected and not easy for Egyptians even to make use of either club; as I discovered by the glances cast in my direction when I came in with one of the few Egyptian members to play tennis."[27] Two months before the outbreak of the war, in June 1914, the new Consul-General Herbert Kitchener made the social exclusion of Egyptians explicit and barred "natives" from membership in the Khedivial Sporting Club.[28] This was a harbinger of the broader discursive exclusions that would take place in the months and years to come.

The systematic denigration of Black Africans was evident in these spaces through the composition of the staff and the types of entertainment on offer. Despite the British crusade against the slave trade, the majority of officers' attendants and servants at the Khedivial Sporting Club were Nubians or Black Africans. Figure 7.2, an image of the interior of Shepheard's Hotel taken in Cairo in 1920, illustrates this visually. All of the seated patrons are white, and all of the servants are Black. A few rare Egyptians, usually themselves the sons of Ottoman officers and their Caucasian concubines, may have been allowed in such spaces in the years before the war. As Samir Raafat puts it in his description of the Gezirah Sporting Club, "the turbaned Nubian sofragis balancing their silver platters of game pie, roast beef, ham chops and cucumber sandwiches" served as "an astute reminder that

---

25. Russell consciously self-identifies throughout his memoir as a "white man" and contrasts his own "tender skin" from that of the "tough, unwashed *Bedu* (i.e. Arab)." Russell, *Egyptian Service, 1902–1946*, 18.

26. Samir Raafat, "Gezira Sporting Club Milestones," *Egyptian Mail*, February 10–17, 1996, http://www.egy.com/zamalek/96-02-10.php, accessed May 28, 2021.

27. Ronald Storrs, *Orientations* (London: Ivor Nicholson & Watson Ltd., 1937), 23.

28. Peter Mansfield, *The British in Egypt* (London: Holt, Reinhart and Winston, 1972), 195.

Figure 7.2 Shepheard's Hotel main dining hall, 1920. *Source*: American Colony. Photo Department, photographer. Egyptian hotels Ltd., Cairo, Shepheard's Hotel. Interior. Main dining hall. Egypt Cairo, 1920 photography. https://www.loc.gov/item/2019693637/.

this was still Africa."[29] Further demonstration of the ideological position of Black Africans in British-occupied Egypt is seen in Figure 7.3, a flyer for a minstrel show put on at the Cairo branch of the YMCA in January 1914. The YMCA, which not only catered mainly to Anglo-Americans in Egypt, but also had a separate Arabic branch in Cairo frequented by Egyptian and Syrian Christians, would have been an easy conduit for American-style segregation to find expression on the Nile. But the important difference between segregation in colonial Egypt and in the United States was that, at least before the First World War, the demographic majority of the country occupied a middle space between two conceptual poles of black and white, somehow closer to the former than the latter, but differentiated enough so as to keep their situation ambiguous.[30]

29. Raafat, "Gezira Sporting Club Milestones," *Egyptian Mail*, February 10–17, 1996.

30. In a 1910 article published in his influential nationalist journal *al-Jarida*, Ahmad Lutfi al-Sayyid illustrated this taxonomy clearly: "Who are the sons of the Nile? They are those who are [to be found] between its source and its mouth. They are those who live in that [distant] torrid region and whose color is black; and those who live in the temperate zone, an whose color is, as you see, somewhere between black and white." See Charles Wendell, *The Evolution of the Egyptian National Image: From Its Origins to Ahmad Lutfi al-Sayyid* (Berkeley: University of California Press, 1972), 261–2.

Figure 7.3 Flyer for Minstrel Show at the Cairo YMCA. *Source*: Kautz Family YMCA Archives, Minneapolis, MN, Y.USA.9-2-22 Box Y.

Drawing a Global Color Line in the First World War

The subtle differentiation between Egyptians and Black Africans in the racial taxonomies of the late nineteenth and early twentieth centuries began to melt away over the course of the short but transformative period of the First World War. Instead of having a special status as "Muslims," and therefore natural subjects of the Ottoman caliph, Egyptians came to be considered similar to other Black, brown, East Asian, and Indigenous subjects of the British and French empires. The color line became evident in Egypt during the war in at least three ways: through the declaration of a protectorate, the mass recruitment of rural Egyptians for the Labor Corps, and the massive influx of foreign soldiers housed in segregated spaces across the country.

When the British declared Egypt to be an official protectorate in November of 1914, they clarified Egypt's position in the empire by placing it in a similar legal position as territories in Africa, Asia, the Caribbean, and the Pacific Ocean. The use of the protectorate as a legal mechanism for imperial expansion and military security in the British Empire grew out of the British experience in colonial India. Beginning in the late eighteenth century, rulers of numerous states surrounding official British Indian territory entered into agreements with the East India Company and, after 1833, the British government of India, in which they exchanged control over their external affairs for "protection." Depending on the history and relative power of each state, they were known variously as British protectorates, protected states, dependencies, dependent states, or "states under British protection."[31] Responsibilities for these states' external policy, and varying degrees of internal policy, were held by political figures living in the country, known as "residents." From 1764 onward, British India's political residency system grew to the north, west, and east until it encompassed nearly 45 percent of South Asia and Myanmar (Burma); part of Thailand (Siam); 35 percent of Southwest Asia, including Bahrain, Kuwait, and some small shaykhdoms in the Persian Gulf; the East African coast; and parts of Central Asia, including Afghanistan and Iran.[32]

In addition to securing the Indian frontiers in a Residency system that spread from the East African coast to Southeast Asia, British imperial officials also used protectorates in the "scramble for Africa." German claims in West Africa initiated a series of events that led to the Berlin Conference of 1885, where a British protectorate was instituted in the Niger River Delta. Ten years later, the East Africa protectorate was proclaimed in today's Kenya, when the British government took over the territory of the Chartered Company of East Africa to secure British interests in Zanzibar. The year before that, a British protectorate had been declared in Uganda, alongside the long-standing chain of dependencies between British Somaliland and Aden.

---

31. James Onley, "The Raj Reconsidered: British India's Informal Empire and Spheres of Influence in Asia and Africa," *Asian Affairs* 60, no. 1 (March 2009): 50.
32. Ibid., 49.

After the declaration of a protectorate in Egypt in 1914, British authorities began an effort to recruit approximately half a million Egyptians, many by force, to work as military laborers in the war. The Egyptian Labor Corps (ELC) began with a group of 3,000 men hired on three-month contracts and sent to Gallipoli to do work such as loading and unloading ships at the island of Lemnos and digging trenches on the peninsula.[33] The much larger effort on the Western Front initially relied on French labor, but by 1915, Allied military authorities began to look to their colonies as sources for what they referred to as "coloured" or "native labour." In 1915, French military officer Charles Mangin announced his intention to recruit a force noir of 500,000 men from the colonies to assist in the war effort as both laborers and infantry troops.[34] Besides importing Indian and Chinese labor, as they had done in the second Anglo-Boer war years before, the British mobilized Caribbean laborers in the British West Indian Labour Corps and organized Black and mixed-race men from South Africa in the South African Native Labor Corps and the Cape Coloured Battalion, respectively.[35]

Sources left behind by the British officers who interacted with Egyptians during the war show how they were racialized alongside Black Africans. E. K. Venables, an ELC officer who left behind extensive correspondence at the Imperial War Museum in London, illustrates this tendency vividly.[36] As a schoolteacher, he kept up with the scientific ideas of his day, including globally circulating theories about biological race. In his unpublished manuscript, he turns an eye to the physiology of the men under his command, describing them as "stickily built, dark-skinned, heavy-jowled, and round skulled, some of the dolichocephalic type, but more approximating the negroid."[37] Here, Venables shows familiarity with the racial science of anthropometry, which attempted to classify human diversity by comparing physical measurements of the body. By the beginning of the twentieth century, the cephalic index—which was obtained by dividing the maximum width of the skull by its maximum length—was the dominant measurement used to classify "racial stocks."[38] By drawing on the cephalic index to classify the men under his command, Venables illustrates how Egyptians were subject to the global discourse of scientific racism. It is significant that Venables comes away from this exercise concluding that most of his men were "approximating the negroid,"

---

33. TNA, FO 141/797/2 No. 2689: General Staff Army HQ (July 23, 1915).

34. Richard Fogarty, *Race and War in France: Colonial Subjects in the French Army, 1914–1918* (Baltimore: Johns Hopkins University Press, 2008).

35. John Starling and Ivor Lee, *No Labour, No Battle: Military Labour during the First World War* (London: History Press, 2009), 95.

36. Imperial War Museum (IWM), Ernest Kendrick Venables Papers (EKV) 1/2: Venables Diaries (March 28, 1916).

37. IWM EKV/2: *They Also Served*, 2.

38. Elise K. Burton, *Genetic Crossroads: The Middle East and the Science of Human Heredity* (Stanford: Stanford University Press, 2021), 32–4.

especially in light of Elise K. Burton's findings that racial classifications were highly fraught and subject to the predominant political considerations of their day.

A British medical officer writing under the pseudonym "Serjeant-Major, RAMC" also grouped ELC men alongside Black Africans. Serving at the largest of the so-called native hospitals—which were segregated hospital units meant to deal especially with the injured men of the ELC—he would have interacted with the men regularly. The way in which he recounted these experiences shows how Egyptians as a group were understood in racial terms by petty officers and other imperial officials during the war:

> The Medical Officer in command of the Kantara establishment possess all the dominant racial traits which have made British rule over Eastern people such a success wherever our flag flies . . . his government of the hospital evidence another quality, much rare though also essentially British—that of *being able to tell one black man from another*, to realize the fundamental divergences of character and temperament between *the various coloured races*, and to adopt his methods accordingly . . . from a fairly extended acquaintance with the lower-class Egyptian—the typical ELC or CTC [Camel Transport Corps] man—he is convinced that upon a true estimation of his peculiar racial qualities depends all our success in governing him both in the present time of war and hereafter.[39] (emphasis added)

By representing Egyptian laborers as "Orientals," the medical officer drew on a long-established distinction between Western selves and Eastern Others in the Western European cultural tradition.[40] But his contrast between the "dominant racial traits" of the (white, British) commanding officer and the "peculiar racial characteristics" of the ELC shows how the older, binary logic of the East/West distinction could be reformulated according to the racial idioms of the early twentieth century. An empirical, scientific approach to delineating racial taxonomy—which the medical officer refers to here as the "essentially British" ability to "realize the fundamental divergences of character and temperament between the various coloured races"— was easily boiled down to a simpler formulation of "being able to tell one black man from another." The men of the ELC—and, by extension, "the lower-class Egyptian" as a racial type—are referred to alternatively as Black men or as part of the "various coloured races." The global color line employed by men like this British medical officer adopted the empirical veneer of science, but, in the same way that Edward Said famously characterized Orientalism, it was still fundamentally an instance of self-definition through Otherization.[41]

---

39. Serjeant Major, RAMC, *With the RAMC in Egypt* (London: Cassell and Co., Ltd., 1918), 293–5.
40. Edward Said, *Orientalism* (New York: Pantheon Books, 1978), 2.
41. Ibid.

It was not just the half a million Egyptians who served in the war who experienced racist abuse; the war also brought such treatment to Egypt's cities and towns. Located at the crossroads of the British Empire and the major theaters of the war in Europe, Egypt became a staging ground for troops, recruits, the wounded, prisoners of war, and laborers. Australian and New Zealander troops encamped outside of Cairo near the pyramids and formed the famed "ANZAC" battalions on the way to serve in Gallipoli. Contingents of the British Indian army were sent to the Western Front through the Suez Canal, and were soon relocated to Egypt, where it was believed that they were more suited to the hot environment of the Sinai/Palestine campaign. As one representative of the YMCA in Egypt during the war put it, "With Cairo, Alexandria and Port Said as centers, Northern Egypt is a vast camp and hospital through which move by tens of thousands the flower of English speaking races and of the Indian Empire."[42] The YMCA established branches at the various fronts associated with fighting in Egypt, including principally Gallipoli and Sinai/Palestine, but these catered mainly to "British and Colonial troops," rather than the Egyptian men of the ELC.[43]

The YMCA also tried to reach troops on rest in Cairo and Alexandria. 84,000 men were stationed in Egypt during the war, almost half of whom were ANZACs. While on leave in Cairo, they visited bars and nightclubs and patronized the city's legal brothels. According to Mario Ruiz, "British officials were especially quick to tie issues of white troops' sexuality with Cairo's reputation of Oriental sensuality and disease as well as widely held fears about racial degeneration."[44] In April 1915, a crowd of drunken ANZAC soldiers rioted in the Wasa'a brothel district, setting fire to couches and buildings and throwing prostitutes from several houses into an alley.[45] Three and a half months later, men of the 2nd Australian Division rioted again. Ruiz finds that "the quotidian matches that erupted between Australians and Egyptians during the war were noteworthy for their racial chauvinism."[46]

Nor were the incoming soldiers limited to Egypt's major urban centers. One of the early campaigns of the war involved skirmishes across the Western Desert in Libya, and after a number of British and Colonial troops engaged in battles as part of this campaign, a contingent of troops remained stationed in Upper Egypt. In February 1916, Bani Suwayf was chosen to be the headquarters of the "Southern Army" of the occupation. A few hundred men were stationed there, with guards on different bridges.[47] The local government hospital was overtaken by the military,

42. YMCA, Y.USA.9-2-22 Box 1, "Montclair's Foreign Representative" (December 21, 1915).

43. YMCA, Y.USA.9-2-22 Box 1, Eady to Mott (September 6, 1915).

44. Ruiz, "Manly Spectacles and Imperial Soldiers in Wartime Egypt, 1914–1919," *Middle Eastern Studies* 45, no. 3 (2009): 357.

45. Ibid., 351.

46. Ibid., 362.

47. TNA, FO 371/2672 No. 182185 Report by Inspector at Beni Suef (September 13, 1916).

and local notables "took it upon themselves" to raise money from the surrounding area to put up shelters for the men and their horses, and to provide fruit, cigarettes, and biscuits for the men in the hospital.[48] There is no reason to suppose that this method of "forced volunteering" was any different from the methods used by state and military officials to recruit men for the ELC, which is to say, it was likely viewed as an imposition at the very least.

John Wintringham, who served with the Lincolnshire Yeomanry unit, was stationed at Bani Suwayf in 1916. In his memoirs, he recounts how, "as soon as we had settled into camp on the edge of the desert, we commenced to put on a 'show of strength', riding through the countryside in all directions and giving the impression that we were much more numerous and ferocious than we really are."[49] Wintringham's unit set up a machine gun range, which they pointed in the direction of a local cemetery.[50] An official report from August recounts the story of a "native who was accidentally shot at night at Mazura for failing to stop when challenged." Although the report insisted "that the accident was entirely the fault of the victim was recognized by all the natives in the neighborhood," it is hard to imagine that stories like this did not influence people's perceptions of the British troops who suddenly occupied their towns.[51]

The First World War, then, witnessed an influx of white troops, a tightening of restrictions in the country, and a massive increase in racialized abuse directed at people in Egypt. Whereas Egyptians had previously occupied an ambiguous position within the British Empire, and they could still claim to be Ottoman subjects in the years before the war, total war against the caliph put an end to any special status accorded to Egyptians when they were racialized as Muslims, especially vis-à-vis Black Africans. Through the declaration of a protectorate, massive recruitment of the "Coloured Labour Corps," and the huge expansion of a segregated and hostile community of white settlers, Egyptians were treated just like Black, brown, East Asian, and Indigenous people across the globe. This was the clearest example of the "global color line" that Egyptians had yet seen, and, just like millions of others who experienced such unprecedented impositions, they launched a revolution in the years that followed.[52]

---

48. Ibid.

49. J. W. Wintringham, *With the Lincolnshire Yeomanry in Egypt and Palestine: 1914–1918* (Grimsby: Lincolnshire Life, 1979), 34–5.

50. Ibid., 34.

51. TNA, FO 371/2672 No. 182185 Report by Inspector at Beni Suef (September 13, 1916).

52. Tim Harper, *Underground Asia: Global Revolutionaries and the Assault on Empire* (Cambridge, MA: Belknap Press of Harvard University, 2021).

"I Will Not Accept Slavery!"

The generation of nationalist intellectuals and activists who lived through the 1919 Revolution was deeply affected by witnessing scenes of their countrymen treated in dehumanizing and racist fashion during the war. The image of ELC recruits being led away from their villages, tied together by a thick rope around the trunk, is a recurring theme in the literature. Historian 'Abd al-Rahman al-Rafi'i—a partisan of the nationalist party and eyewitness to the First World War—consistently related the treatment of ELC workers to animals in his *Thawrat 1919* (1947). They were "tied by ropes and driven away like cattle . . . and moved by train in animal pens."[53] Men were grabbed from their homes and gathered "like cattle," being whipped if they refused to join.[54] For those working in the Sinai, al-Rafi'i described them as dying "like flies" in the desert.[55] Animalistic similes appear in other nationalist histories of Egypt, such as 'Ali Barakat's essay on the occasion of the ninetieth anniversary of the revolution, where he wrote of the ELC: "men of the government would enter into the villages and wait for the *fallahin* to return to their homes at sundown and gazed out at them *like cattle* and seized the best suited of them for service."[56] To commemorate the fiftieth anniversary of the revolution, Egyptian social historian Amin 'Izz al-Din wrote about the ELC in the illustrated magazine *al-Mussawir*, and his article was accompanied by drawings of men tied together (see Figure 7.4)).

Comparing the treatment of the ELC to animals emphasizes the dehumanizing aspects of British colonial policy that were made acute in this unique moment. By relating conscripted Egyptian laborers to "cattle" (*ana'am*) or "flies" (*dhubaba*), al-Rafi'i and Barakat point out how the men of the ELC had been reduced to what Giorgio Agamben calls "bare life."[57] This is the ability of the state to accord onto some people a status shorn of any metaphysical significance as humans, transforming them into mere bodies. A similar operation occurs with the race concept, which reduces humans to just another type of animal to be studied through empirical observation. The race concept, and especially what Ivan Hannaford calls "the racialization of history," posits an alternative version of human genesis from those on offer within Abrahamic religious traditions. This origin story was more in concert with the scientific discourses that came to serve as at least a partial ground for the truth in the eyes of an ascendant generation at the turn of the twentieth

---

53. 'Abd al-Rahman al-Rafi'i, *Thawrat 1919: Tarikh Misr al-Qawmi min 1914 illa 1921* (Cairo: Dar al-Ma'arif, 1947), 70.

54. Ibid., 71.

55. Ibid.

56. 'Ali Barakat, "Al-Rif al-Misri fi Thawrat 1919," in *Tisa'un 'Aman 'ala Tawrat 1919* (Cairo: 'Amal Nadwat Markaz Tarikh Misr al-Mu'asr, March 19, 2009), 53.

57. Giorgio Agamben, *Homo Sacer: Sovereign Power and Bare Life*, Translated by Daniel Heller-Roazen (Palo Alto: Stanford University Press, 1998).

Figure 7.4 "Al-Shughul fi-l-Sulta" (Working for the Government). *Source:* Amin 'Izz al-Din, "Awwal Dirasa," *Al-Mussawir* (March 1969).

century.[58] What the recruitment of ELC laborers illustrated for nationalist historians, then, was the racialization of Egyptians. Instead of being appreciated as metaphysically significant humans, Egyptians from the countryside were being treated like animals in public space as their more urbane compatriots looked on.

58. Hannaford, *Race*. El Shakry, *Great Social Laboratory*.

Memoirs and diaries of prominent statesmen make it clear that they witnessed such scenes and were deeply influenced by them. A persistent theme focuses on how the men of the ELC were seized by force and compelled to join up, not of their own free will, but by violent compulsion. In his diary-style memoirs, Saad Zaghloul writes of frequent trips to the countryside. On one such occasion, on May 28, 1918, he notes that recruiting authorities "kidnap people from the markets, streets, mosques, and courthouses, and they call on them to sign something saying that they request to volunteer! And those who refuse to sign get beaten until they do sign!"[59] In her well-documented research on the First World War in Egypt, Latifa Salim recounts a speech in which Zaghloul invoked the image of a British soldier "driving Egyptians handcuffed in iron shackles."[60] Furthermore, Salim quotes a story from an unpublished section of Zaghloul's diaries from November 1918—the same month the *wafd* was founded—about a group of ELC recruits in Minya who tried to resist recruitment but were beaten back by a group of soldiers and policemen, and marched away toward a holding cell "handcuffed in iron shackles."[61] In his recollections of the ELC, then, Zaghloul seems to consistently refer to the violent means through which men were recruited.

One reason why Zaghloul may have dwelled on this subject is because it exposed the hypocrisy of what the British insisted on referring to as "volunteering." By likening the recruitment campaigns to "kidnapping" (*khataf*), Zaghloul hoped to illustrate that the men of the ELC did not enter of their own free will. This aspect of ELC recruitment was also analyzed by the statesman Ahmad Shafiq in his historical study and memoir, *Hawliyyat Misr Siyasiyya* (1926). Shafiq had resigned from his governmental post in protest when the First World War broke out, spending the duration of the conflict in Istanbul alongside the ex-Khedive, 'Abbas Hilmi II. When he returned, he set himself to the task of researching his book, and began consolidating his notes and diaries into a ten-part series of memoirs. Part one only begins speaking in granular detail when it gets to the First World War. In discussing the "gathering of Egyptian workers," Shafiq narrates a sad story of one recruit who wanted so badly to escape that he threw himself from a moving train, and another story in which, as the recruits were passing by "in shackles," a witness to the scene asked with a thick hint of irony: "these are supposed to be 'volunteers'?!" Like Zaghloul, then, the witness in Shafiq's story underlines the hypocrisy of British rhetoric surrounding the ELC. Shafiq blames his former governmental colleagues who stayed on and worked with the British after the declaration of the protectorate, lamenting that "all of the administration

---

59. Sa'd Zaghlul, *Mudhakkirat Sa'd Zaghlul, vol. 7* (Cairo: al-Hay'a al-Misriyya al-'Amma li-l-Kitab, 1988, 36).

60. Latifa Salim, *Misr fi-l-Harb al-'Alimiyya al-Ula* (Alexandria: al-Hay'a al-'Amma li-Maktabat al-Iskandariyya, 1984), 253.

61. Ibid., 252.

of the government was forced to fulfill the heavy requests [for ELC labor] on the backs of the villagers (*li-kahil al-bilad wa-l-'ibad*)."⁶²

While Shafiq is correct in pointing to the irony of British efforts to portray ELC recruiting as "voluntary," his emphasis on the wretched condition of people caught up in coercive labor regimes exists in tension with some of his earlier writing on the subject. After all, before his transformation into a historian and chronicler toward the end of his life, Shafiq was best known for publishing a polemical treatise defending the Islamic practice of slavery, titled *L'esclavage au point de vue Musulman* (1891). In it, he answered back charges from a Belgian newspaper that "for the Muslims, the hunt for slaves is a right and almost a duty; a right because they believe and teach that the Black is not of the human family, holding the middle ground between human and animal."⁶³ Instead, Shafiq insisted, "far from considering the slave an animal, the Qur'an recommends that Muslims treat them with graciousness and benevolence, which is what the Europeans, even those who live in the Orient . . . ignore up to the present."⁶⁴ In this earlier piece, then, Shafiq describes a uniquely Islamic form of slavery that adheres to what Ehud Toledano calls "the good treatment thesis," emphasizing the differences between Western and specifically American slavery and a supposedly gentler, more benign version of enslavement practiced in Muslim lands.⁶⁵ But Toledano's research, as well as the work of others, shows how "the significance of past enslavement in present-day politics in the United States . . . [is] no less relevant . . . [than] the debate on enslavement in the Mediterranean world."⁶⁶

After familiarizing myself with the historical literature on race and slavery in America and the Ottoman Empire, the good treatment thesis propagated by Shafiq reminds me of the "Lost Cause" narrative in the historiography of the US South. Proponents of the Lost Cause ignore the central role of slavery in the Confederacy, focusing instead on the so-called antebellum culture of honor as the dominant value system that held the political project of the South together. They argue that enslaved Blacks were well treated and happy with their lot.⁶⁷ In an unpublished article criticizing nostalgia for the so-called Cosmopolitan Alexandria of the late nineteenth and early twentieth centuries, Robert Vitalis has already made the point that much of the discourse typified by authors like Lawrence Durrell is similar to the Lost Cause, in that both are "mythologies as attempts to rewrite the past of what coincidentally were two cotton export economies in ways that deny the reality of

---

62. Ahmad Shafiq Basha, *Hawliyyat Misr al-Siyasiyya*, vol. 1 (Cairo: Matba'a Shafiq Basha bi-Shari'a Sami Raqm 28: 1926), 91.

63. Ahmed Chafik Bey, *L'esclavage Au Point De Vue Musulman* (Cairo: Imprimerie Nationale, 1891), 5.

64. Ibid.

65. Toledano, *As If Silent and Absent*, 17.

66. Ibid., 8.

67. Adam H. Domby, *The False Cause: Fraud, Fabrication, and White Supremacy in Confederate Memory* (Charlottesville: University of Virginia Press, 2020).

hierarchy that sustained them and that exonerated those once on top from any responsibility for the loss that they endured."[68] But while Vitalis is interested in how so-called indigenous Egyptians fit in Alexandria in the stories of European colonies and families with consular protection mourned by Durrell, I intend to make a comparison here between two historical narratives about slavery—the Lost Cause and the Shafiq-style "good treatment hypothesis"—in order to interrogate what representations of slavery can tell us about Egyptian nationalist attitudes towards Black Africans during the 1919 Revolution.[69]

What both the Lost Cause and the good treatment thesis tend to ignore is what the historical record tells us about actually existing slavery in the US South and Ottoman Egypt, respectively. While slave testimonies from Egypt are much harder to come by than those in the American South, Toledano's research into court records and consular archives in the nineteenth century shows that many slaves in Egypt and across the Ottoman Empire tried to escape and resist their masters with any means at their disposal.[70] Similarly, Troutt-Powell's analysis of Egyptian popular culture—and of the few extant narratives written by enslaved Black people in Egypt and Sudan—has uncovered a persistent link between Blackness, the condition of enslavement, and Trans-Saharan African origin in Egypt during the late nineteenth and early twentieth centuries.[71]

So when, for example, the nationalist activist 'Ali Sha'rawi protested to the acting High Commissioner Reginald Wingate in a famous meeting on November 13, 1918, "I will not accept slavery and my soul will not be satisfied living under its yoke!"[72] We should not think he was employing the metaphor of slavery simply to describe the relationship between the British and Egyptians as coercive, nor should we assume that he was drawing attention to commodification of the Egyptian national body in global financial markets.[73] For at least a generation, intellectuals in Egypt had lived with the "uncomfortable realization that, in the eyes of western European culture, Egypt stood somewhere closer to Africa than to Europe."[74] But it was the unprecedented British actions during the First World War—the

---

68. Robert Vitalis, "Alexandria without Illusions," unpublished paper, 2008. I thank Prof. Vitalis for sharing this excellent essay with me privately, and I hope it can find a home in a published work someday.

69. Many members of the Greek, Italian, British, Maltese, and other European colonies in the city—not to mention Syrians, Levantines, and Jewish bourgeoisie who had secured foreign status in Egypt's complex laws of extraterritoriality—were actually born and lived their whole in Egypt. See Vitalis, "Alexandria without Illusions," 9.

70. Toledano, *As If Silent and Absent*.

71. Troutt-Powell, *A Different Shade of Colonialism*.

72. Markaz al-Watha'iq wa-l-Buhuth al-Tarikhiyya li-Misr al-Mu'asr, *Khamsun 'Aman 'ala Thawrat 1919* (Cairo: Mu'assasat al-Ahram, 1969), 135.

73. See Aaron Jakes, *Egypt's Occupation: Colonial Economism and the Crises of Capitalism* (Palo Alto: Stanford University Press, 2020), 222.

74. Troutt-Powell, *A Different Shade of Colonialism*, 79.

mass recruitment of rural Egyptians for the so-called Coloured Labour Corps, the declaration of the protectorate, and the massive influx of European soldiers—which put the structural similarities between Egyptians and Black Africans vis-à-vis the British Empire in the starkest relief.

Rather than developing this commonality in the direction of pan-African solidarity, the slavery metaphor as used by Sha'rawi and other nationalist writers in his generation produced politically mobilizing force from its assertion of British mischaracterization of Egyptian race in drawing a false equivalence between Egyptians and Black Africans.[75] Sha'rawi himself grew up in a milieu where slavery was common, and though his wife—the famous Egyptian feminist activist Huda Sha'rawi—was born to a Caucasian concubine, the majority of slaves in Egypt during his lifetime were Black people (*sudani*).[76] During the war, the old *casta*-style distinctions between Egyptians and Black Africans, which were upheld during the British colonial period despite the imposition of white supremacy, had melted away, and this left some nationalist activists and intellectuals shocked and dismayed. It is true that anti-Blackness is just one of many possible structures of feeling invoked by using the slavery metaphor in Egypt around the time of the 1919 Revolution, but it is one that would have proved politically meaningful and that we would be wrong to ignore.

For political leaders like Zaghloul engaged in conversations with an international audience, the decisive role that Egyptians and other nonwhite peoples played in the war effort offered a powerful rhetorical weapon. In one letter, Zaghloul insists that such a policy had upended the global order of white supremacy by illustrating the extent to which the metropole relied on the colonies, rather than the other way around. In a letter to the British House of Commons, Zaghloul wrote:

> In appealing to her dominions, her colonies, and the non-European races over whom she was ruling, for aid in blood and treasure, the British made it perfectly clear that in their opinion the world was no longer big enough to contain two moralities, one for Europe and another for Asia and Africa.[77]

---

75. In remarks he made to the Egyptian newspaper *al-Mu'ayyid* on the Fourth of July in 1896—which were explicitly in celebration of the American Revolutionary project—a nationalist from an earlier generation, Mustafa Kamil, made it clear that he associated the condition of enslavement with Blackness, and taunted his Egyptian compatriots for being less willing to fight for their rights than the Mahdi's soldiers in Sudan: "If you listen to your conscience, you will learn that you are among the poorest of nations and that the Black Africans (*zunuj*) that you used to use as slaves have become more vigorous than you in preserving their national rights!" 'Ali Fahmi Kamil, *Mustafa Kamil Basha fi 34 Rabi'an*, Vol. 5 (Cairo: Matba'a al-Liwa', 1908), 77.

76. Cuno and Walz, *Race and Slavery in the Middle East*, 8.

77. Zagloul, *The White Book: Collection of Official Correspondence from November 11, 1918 to July 14, 1919* (Paris: The Delegation, 1919), 42.

The global circulation of migrant laborers and soldiers in the war perforated the conceptual and spatial barriers that had previously separated "Europe" from "Asia and Africa," creating a networked space that was incongruent with the racialized logics of the global color line. The creation of this new spatial imaginary entailed shared experiences of sacrifice during the war, which could become the basis for a global shift away from white supremacy and toward independence (*istiqlal*) for every racial/national community (*umma*) that had been victimized by it.

Conclusion

In rejecting a world with two moralities, "one for Europe and another for Asia and Africa," Zaghloul was speaking out against the rising tide of white supremacy that defined his generation. But it is curious, here, that he omits the Americas. After all, African Americans like Frederick Douglass and W. E. B. Du Bois had been speaking out against the color line for years before the 1919 Revolution. But while Douglass traveled to Egypt in the 1870s with an eye to comparison with his home country,[78] and Du Bois wrote on the Egyptian Revolution of 1919,[79] their contemporaries in Egypt did not develop a sense of reciprocal solidarity. In an attempt to reverse this impulse, this chapter has tried to determine what we can learn when we apply the lessons of African American history, which produced some of the most perceptive theorists of global race in the late nineteenth and early twentieth centuries, to the context of British colonial Egypt.

One important lesson is that the consolidation of white racial identity matters for a proper understanding of the late imperial age. Surveying the memoirs and unpublished correspondence of British soldiers, American missionaries, and "Anglo-Egyptian" government employees, it is clear that they thought of

---

78. Visiting Egypt in 1887, Douglass wrote, "I do not know of what color and features the ancient Egyptians were, but the great mass of the people I have yet seen would in America be classified as mulattoes and negroes. This would not be a scientific description, but an American description. I can easily see why the Mohomidan [*sic*] religion commends itself to these people, for it does not make color the criterion of fellowship as some of our so called Christian nations do." Douglass, *Frederick Douglass Diary Tour of Europe and Africa*, September 15, 1886. The manuscript/mixed material can be found on the Library of Congress website, https://www.loc.gov/item/mfd.01001/.

79. In the June 1919 edition of the NAACP's official journal, *The Crisis*, Du Bois wrote, "the sympathy of Black America must of necessity go out to color India and colored Egypt," see W. E. B. Du Bois, "Egypt and India," *The Crisis* (June 1919), 62. My research suggests that Egyptian nationalists of the 1919 generation would not have appreciated this way of referring to them. See Bayan Abubakr, "The Contradictions of Afro-Arab Solidarity(ies): The Aswan High Dam and the Erasure of the Global Black Experience," *Jadaliyya* (September 24, 2021), https://www.jadaliyya.com/Details/43334/The-Contradictions-of-Afro-Arab-Solidarityies-The-Aswan-High-Dam-and-the-Erasure-of-the-Global-Black-Experience.

themselves as *white people* first and foremost and conceptualized their political project in Egypt in terms of white (or Anglo-Saxon) racial supremacy. They created segregated spaces like the Shepheard's Hotel and the Khedivial Sporting Club, and they instituted racial hierarchies in the army and the government ministries. When they faced the exigencies of war, they only further entrenched these hierarchies. British officials terminated official Ottoman sovereignty, declared a protectorate, and forcibly recruited hundreds of thousands of young men from the Egyptian countryside to serve behind the lines as laborers supporting the war effort. The racist culture that permeated the troops traveled with them when they were on leave in Egyptian cities, leading riots and abuse heaped on the residents of Cairo, Alexandria, the Suez Canal zone, and Bani Suwayf.

Another important lesson that historians of modern Egypt can learn from the African American experience is to pay attention to the afterlives of actually existing slavery. Tens of thousands of African slaves made their way into Egypt via Sudan every year until the last decade of the nineteenth century. This inculcated a popular association between Blackness and slavery in Egypt by the time of the First World War. Egyptian intellectuals writing in Arabic could match British officials writing in English in their disdain for "African savages," as Abu Shadi put it in the petition that opened this chapter. When British influence was first taking root in Egypt, distinctions between Egyptians on the one hand, who were identified primarily as Muslims or "Mahommedans," and Black Africans on the other hand were typified in the rare exceptions made for Egyptian membership into exclusive social clubs, where they could be served by Black "sofragis." They were backed up with the intricate taxonomies of race in global scientific thought. But during the war, such theoretical distinctions between Egyptians and Black Africans were clearly erased in practice when hundreds of thousands of Egyptians from the countryside were "kidnapped" and sent away to work in chains. This forced "enslavement" of Egyptians entailed a racialization of the entire country alongside Black Africans. Representations of Egyptians as having been "enslaved" by the British drew their mobilizing force in part from a culture that had been steeped in specifically racialized understanding of slavery that was violated by the ELC and the declaration of a protectorate in Egypt.

Overall, the relationship between the 1919 Revolution and global white supremacy, which was co-terminus with the appearance of the global color line, was fraught. By taking to the streets in protest against the British presence, Egyptians rejected the white supremacy that had been implemented in their country over the course of decades. This project was partial and unfinished, and would continue throughout the twentieth century. But the racial caste system imposed by the British was grafted on top of a social order that entailed exclusion and oppression of Black people. Egypt's experience as a springboard for Ottoman colonization of the Sudan in the nineteenth century set the stage for it to become particularly dependent, both economically and culturally, on the Trans-Saharan slave trade. Even after the slave trade was abolished, and, in many senses, because abolition was so tied up with the arrival of British power, slavery continued surreptitiously, and a cultural link between the condition of enslavement and Blackness was maintained. The unilaterally imposed settlement that emerged out of the 1919 Revolution separated a now quasi-independent Egypt from its former colony in the Sudan, and nationalist activists spent a good deal of energy trying to reassert their exclusive right to colonize their former empire in the decades that followed.[80] And while Raphael Cormack's recent research into Cairene nightlife in the 1920s exposes a vibrant jazz scene that incorporated many African Americans who felt out of place in the country of their birth, these cultural forms coexisted alongside so-called jungle films that served to "entrench African otherness" in interwar Egypt.[81] It is clear that much research still has yet to be done in colonial and postcolonial Egypt taking white supremacy and anti-Blackness seriously as analytical starting points.

Note: This material appears partially in my book *The Egyptian Labor Corps: Race, Space, and Place in the First World War* (Austin: University of Texas Press, 2021). I thank the University of Texas Press for permission to publish certain selections here.

80. Troutt-Powell, *A Different Shade of Colonialism*.
81. Raphael Cormack, *Midnight in Cairo: Divas of Egypt's Roaring '20s* (New York: W. W. Norton & Co., 2021); Ifdal Elsaket, "Jungle Films in Egypt: Race, Anti-Blackness, and Empire," *The Arab Studies Journal* 5, no. 2 (Fall 2017): 8.

Chapter 8

POLITICS FROM AFAR

EGYPTIANS IN EXILE DURING TWO REVOLUTIONS (1919 AND 2011)

Taqadum Al-Khatib

Introduction

This chapter traces the strategies employed by oppositionists who left Egypt in the years surrounding the 1919 Revolution, and those who did so after the 2011 uprising and then the 2013 coup. Most scholars who have studied contemporary Egyptian opposition groups in exile have not taken into account their predecessors in Europe at the beginning of the twentieth century, especially in Germany and Switzerland. Egyptian intellectuals had sought in these two countries to better understand the concept of nationalism in order to advance the decolonization processes and strengthen the independence movement in their home country. Egyptian groups currently in exile in Europe chose it as a site for their political struggle against the post-July 2013 authoritarian regime because it offered sanctuary and the opportunity to analyze and act upon oppositional ideologies and political strategies. In these regards Europe has been a more conducive environment than either Turkey or Qatar.

Methodology

This chapter addresses exiled groups in two different periods, providing comparisons between them in order to shed light on Egyptian diasporas, national liberation movements, and the impact of host states' policies toward the activities of Egyptian exiles. The first group—Egyptian activists who were exiled in the period leading up to the 1919 Revolution—was rooted in the idea of striving for political sovereignty on behalf of a nation.[1] The contemporary political diaspora

---

1. Yossi Shain, *The Frontier of Loyalty: Political Exiles in the Age of the Nation-State* (Ann Arbor: University of Michigan Press, 2005), 6.

consists of those opposed to the military government that seized power in the wake of the 2011 uprising, whether out of Islamist, liberal, or other beliefs. Both diasporas included those with sharp political and ideological differences. This chapter compares the two in an effort to underscore the importance of media and political organization, whether among Egyptian groups during their exile in Europe (particularly in Germany and Switzerland) during the period of the 1919 Revolution, or by groups residing in Turkey and Western Europe since 2013. It will also show how the current diaspora opposition groups have utilized similar tactics to those employed by their predecessors during the period of the 1919 Revolution. It thus combines a bottom-up perspective on migrants and their transnational political practices at the microlevel with a policy perspective at the macro level. It looks at both individual activities and the institutional and policy contexts in an effort to explain why diaspora mobilizations take different forms in different contexts. In order to understand the dynamics of Egyptian political diasporas in the two eras, three methodological elements have been combined: informative-narrative interviews with contemporary transnational activists in different localities, analysis of documents obtained from the German archives, and comparative-historical analysis.[2]

Defining the Egyptian Diaspora

This assessment deploys a conception of diaspora that stresses an orientation toward, and engagement with, homeland politics.[3] The term "Egyptian diaspora" in this chapter, therefore, refers specifically to Egyptians living abroad, whether temporarily or permanently, who were mobilized and actively engaged in the decolonization process during the 1919 Revolution, or, in the contemporary period, who are engaged in transnational politics focused on Egypt. While the word "diaspora" does invoke notions of home, physical migration from one place to another, national consciousness, collective identity, shared solidarity, and orientation toward the homeland,[4] people within diasporas may have or take on many identities, including both those affiliated with homeland identities and new identities formed in diaspora.[5] Diasporas in the globalization era form and reform

---

2. Matthew Lange, *Comparative-Historical Methods* (London: SAGE Publications Ltd, 2012), 1.

3. T. Lyons and P. Mandaville, "Think Locally, Act Globally: Toward a Transnational Comparative Politics," *International Political Sociology*, no. 4 (2010): 124–41.

4. Joshua Kaldor-Robinson, "The Virtual and the Imaginary: The Role of Diasporic New Media in the Construction of a National Identity during the Break-up of Yugoslavia," *Oxford Development Studies* 30, no. 2 (2000): 187–77

5. Stuart Hall, "Cultural Identity and Diaspora," in *Colonial Discourse and Post-Colonial Theory: A Reader*, ed. Partik Williams and Laura Chrisman (London: Harvester Wheatsheaf, 1994), 227–37.

within the dynamic global context operating politically at the transnational level and engaging with key international actors.[6] The aims of diaspora politics are to (1) influence the political situation in the country of origin or the symbolic homeland, either by establishing links with political actors, organizations, and institutions in that country or by supporting actors and movements on the ground symbolically; (2) influence public opinion in the country of residence about political events in the country of origin; and/or (3) provide alternative sources of information on the political situation in the country of origin.[7]

Research Questions

This chapter addresses the following questions: Who constituted the diaspora groups which pursued transnational political activities and what activities, particularly in Western Europe (Germany and Switzerland) and Turkey, did they engage in? How did those governments respond to these activists resident in their countries? What networks were generated by these groups to pursue their political objectives? How were political connections organized across borders? How have these networks been used to influence politics in Egypt? What communication tools were used for political mobilization? Are contemporary groups inspired by the era of the 1919 Revolution, and have they adopted similar strategies to counter today's authoritarian regime? Did the German support for those groups have real significance, and if so, in what way? Is the Turkish/Qatari support for the contemporary Muslim Brotherhood equivalent to the German support for early twentieth-century groups, or is it fundamentally different? What does this Turkish influence mean for the future of the Brotherhood especially?

This chapter explores the media experience and the publication of newspapers by the opposition in exile during the period of the 1919 Revolution (e.g., those of Shaykh ʿAlī al-Ġayyātī and Manṣūr al-Kādī) and compares it to the experience of the current Egyptian opposition in exile (e.g., *Al-Sharq* television channel and the establishing of political organizations). The second example will focus on one of the political entities established by the opposition in exile during the 1919 Revolution, and the role of the Egyptian National Party (ENP) (al-Ḥizb al-Waṭanī), particularly its second branch, which was established in Berlin under Muḥammad Farīd's leadership, and will compare it to the experience of the current Egyptian opposition in exile (e.g., the Egyptian Human Rights Forum—the EHRF—as an example).

---

6. Robin Cohen and Carolin Fischer, eds., *Routledge Handbook of Diaspora Studies* (London: Taylor and Francis Group, 2019).

7. Lea Müller-Funk, *Egyptian Diaspora Activism During the Arab Uprisings. Insights from Paris and Vienna* (New York: Routledge, 2019), 5.

Factors Affecting the Efficacy of Diasporic Activity

In the vast literature on diasporas, two dominant approaches can be identified. The first sees diaspora communities as actors within transnational processes, while the second treats diasporas more like social movements on a transnational level. In his book *The Frontier of Loyalty: Political Exiles in the Age of the Nation-State*, Yossi Shain identifies three major elements playing a role within the relationship between exiled groups and their compatriots abroad, which vary dramatically from one case to another and are affected by variables such as the organization's own character, the host state's policies toward the exiles' activities, and the home regime's counteractivities to discourage dissent among the national community abroad.[8] These three interconnected factors impact the efficacy of diasporic influence. The sociopolitical nature of the host country determines the ability of a diaspora to organize influence and to exert indirect influence on its homeland and also has an effect on the character of the diaspora itself. There might be cases in which such regimes seek to exploit a diaspora to advance their own foreign policy interests (e.g., the German and Turkish governments and the Egyptian exile community during the 1919 Revolution and in the post-2013 period, respectively). To exert effective influence on homeland politics a diaspora must be united in its position on the issue. Different groups within the community might have diverging views, and if the diasporic community is divided, its influence is weakened or might be diffused in different directions.[9]

Host Countries, Motivations, Methods, and Consequences

Western European countries (especially Germany and Switzerland) and Turkey are the key host countries for the Egyptian diaspora, the former in both the early twentieth century and at present, and the latter primarily in the current period. German support for Egyptian nationalists in the period around 1919 was motivated by its broader policy during the rule of Kaiser Wilhelm II to support radical movements and nationalists against colonialism around the world. In addition, during the First World War, Germany and the Ottoman Empire had cultivated pan-Islamic propaganda in an attempt to mobilize Muslims against their (colonizing) enemies, and Germany presented itself as more appealing in terms of both the anti-fascist and anti-imperialist contexts. Also, Germany sought greater influence with the young Egyptian students in Berlin and Switzerland. German funding of student groups and of individual exiles played a decisive role in this situation.[10] German funding differed in accordance with the funded person's

---

8. Shain, *The Frontier of Loyalty*, 52.
9. Ibid.
10. Mahmoud Kassim, *Die diplomatische Beziehungen Deutschlands zu Ägypten 1919–1936* (Münster-Hamburg: LIT- Verlag, 2000), 41.

political weight; for example, documents reveal that Germany gave the Egyptian Khedive Abbas II around five million Goldmarks over two years.[11]

The exiled groups during the 1919 Revolution consisted of the leaders of the national movement, like Muḥammad Farīd and Shaykh ʿAbd al-ʿaziz Ǧāwīš, and a large number of students who had moved from Istanbul to Berlin. The student movement in Berlin, along with the leaders of the ENP, had played a crucial role in the mobilization of Egyptians to make their national demands known to a wider European public, in hopes of securing sympathy for the cause. But despite its members' political and cultural divisions and economic disparities, they were able to create common ground around their shared goal of fuelling the decolonization process and strengthening the independence movement in their home country. The sociopolitical nature of Germany at that time as a host country affected the character of the Egyptian exiled groups there. There were at least two competing streams in the ENP: Shaykh ʿAbd al-ʿaziz Ǧāwīš, who represented the Islamic wing, which insisted on close ties with Turkey (the Ottoman Empire), and Farīd, who represented a more secular, pragmatic orientation, which aimed at complete autonomy for Egypt. Farīd was thinking of a pan-Islamic union modeled on the same lines as the Pan-Germanic Union, to be founded after the war and led by the Ottomans, but with each Muslim country enjoying autonomy and sharing equal rights with the Turks. He believed that an alliance between the Germanic and Islamic unions would be a stronghold against imperialist European power.[12] The change in the attitude of Farīd and others was due to the influence of the more open and liberal society in Germany, which they embraced.

Turkey/Qatar's present-day support for the Egyptian diaspora (especially the Muslim Brotherhood) after the 2013 coup d'état bears significant similarities to the German support for the Egyptian opposition during the early twentieth century, as the following section will outline. Turkey and Qatar granted refuge to a number of important Brotherhood leaders who had fled Egypt. Turkey has found common cause with Qatar most of all, as the two countries share a similar preference for Sunni Islamist movements, like the Muslim Brotherhood. Turkey's ruling Justice and Development Party (AKP) is a political party with clear Islamic roots, one which has focused its foreign policy around Turkey as an Islamist regional player. There is also continuity from the era of the Ottoman Empire to today's AKP, which has repackaged similar appeals to mobilize Muslim political activists against autocratic regimes. As for Qatar, its flagship media company, Al Jazeera, has housed Egyptian Muslim Brotherhood leaders in a five-star Doha hotel and granted them regular airtime to promote their cause in the wake of the coup of 2013. Al Jazeera also aired the Brotherhood's ongoing anti-coup protests in Egypt

---

11. PAAA, [The Archive of the Germany Foreign Ministry] R15047 (November 7, 1915).

12. Muḥammad Farīd, *Muḏakirātī baʿd al-Hiǧra* (Memoirs), note No. 4, 132. Also Raouf Abbas Hamed, *Germany and the Egyptian Nationalist Movement 1882–1918*, New Series, Bd. 28, Nr. 1/4 (1988): 24.

and in almost all cases allegedly paid the Brothers for the footage.[13] The roots of Qatari support for the Brotherhood precede the Arab Spring and are based in the overlap of its state interests with those of the Brotherhood—"large, well developed, deeply rooted in society, and multinational."[14]

As mentioned earlier, the sociopolitical nature of the host country plays a role in the ability of a diaspora to organize and influence its homeland. This is borne out by the current situation of the Egyptian opposition in Turkey, especially after the recent moves by Ankara and Cairo toward a diplomatic rapprochement. As a consequence of this thaw in relations, two Muslim Brotherhood-affiliated television presenters—known for their anti-Egyptian-regime rhetoric—were put on "open leave" after their politically charged shows were axed from Islamist-oriented television stations *Al-Sharq* (The East) and *Mekameleen* (We Continue).[15]

But there is also an important question about what this Turkish influence means for the future of the Brotherhood. One outcome could be the promotion of a "Turkish model" of Islamic governance in Egypt. In Turkey, this model has meant a blend of Islam and democracy, which voters have embraced and the military has accepted. Another possible outcome could be the end of the Muslim Brotherhood as a conservative, youth-based movement, as it loses its youth to the more open and liberal society they are embracing in Turkey.[16]

In general, disputes between opposition forces during the 1919 Revolution revolved around their loyalty to the Ottoman Empire or to the complete independence of Egypt. They saw their most important task to be creating international sympathy for their "Egyptian Question." To this end, they organized various congresses in Western European countries as early as 1910, took part in other political events, passed countless resolutions, and published numerous articles, brochures, and so on. In addition, they founded newspapers, most of which only lasted for short periods of time. They also conducted intensive contacts with well-known political figures in several Western countries who actively opposed Great Britain.[17]

---

13. Eric Trager, "The Muslim Brotherhood Is the Root of the Qatar Crisis. The Saudi-led Bloc Has Made 13 demands of Doha, but They're Mostly about Resolving One Issue—and Time is Almost up," https://www.theatlantic.com/international/archive/2017/07/muslim-brotherhood-qatar/532380/ (July 2017) (accessed March 12, 2021).

14. David B. Roberts, "Reflecting on Qatar's 'Islamist' Soft Power," Berkley Center, April 2019. https://www.brookings.edu/wp-content/uploads/2019/04/FP_20190408_qatar_roberts.pdf. (accessed March 12, 2021).

15. Arab News, "Muslim Brotherhood-affiliated political show hosts axed in Egypt," April 11, 2021. https://www.arabnews.com/node/1841076/media (accessed April 15, 2021).

16. Omer Taspinar, "Turkey: The New Model?" Brookings Institution, July 28, 2016, https://www.brookings.edu/research/turkey-the-new-model/ (accessed April 9, 2021). To reach this conclusion, I conducted interviews over the phone with mid-level Brotherhood leaders and members in Egypt, Turkey, and Qatar.

17. Ibid.

Germany and the Nationalist Movement

As far as Egypt was concerned, Germany initially showed no sympathy for the Egyptian nationalist movement either before or after the British occupation. Nevertheless, Muṣṭafa Kamil (1874–1908), the leader of the nationalist movement and founder of the Egyptian Nationalist Party, hoped to change the German neutral attitude in favor of the Egyptian Question.[18] His continuous attempts to persuade Germany to intervene in favor of Egypt played an important role in changing Berlin's attitude on the issue. Kāmil, who was from a wealthy family, used his trips to Europe to present his political intentions, which he wanted to realize with the help of France. He also visited Berlin several times, the first time in 1896. Writing in the newspaper *Die Post* on October 17 of that year, he explained the purpose of his visit:

> A patriotic duty brings me here. The sad situation of my unhappy fatherland showed me what kind of duties I, as a man, have to fulfil towards the country of my fathers. I have many friends who, like me, are ready to fight the British, who, in contravention of all sworn treaties and the most solemn promises, persist in their brutal and illegal occupation of our fatherland.[19]

Kāmil proposed to Khedive Abbas II that the ruler extend an invitation to the Kaiser's family to visit Egypt in the winter of 1896, but the Khedive declined to act on the suggestion, preferring not to incite the hostility of the British.[20]

On April 9, 1897, Kāmil wrote once again in *Die Post*, this time to complain that he had heard from German politicians that "Germany was not interested in the Egyptian question; it was a matter for the French." Kāmil called this attitude a mistake. By contrast, he said, the Egyptian Question was an international one. When Great Britain and France finally agreed on their colonial interests in the Entente Cordiale in 1904, the Egyptians turned away, bitterly disappointed, and focused all the more on Germany. Apparently, Kāmil took seriously Kaiser Wilhelm's speech in Damascus on November 8, 1898, in which he had assured the Muslims that "the German Emperor will be their friend at all times."[21] The Egyptian saw help for Egypt in a German-Ottoman alliance, but during his next visit to Germany in 1905, Kāmil wrote in the October 23 edition of the *Berliner Tageblatt* to ask soberly: Can Germany lay claim to the friendship of Islam if it gives Egypt a price and England allows it to usurp supreme power over all of the Muslims? "If Islam," he implores the foreign policy-makers of the German empire, "has one wish today, it is to see Germany take an attitude on the Egyptian Question

---

18. Hamed, *Germany and the Egyptian Nationalist Movement 1882–1918*, 11.

19. Frank Gesemann, Gerhard Höppm, and Haroun Sweis, *Araber in Berlin. Miteinander Leben in Berlin* (Berlin: Im Auftrag der Ausländerbeauftragten des Senats, 1998), 12.

20. Hamed, *Germany and the Egyptian Nationalist Movement 1882–1918*, 12.

21. Ibid.

that is at the same time favourable to the interests of Islam and to your Germany." Muṣṭafa Kāmil did not see it again. The ENP, which he founded shortly before his death in 1907, long remained committed to the illusion that Egypt's best chances of liberation from British rule would come with the help of Germany and the Ottoman Empire.

Kāmil's friend Dr. Maḥmūd Labīb Muḥarram, who had settled in Berlin in 1910 and had married a German woman, acted in the same vein. In conversations with politicians and in newspaper articles, he campaigned for the German-Ottoman alliance, but above all for Germany's support for the Egyptians and Libyans, against whom Italy waged a colonial war in 1910. In the same year, when Muḥammad Farīd visited Berlin, he was warmly received by German intellectual circles. He was invited to a meeting organized by the Colonial Club to lecture on the Egyptian Question. The meeting opened with a speech by Dr. Weigelt, who expressed the Germans' sympathy with the Egyptian nationalist cause, then followed by Farīd and Muḥarram, who delivered his speech in German in an address directly to the German people. The meeting was reported by the German press, and Farīd was satisfied with the results.[22] In this activity, Muḥarram tried to involve other Egyptians living in Berlin, particularly students who had returned to Germany since 1909; in 1912 there were already twenty.[23] For this purpose he founded the "Egyptian League" in 1911, the first organization for Arabs living in Germany.[24] Muḥarram died in Berlin on September 4, 1913.[25]

The ENP, still looking to Europe for assistance, continued to place a greater emphasis on propaganda and persuasion than on direct action. It hoped to organize a larger following in Egypt in order to make its claims seem more creditable to both European politicians and public opinion. Spurred on by the increased sympathy of the left wing in England and the founding of the Egyptian Committee in Parliament, the ENP elected to issue English and French editions of its nationalist newspaper.[26]

At the beginning of the First World War, Muḥammad Farīd moved to Istanbul, and there he was informed by the German secretary of the Orient that Germany was ready to supply the Egyptian nationalists with armaments and military experts

---

22. Ibid, and Muḥammad Farīd, *Muḏakirātī baʿd al-Hiǧra* (Memoirs), note No. 2, 50.

23. Gerhard Höpp, "Zwischen Universitäten und Straße. Ägyptische Studenten in Deutschland 1849–1945," in Die Beziehungen zwischen der Bundesrepublik Deutschland und der Republik Ägypten, ed. Konrad Schliephake and Ghazi Shanneik (Würzburg, 1990), 31.

24. Ibid.

25. *Muḥammad Farīd* has eulogized him in his memoirs. More about *Maḥmūd Labīb Muḥarram* and *Farīd*'s eulogies in ʿAbd-ar-Raḥmān ar- Rāfiʿī: *Muḥammad Farīd* (1984), 341.

26. Robert L. Tignor, *Modernization and British Colonial Rule in Egypt 1882–1914* (Princeton: Princeton University Press, 1966), 249–91.

if they could revolt against the British. This generous offer was never realized.[27] On the other side, the Germans were thinking of a surprise offensive against the Suez Canal to disrupt British communications throughout the entire Near East and thereby undermine the Allied war effort in Europe. As a result, the Egyptian nationalists formed a revolutionary committee in Istanbul on September 13, 1914 (including Farīd and Shaykh 'Abd al-'aziz Ğāwīš, as well as Khedive Abbas II) and sent some of their members to Cairo accompanied by German soldiers to make all the necessary preparations to liberate the country and bring Khedive Abbas II back to power.[28] The Germans suggested that the German spies in Cairo were spreading false news that the German and Turkish forces had defeated the British forces, with the aim of provoking the Egyptian army present in Cairo and Sudan. When this rebellion was to have occurred, the Suez Canal and the waterway in Port Said would have been closed in parallel, as would the water stations that control the flow of water to the canal, the telephone exchanges, railroad lines, bridges, telegraph lines, military barracks, and the ports of Alexandria, Port Said, and Suez.[29] Khedive Abbas II proposed destroying the five water switches that control the water flowing into the Suez Canal.[30] Farīd had suspicions about the Germans' intentions, concerned that they would not think about Egypt's liberation and the organization of an armed Egyptian resistance against the British if the military campaign could fulfill their strategic objectives. At the same time, he had similar suspicions about the intentions of the Ottoman Committee of Union and Progress (CUP) toward Egypt. The leading figures of the CUP government wanted in fact to withdraw the privileges bestowed on Egypt by the firmans of 1841 and 1873 and turn her into a mere province controlled by the Turkish government in Istanbul. Such intentions widened the gap between the CUP and the leader of the ENP.[31]

The question of the independence of Egypt and the perception that Farīd and the Egyptian nationalists had adopted of the relations between Egypt and the Ottoman Empire put Farīd in danger. One of the documents in the German archives mentions that *Farīd* traveled to Switzerland in December 1915 to attend a meeting organized by Egyptian youths in Geneva. Upon his return to Turkey, he was arrested by the Turkish authorities and interrogated as punishment for his clear positions on Turkey at that meeting.[32] After his release from prison, Farīd expressed his position on the Turks in front of one of his comrades who tried to speak Turkish; Farīd replied to him angrily: "Do not speak to me in that damned language. I am tired of the Young Turks."[33]

27. PAAA 15044, 310, and *Muḥammad Farīd*, (Memoires), 88.
28. PAAA 15046, P. 43.
29. PAAA 1504, October 1914, 62.
30. Maybe that was the reason the British announced the deposition of Khedive Abbas II for collaborating with their enemies (Ibid).
31. Hamed, *Germany and the Egyptian Nationalist Movement 1882–1918*, 18–19.
32. PAAA 15050. P116. 26.02.1917.
33. Ibid.

This tension between the CUP and the leader of the ENP was the reason why Farīd transferred his headquarters to Berlin. From there, Farīd resumed his activities, conducting intensive contacts with well-known political figures in several Western countries who actively opposed Great Britain. Farīd was planning to convince the German foreign minister Arthur Zimmermann of the necessity of a second campaign against the Suez Canal after the failure of the first one, but Zimmermann told him that the military situation would not allow even consideration of such a campaign, and that waging submarine war against Britain and France would bring them to their knees. Germany was thus able to dictate whatever settlements she liked, including that of Egypt.[34]

Feeling that Germany had become less interested in the Egyptian Question, Farīd and the Egyptian nationalists appealed to German political parties and influential politicians for support. A German-Egyptian Society was to be founded in Berlin, and a new Egyptian party was to be established in Switzerland.[35] Under the name "The Society for the Liberation of Egypt e.V. Berlin," a new organization was created: "The Society for the Liberation of Egypt aims to liberate the Nile Valley from the English yoke in order to restore the status quo ante as it was before the conquest of English Egypt in 1882."[36] The nationalists' leaders approached several German politicians, asking them to become members of this new organization. They received affirmative answers from eminent statesmen such as Admiral Alfred von Tirpitz, the liberal leader Gustav Stresemann, the conservative leader Westarop, and the Kaiser's brother-in-law, von Schleswig Holstein, who agreed to be president of the society.[37]

Farīd, who was thinking of a pan-Islamic union modeled on the same lines as the Pan-Germanic Union led by the Ottomans, but with each Muslim country enjoying autonomy and sharing equal rights with the Turks, refrained from committing himself to the German Islamic propaganda when he was approached by the German Foreign Office to take part in editing *Al-Jihad*, a German organ issued in 1915 that was published in various languages relevant to the Islamic world, including Arabic.[38] Meanwhile, Shaykh ʿAbd al-ʿaziz Ğāwīš, who represented the Islamic wing which insisted on close ties with Turkey (the Ottoman Empire), committed himself to the Ottoman Empire by publishing the newspaper *Die Islamische Welt* for the CUP in Berlin.[39]

After the rise of the Wafd Party in Egypt and the death of Farīd in 1919, the ENP remained active as individuals in Europe and as a party in Egypt until all

---

34. Hamed, *Germany and the Egyptian Nationalist Movement 1882–1918*, 21.
35. Kassim, *Die diplomatische Beziehungen Deutschlands zu Ägypten 1919–1936*, 39.
36. Ibid.
37. Ibid, 23.
38. PA-AA, R 20938.
39. Arthur Goldschmidt, "The Egyptian Nationalist Party 1882–1919," in *Political and Social Change in Modern Egypt: Historical Studies from the Ottoman Conquest to the United Arab Republic*, ed. P. M. Holt (London: Oxford University Press, 1968), 329.

political parties were abolished after the 1952 military coup, and as a result they ceased to constitute an important bloc in Egyptian politics.

German Involvement in the Events of the 1919 Revolution

The documents in the German archives reveal many details about German support for the Egyptian opposition in the early twentieth century and also explain Germany's perspective and attitude toward the 1919 Revolution, which unfolded when Egyptian nationalists, led by Saad Zaghloul, sought a hearing at the peace conference in Versailles in 1919–20 but were denied participation. The nationalist bloc had hoped to make the case that Egypt deserved its political independence under the principle of national self-determination enunciated by US president Woodrow Wilson as one of his well-known fourteen points.[40] The Germans were given harsh peacemaking conditions by the Allies and had to pay staggering reparations to France and Britain for the alleged damages done to these countries during the First World War. Given this context, German diplomats and the other pro-German residents in Egypt and elsewhere doubtless had a much different perspective on the Egyptian nationalist program than the British and the French.

Great Britain and France were very concerned about the possible consequences of this propaganda and invested considerable effort and funds in intercepting it and countering its arguments.[41] They sought to foster their "own Muslims," who were well versed in Islamic and pan-Islamic argumentation and who could refute the other side with authority. One example is Shaykh ʿAlī al-Ġayyātī, who argued that the Ottoman Caliphate had no legitimacy and that Sharif Ḥusayn, a direct descendant of the Prophet Muhammad and a member of the Prophet's Quraysh tribe, was the appropriate person to assume such a position and functions.[42] This history of European involvement in such issues raises a question about the 1919 Revolution, and whether it was a pure Egyptian revolution, or whether German agents played a role, both directly and indirectly, in supporting the leaders of this revolution.

Herbert Diel, a German Middle East expert who was also an official at the German Imperial Foreign Office,[43] drew up a lengthy memorandum in March

---

40. Arthur Goldschmidt, *Historical Dictionary of Egypt* (Lanham: The Scarecrow Press, 2013), 171.

41. Jacob M. Landau, *Pan-Islam. History and Politics* (London: Routledge 1990), 121.

42. Ibid.

43. Herbert Diel (March 27, 1886–September 12, 1955) had been working at the Foreign Office since 1909. First, he worked as a dragoman at the embassy in Morocco. Following a stopover in Constantinople and at the Foreign Office in Berlin, from 1918 to 1919 he worked at the embassy in Bern. He retired in 1944.

1919 on the events that had taken place in Egypt.⁴⁴ He tried to provide evidence to observers of the Egyptian scene that this was a "pure Egyptian revolution."⁴⁵

However, there were other voices who disagreed with Diel. The French-language newspaper *Matin* was quoted presenting the proposition that the initial sparks of the organized uprisings were orchestrated from Berlin. According to the newspaper report, the decisions were made in the Hotel Adlon in Berlin by nationalist politicians including Irishman Chatterton Hill, Chempakaraman Pillai of India, and Egyptian ʿAlī ʿIilwī.⁴⁶ The possibility that this supposition by *Matin* was accurate cannot be completely discounted, but with a probability bordering on certainty, it can be assumed the newspaper was referring to a protest meeting that took place in Berlin at the beginning of April 1919 at the Hotel Adlon,⁴⁷ organized by the ENP.⁴⁸

Tools and Methods

As mentioned earlier, in the years prior to the 1919 Revolution, Egyptian opposition activists in exile founded newspapers and political entities in order to garner sympathy in Europe for their opposition to British colonial rule, especially in Germany. In Geneva, Dr. Manṣūr Rifʿat established the Egyptian Patriot Club, Muḥammad Fahmī established the Young Egyptian Committee, and ʾAḥmad al-Dardīrī established the Egyptian Student Association (Sphinx), while

---

44. See PAAA 1503, 123–30.

45. See PAAA 1503, 123–30. The Egyptian writer and journalist *Muṣṭafa ʾAmīn* wrote that the British were surprised by the apparently well-organized uprisings. Because of their good organization, the British drew the wrong conclusion that Germany was involved in the uprisings in the background. In retrospect, he emphasizes once again that the revolution of 1919 was a purely Egyptian one. See also Kassim, *Die diplomatische Beziehungen Deutschlands zu Ägypten 1919–1936*, 35–45.

46. PAAA 15053, 134, and Kassim, *Die diplomatische Beziehungen Deutschlands zu Ägypten 1919–1936*, 35–45.

47. Hotel Adlon owes its name to its original owner, Lorenz Adlon, a native of Mainz and a Berlin restaurant manager of good repute. Adlon invested twenty million Goldmarks and two years in the creation of the hotel, which opened on October 23, 1907. Hotel Adlon's first (and most loyal) guest was Emperor Wilhelm II, the last Kaiser of Germany. His desire and request to be the first guest to enter the hotel was honoured on its opening day. He treated Hotel Adlon as if it were one of his palaces. He even paid the hotel an annual retainer (equivalent to €75,000 in the present day) to ensure there were always rooms available for his personal guests upon demand. For more information about the hotel, see: https://www.historichotels.org/hotels-resorts/hotel-adlon-kempinski/history.php (accessed September 10, 2020).

48. PAAA 15053,134.

'Alī al-Ġayyātī[49] and Manṣūr al-Kādī both established independent newspapers. In Berlin, Muḥammad Farīd played a crucial role in establishing and strengthening nationalist sentiment among the Egyptian opposition groups in exile.

Both al-Ġayyātī and al-Kādī,[50] however, felt more committed to their own convictions than to any of the other groups of Egyptian nationalists that had previously been effective in Switzerland and contributed to the propagation of their nationalist ideas; both were also of greater importance because of their ability to publish their own newspapers. In the years after the First World War, both men clearly expressed in the *Gazette de Lausanne* their support for the Egyptian cause, writing a series of in-depth articles on the topic, often published on the front page.[51] The principle of self-determination proclaimed by President Woodrow Wilson during the Paris Peace Conference in 1919–20 brought unprecedented opportunities for the colonized and marginalized, including Arabs, Jews, Armenians, Kurds, and many other populations, allowing them to take their struggle against imperialism to the international arena.[52] The conference issued a statement recognizing the British protectorate over Egypt in Article 147. Recognizing Egypt as a protectorate was a great victory for the Egyptian delegation, which was led by Saad Zaghloul. But a few days before the peace conference, violence erupted in Egypt, and as a result the prime minister resigned, and Egypt was left without a government. London decided to send a commission, headed by Lord Milner, to examine the causes of the unrest and to report on the establishment of constitutional government which, under the protectorate, will be the best calculated to promote its peace and prosperity, the progressive development of self-governing institutions and the protection of foreign interests, complying with the requests for independence was not considered.[53] Through his continued writings, and more importantly his magazine *La Tribune d'Orient*, published in Geneva, al-Ġayyātī sought to attract the attention of both European public opinion and that of the members of the

---

49. *Shaykh 'Alī al-Ġayyātī* was an Egyptian graduate of al-Azhar who lived in Switzerland during the First World War and wrote for the French and pro-Entente Arabic press. There, he studied social sciences and also worked as a correspondent for the Egyptian newspaper Al-Mu'yyad. In order to avoid prosecution for the publication of his nationalist-patriotic poetry collection, he fled Egypt on July 5, 1910. *Muḥammad Farīd* wrote the introduction to *al-Ġayyātī's dīwān* (collection of poems), which resulted in his prosecution, despite denying that he had ever read the poems.

50. Marc Trefzger, *Die nationale Bewegung Ägyptens vor 1928 im Spiegel der schweizerischen Öffentlichkeit* (Basel und Stuttgart: Verlag von Helbing & Lichtenhahn, 1970), 113.

51. Landau, *Pan-Islam*, 120–1.

52. Erez Manela, *The Wilsonian Moment, Self Determination and the International Origins of Anticolonial Nationalism* (Oxford: Oxford University Press, 2009), 4.

53. Quoted by Goldschmidt Jr, *Historical Dictionary of Egypt*, 70.

League of Nations residing in Geneva, in an attempt to promote the cause of Egypt and other Arab nations.[54]

When the Egyptian delegation—which in London had been able to reach an agreement with Lord Milner on the basis of a prior agreement between Great Britain and Egypt once recognized as "independent"—submitted the so-called Milner-Zaghlūl Project to the relevant circles in Egypt for assessment, al-Ġayyātī wrote in the *Gazette de Lausanne* calling for an acceptance on the basis of understanding. Only one month later, however, he had to express his deep disappointment at the break-off in Anglo-Egyptian negotiations in another article, and when Lord Milner's resignation made the victory of the imperialist forces in Britain over the Milner Commission all the more clear, al-Ġayyātī urged his compatriots to multiply their efforts again by means of presenting the new situation and assured the British that nothing would stop the Egyptians in their struggle for freedom and independence.[55]

Wilson's inspirational vision of free self-determination and the complete equality of nations continued to be used by Egyptian politicians and activists to underpin their arguments in the struggle for a free and independent Egypt. This was not only shown by the materials published by Egyptians in Switzerland since 1917, but also the fact that, despite all disappointments because of the policies of the victorious states in the First World War, and because of the successful turning away from Wilson's principles, al-Ġayyātī still provided the headline for *La Tribune d'Orient*, published from 1922, from Woodrow Wilson's statement announcing the basic lines of his fourteen-point declaration on January 8, 1918.[56]

After 1919, al-Ġayyātī came to the decision that the leadership of the Egyptian independence movement had to be left entirely to the nationalists who had stayed in their homeland during the war. Al-Ġayyātī sought to attract the attention of both European public opinion and that of the members of the League of Nations residing in Geneva, in an attempt to promote the cause of Egypt and other Arab nations.

At the end of February and the beginning of March of 1917, several Swiss newspapers reported on *Le Nil* (published by Mansūr al-Kādī[57]), saying that this new bimonthly magazine would "represent the interests of the nationalist Egyptians," and was intended "to bring together the various Egyptian groups in

---

54. Trefzger, *Die nationale Bewegung Ägyptens vor 1928 im Spiegel der schweizerischen Öffentlichkeit*, 113.

55. Ibid, 115.

56. Ibid, 40.

57. *Mansūr al-Kādī*, born in Alexandria in 1890, lived in Lausanne, Switzerland, from May 1917 to the end of 1925. In 1927, *al-Kādī* began publishing his newspaper *Le Nil* but was soon hindered by his lack of financial resources. His studies in high commerce at Lausanne University were also stymied by lack of funds. *Le Nil* covered Ancient Egypt and was mainly distributed in academic circles.

Switzerland and to orient the audience about Egypt."[58] The ʿUrābī revolution in 1881 had proclaimed the slogan "Egypt for the Egyptians," which was the same motto used during the 1919 Revolution.[59] *Le Nil* had consistently reaffirmed the demand "Egypt for the Egyptians," as a predominant unified goal for the Egyptian people. In addition to the hope of triggering an awakening among the Egyptian people, the magazine also reflected the hopes of Egyptian nationalists to pursue and realize the principle of self-determination first proclaimed by Woodrow Wilson.[60]

In 1908, the permanent committee of the Young Egyptian Committee was constituted and officially declared, and from that time, Muḥammad Fahmī pursued the firm intention of making Geneva the headquarters of the nationalist association, which he had personally cofounded. As chairman of the committee, he was able to assume a leading position among the Egyptians residing in Geneva, and elsewhere in Switzerland and Europe. Like many other Egyptian nationalists, however, after the First World War, when unrest broke out in Egypt, he had to renounce his claim to leadership within the Egyptian nationalist movement in Europe and continue the national struggle to gain autonomy and complete independence for Egypt under the banner of the Wafd Party, headed by Saad Zaghloul.[61]

When Fahmī appeared in public in 1908 as the president of the Young Egyptian Committee, his nationalist activities initially extended to advertising, mobilizing, and conducting meetings and congresses of Egyptian youth. Through these events, he aimed both to unify the Egyptian nationalists and students living in Europe around a common approach and to promote the national demands of the Egyptians among the European and Swiss public.[62]

---

58. PAAA 1550, 106.

59. As long as ʾIsmāʿīl reigned, the desire to get rid of the Khedive constituted a clear convergence of interests—even if the first signs of divergence within the lodges appeared between supporters of *Halīm* and *Tawfīq*, as *al-Afghānī* testifies too, according to the documents discovered. But after *Tawfīq's* investiture, the split between different partisanships must have been stark, with a clear division between pro-Khedive (and therefore pro-British) and pro-ʾUrābī or anti-imperialists; the inept *Tawfīq* became, in fact, the screen through which British rule of Egypt was exercised, exasperating the masses by continuing to oppress them.

60. In his book *The Wilsonian Moment: Self Determination and the International Origins of Anticolonial Nationalism*, Erez Manela writes that Egyptian nationalist icon Saʿd Zaġlūl, as well as a long list of leading politicians, parties, professional organization, women's groups, student groups, Egyptian organizations abroad, and even private Egyptian citizens, moved to write to the president of the United States when he arrived in Paris for the peace conference. For more on this, see *The Wilsonian Moment, Self Determination and the International Origins of Anticolonial Nationalism*.

61. Ibid.

62. Ibid.

At the end of November 1908, the leading Swiss newspapers began for the first time to cover a congress by the Young Egyptian Committee set to take place in Geneva the following year. In addition, in May 1909, Fahmī, as president of the committee, issued a special appeal in the press, inviting not only Egyptians but also Europeans interested in the topics of Egypt and the cause of the Egyptian people. The Second Congress of Youth in Geneva was held on September 13 to 15, 1909, and brought together Egyptian nationalists, who later became widely known in Europe, alongside members of the British Labour Party and Irish nationalists. The Congress was able to draw the attention of the Swiss press to a large extent, not least because of the participation of the British Labour leader Keir Hardie.[63] Reports about the Congress were published in several newspapers in the French part of Switzerland.[64]

Fahmī, for his part, built on the efforts of Farīd and the ENP at the international socialist congresses held in Bern and Lucerne in 1919 and therefore held another congress in the summer of 1920 while in London after the return of the Milner Mission from Egypt,[65] while negotiations were already underway about the regressive shape of Egypt's autonomy. It was still appropriate to appear before a new international socialist gathering to promote the Egyptian Question.[66] The assembly received his remarks favorably and decided to support the Egyptian demands for independence. This was then announced in the press, and in the "Resolution on the Rights of the Peoples" adopted by the 1920 congress, the independence of Egypt was demanded first. Thus, Fahmī could feel the satisfaction of a certain success during his last major public appearance, because he could at least trust that the numerous influential British socialists who appeared at that meeting of the Second International would pursue emancipation efforts after they returned home and would continue to vote in favor of Egypt, according to the resolution passed in Geneva.[67]

---

63. James Keir Hardie, the founder of the British Labour Party, was born on August 15, 1856, in Newhouse, Scotland. He became an important Scottish politician, a pioneer of socialism in the UK and an influential trade unionist. He was a crucial political figure who became the first Labour Member of Parliament and established the movement that has been a mainstay in British politics ever since. Hardie contributed strongly to Egyptian and Indian struggles for freedom. See https://www.historic-uk.com/HistoryUK/HistoryofBritain/Keir-Hardie/ (accessed September 7, 2020)—Prabha Ravi Shankar, "Socialist Labour leader James Keir Hardie (1856–1915) contribution to India's struggle for Freedom," *Proceedings of the Indian History Congress* 60 Diamond Jubilee (1999): 675–83.

64. Trefzger, *Die nationale Bewegung Ägyptens vor 1928 im Spiegel der schweizerischen Öffentlichkeit*, 45.

65. Ibid.

66. Ibid.

67. Ibid.

Creating a Political Party

To combat the Egyptian exiles in Switzerland, the British government dedicated itself to gaining support among Egyptian expatriates and to sowing discord among them.[68] It had focused on trying to recruit perhaps the closest associate of Muḥammad Farīd. This was ʾIsmāʿīl Labīb, the vice-chairman of the ENP.[69] On the other hand, in November 1917, a British national in Switzerland had secretly negotiated with other several Egyptians on the formation of a new party. The British wanted to win the Egyptian opposition over to this task, especially those who had enough prestige with the broader Egyptian population to be able to exercise influence.[70] The first, immediate purpose of forming a party was to build an Egyptian army of their own.[71] The British government tempted them with a great promise: the prospect of an Egyptian government of its own in an autonomous state.[72] In 1917, the new party, the Young Egyptian Liberal Party, was launched publicly.

Of course, a pro-German and generally pro-Turkish position prevailed within the ranks of the newly founded party. However, the Young Egyptians, like many politicians from the ENP, were divided on Turkey. When the Turks had fought against the British in a joint military alliance with Germany, they had found broad support among the Young Egyptians, but this support had increasingly diminished with the dwindling prospect of military success.[73]

After the founding of the Young Egyptian Liberal Party, publications were planned in which Egyptian students in Switzerland would publicly revoke their previous sympathy for Germany and Turkey. From the British side, there were real, formulated proposals for publications on topics such as whether Turkey itself would be under "unbearable conditions," or whether there would be a cultural "inferiority" compared to the Egyptian level, or that Germany had only "bad intentions" toward Egypt.[74] From this, even those Egyptians previously opposed would have simply drawn the conclusion "that the salvation of our beloved fatherland lay only in uniting with England, but then again, they weren't the decisive people."[75]

---

68. P. 51.
69. PAAA1505, 63.
70. PAAA 150551, 20.11.1917, 51.
71. PAAA 15051, 51.
72. PAAA 15051, 0.53, P.64. Kassim, *Die diplomatische Beziehungen Deutschlands zu Ägypten 1919–1936*, 40.
73. ʿAlī al-Ġayyātī argued that the Ottoman Caliphate had no authenticity and that Sharīf Ḥusayn, a direct descendant of the Prophet Muhammad and a member of the Prophet's Quraysh tribe, was the appropriate person to assume these functions. See Landau, *Pan-Islam*, 120. Also: PAAA 15050, 139–42.
74. PAAA 15051, 52.
75. PAAA 15051, 8.2.1918, 90f, also Kassim, *Die diplomatische Beziehungen Deutschlands zu Ägypten 1919–1936*, 41.

Given this rise in conflicting views on Britain's future role in Egypt, it was only natural that Germany would seek greater influence among Egyptian students in Switzerland. Funding played a decisive factor in this. An informant from the German legation in Bern addressed this point: "Another [. . .] reason seems to me to be that we keep our pockets more buttoned than the Entente. France and England seem to be important enough to capture the mood of the Orientals."[76]

In the winter of 1917/18, the British, however, believed that the founding of a party should not be promoted too quickly, because the Egyptians had not yet shown sufficient support for it.[77] The decisive basis for the ultimate failure of the party was in fact the great difficulty in finding influential political figures among Egyptian exiles to back it. In the months that followed, after the British deliberations on founding a new political party became known, German efforts also concentrated on Labīb, the vice-chairman of the ENP, with the sole objective of defeating the British plan.

In the early summer of 1919, the idea of a new political union of politicians in exile in Egypt appears for the first time in the German documents. It was clear from the start that these considerations were clearly based on a German initiative.[78] But since the ENP already existed, the German considerations for the establishment of a new party concentrated on the leading politicians of this party, especially Farīd, who was involved in an Islamic union that should be part of the Ottoman tradition (led by Ğāwīš), and the leader of the Young Egyptian Committee, Fahmī in Geneva. The greatest difficulty for Germany was undoubtedly in overcoming the sometimes downright contradicting views expressed by the leaders of the various factions within the ENP. In addition, Germany, the driving force behind the new party, could in no way be exposed in public as occupying this role, as that would completely endanger the German plan, which envisaged the new party as a mere means to secure German influence in a future Egypt. It is precisely for this reason, as is well known, that the German Foreign Office wanted to establish a new German-Egyptian company in Berlin, an idea that had been promoted at around the same time.

However, after three months of preparation, the planned German-Egyptian party, which was scheduled to be launched at an Egyptian diaspora event in Switzerland, was never brought to fruition.[79] Why did the German-Egyptian party project fail?

A number of factors contributed to this failure. The most serious point was certainly the ultimately irresolvable contradictions of the existing Egyptian groups both inside and outside the ENP. Another argument against founding a party for

---

76. PAAA 15050, PAAA 15053,10, also Kassim, *Die diplomatische Beziehungen Deutschlands zu Ägypten 1919–1936*, 40.
77. PAAA 15051, 59.
78. PAAA 15052, 20.06.1918, 32.
79. Ibid., 79.

the Egyptians involved was Germany's military and political alliance with Turkey.[80] Finally, there was a significant obstacle in the fact that Germany was under no circumstances to be exposed as the real mastermind behind the entire project. As mentioned earlier, there were at least two competing streams in the ENP. There were also the total opponents of the Ottoman Empire, who wanted to live under British occupation rather than under Turkish rule. This included ʾAlī Šamsī. The German planners of the party project naturally had to take these circumstances into account. The plans were finalized in several preparatory meetings between representatives of the Orient Department of the Foreign Office and Egyptians in Berlin.[81] The most important people in the political groups were to be integrated through the formation of "branch committees" in Istanbul and Switzerland. Farīd was to take over the chairmanship of the entire organization. In Turkey, Ǧāwīš was to take over the leadership of the local branch committee, and in Switzerland, ʾIsmāʿīl Labīb would do the same. In the case of Labīb, one must not forget that the British had planned just six months earlier to put him in the same position. Above all, Germany hoped that this distribution of tasks would include the alleged opponents of the overall project.

Party formation in Switzerland was bedeviled by these divisions. The German diplomat Otto Günther von Wesendonk,[82] who was part of the Political Department of the Foreign Office, assumed that the primary difficulties facing opposition organization in Switzerland would result from the activities of the young Egyptian Fahmī.[83] According to von Wesendonk, he and his followers were real opponents of any ties with Turkey.[84] The biggest hurdle for the project was finding a suitable candidate among the leading Egyptians in exile in Switzerland. In any case, the Foreign Office did not want to give up the project. The delegate from the Foreign Office therefore emphasized that until Farīd and the others arrived in Switzerland, they should take matters into their own hands, negotiate with Šamsī, Fahmī, and Labīb, and, if necessary, present the Egyptians in Switzerland with a fait accompli.[85] However, Fahmī rejected the Germans' request out of his personal "dislike" for Farīd. Labīb had initially favored the Foreign Office, but the allegations that he might be a British spy were still too serious and made him unfit for this major

80. Ibid., 75.
81. Ibid.
82. Otto Günther von Wesendonk (October 3, 1885–June 28, 1933). He joined the foreign service in 1908. It is noteworthy that he was dismissed from service in the Reich in early 1914 because he had married a foreigner. After the outbreak of the First World War, however, he was reassigned to the Political Department of the Foreign Office. For more about him see Johannes Hürter, *Biographisches Handbuch des deutschen Auswärtigen Dienstes 1871 - 1945. 5. T - Z*, Nachträge, ed. *Auswärtigen Amt, Historischer Dienst.* vol 5: Bernd Isphording, Gerhard Keiper, Martin Kröger (Schöningh, Paderborn u. a., 2014).
83. Kassim, *Die diplomatische Beziehungen Deutschlands zu Ägypten 1919–1936*, 39.
84. Ibid.
85. Ibid.

task. Only Šamsī remained, but he declared that the formation and leadership of a national Egyptian group in Switzerland would not be accepted by diaspora Egyptians.[86] Šamsī justified his rejection by citing the intention of the planned party to achieve the old state of 1882 for Egypt. He suggested that, at least at this point, none of the Egyptians in exile would understand this goal. In the German report on Šamsī's rejection, this is discredited as a "tactical" argument.[87] Berlin's reaction to this negative attitude was, naturally, extremely critical, and they no longer wanted to "support" Šamsī in the future.[88] In any case, these reactions did not change the fact that the German plan to found a new ENP in exile had failed.

Diaspora Youth Politics in Times of Political Turmoil (post-2013)

This section focuses on the practices and narratives of belonging among the main actors of two Egyptian groups, as well as their activities, in Turkey and Western Europe in the period after the events of 2013. The activities of these groups (founding Al-Sharq television channel and establishing political entities, such as the Egyptian Human Rights Forum) after 2013 can be mostly characterized as indirect transnational activities. Members wanted to influence public opinion on political events happening in Egypt and provide alternative sources of information on the political situation in the country of origin, as well as to influence public opinion in the country of residence about political events in the country of origin.[89]

In the period after 2013, however, political remittances[90] have had a direct effect on the politicization of migrant communities abroad. Ultimately, it is clear that political remittances flowing from Egypt influenced the type of activism which the groups pursued in the receiving context.[91] Their activism could be described as moving from direct involvement in political movements in their home country during the (post-)revolutionary phase (2011–13) to engage in community associational life in the period after 2013.[92]

However, the type of diaspora activism that these groups pursued was also influenced by the context in which it took place, a key feature of transnationalism (the sociopolitical nature of the host country). The current diaspora opposition groups have utilized similar tactics to those employed by opposition groups

---

86. PAAA, 15053, 1918, 8.
87. Ibid.
88. Ibid.
89. Müller-Funk, *Egyptian Diaspora Activism during the Arab Uprisings*, 5.
90. Political remittance is about how migrants and diaspora networks contribute to the political changes in the country of origin.
91. Lea Müller-Funk, "Fluid Identities, Diaspora Youth Activists and the (Post-) Arab Spring: How Narratives of Belonging Can Change over Time," *Journal of Ethnic and Migration Studies* 46 (2020): 1114–20.
92. Ibid.

during the period of the 1919 Revolution. They realized the importance of the media in the current globalized world. As a result, a number of Egyptian exiles created various Arabic media and online platforms, some of which gained considerable audiences, both inside Egypt and in the diaspora. These online outlets have been very critical of the Egyptian regime and its political practices, both internally and internationally. Popular outlets include the satellite television stations Al-Sharq (The East) and Mekameleen (We Continue), both broadcasting from Turkey using a French satellite. Al-Sharq station is headed by Ayman Nour, a prominent Egyptian politician who was a member of the Egyptian parliament and a presidential candidate in the era of Hosni Mubarak and is also founder and chairman of the Ghad Party. The Al-Sharq and Mekameleen stations have some ties to the currently outlawed Muslim Brotherhood and disseminate its discourse and political views. Two of Al-Sharq's most popular programs are *Ibn al-Balad*, hosted by Egyptian actor Heshm 'Abdalla, and *Ma'a Mo'taz*, hosted by the prominent presenter Mo'taz Maṭar. The former's political position is far from the views of the Muslim Brotherhood, while the latter is aligned with the organization.

The sources of funding for these channels are not clear but reportedly may come from the Muslim Brotherhood and the Qatari government.[93] This mixture of Islamist and secularist talk show hosts suggests that the owners of these channels are aiming to (1) attenuate the political polarization which has taken root after the battle orchestrated over Egypt's 2011 referendum and the 2012 constitution; (2) challenge the new regime's legitimacy after July 2013 by taking advantage of a sympathetic political environment in Turkey; (3) form a unique platform for the large number of Egyptian opposition members who have no voice and no place in the local media outlets in Egypt, which allow only the regime's narrative; and (4) to function as a forum for the opposition from different political backgrounds in order to play a key role in mobilizing Egyptians in exile. Despite attempts by the Egyptian regime to pressure Europe and Turkey to close these channels,[94] they have succeeded in playing a significant role in organizing and maintaining the group's supporters, garnering new followers, and offering counternarratives.[95]

Since Egyptian President Abdelfattah Al-Sisi seized power in 2013, he has opted to eliminate the basic structures and components of politics such as functioning political parties, an independent parliament, and civil society organizations. He has also eliminated all his political opponents, preventing them from acquiring social

---

93. Egypt Independent, "Employees at Turkey-based *al-Šarq* news channel admit Qatari financing," April 20, 2018, https://egyptindependent.com/employees-at-turkey-based-al-sharq-news-channel-admit-qatari-financing/ (accessed September 1, 2020).

94. Middle East Monitor, "Egypt Urges European ambassadors to Close Pro-Muslim Brotherhood Satellite Channels," February 4, 2015, https://www.middleeastmonitor.com/20150204-egypt-urges-european-ambassadors-to-close-pro-muslim-brotherhood-satellite-channels/ (accessed September 1, 2020). See also Beverley Milton-Edwards, *The Muslim Brotherhood, the Arab Spring and its Future Face* (London: Routledge, 2016).

95. Ibid.

or institutional positions through which they might be able to challenge him. He has also designated the Muslim Brotherhood a terrorist organization and in doing so has relied on the state's institutions in an attempt to legitimize and consolidate his unchallenged power. While the process of attempting to depoliticize the masses continues, channels such as Al-Sharq and Mekameleen have had a direct impact on the politicization of diaspora communities abroad, as well as inside Egypt by providing alternative information and views from those provided by regime-friendly channels. Their viewership includes not only Egyptians at home and abroad but also viewers from the wider Arab World, a fact which worries the government, as does their success in poaching viewers from the regime channels. The opposition channels have also been prominent in prompting discussions about major issues of national security in Egypt. During the controversy over the concession of the Red Sea islands of Tiran and Sanafir to Saudi Arabia in 2016, for example, opposition media broadcast the testimonies of expert academics regarding Egypt's ownership of the islands. They have also shed light on the Grand Ethiopian Renaissance Dam crisis and its effects on the River Nile.

As noted earlier, the sociopolitical nature of the host country determines the ability of a diaspora to organize influence and to exert indirect influence on its homeland and also has an effect on the character of the diaspora itself. In this context, the sociopolitical nature of the host countries in which the Egyptian diasporas are located, especially in Western Europe, is liberalism. The European model has opted to strengthen domestic institutions through which individuals and groups in civil society can express their views. As the European liberal system demonstrates, robust and independent institutions such as NGOs, the legislature, and the judiciary, as well as the conditions that allow for free expression of public opinion, are a critical link in creating a functioning system.[96] The Egyptian diaspora, especially the human rights groups, thus enjoy the privileged status of other transnational actors, being able to exert influence as an interest group in both the homeland and the host country and affecting the homeland because of their influence in the host country.

This situation led a group of Egyptian human rights defenders (leftists and secularists) based in Western Europe to establish the Egyptian Human Rights Forum in March 2019 as an independent NGO.[97] According to its charter, the forum aims to mobilize Egyptian human rights defenders and activists in diaspora and inside Egypt, by working with its members to develop collective positions and to comment in social media on Egypt's political, economic, and legislative developments.[98] The forum has attempted, mainly through personal connections, to establish contact with NGOs in Egypt such as the Cairo Institute for Human

---

96. Andrew Moravcsik, "Explaining International human Rights Regimes: Liberal Theory and Western Europe," *European Journal of International Relations* 1, no. 2 (1995): 157–89.

97. https://www.egyptianforum.org/index.php/about/(accessed September 8, 2020).

98. Skype interview with one of the members of the EHRF in France (August 22, 2020).

Rights Studies and the Egyptian Commission for Rights and Freedoms. The forum has also collaborated with international organizations such as EuroMed, Amnesty International, and Human Rights Watch, to mobilize member states of the United Nations Human Rights Council in Geneva when Egypt's human rights record was subject to Universal Periodic Review on November 13, 2019.[99]

Conclusion

In general, the activities of the Egyptian diaspora illustrate that exiled communities are affected by the nature of the host country in which they operate. In Europe, the Egyptian opposition is freer to exert effective influence, while in Middle Eastern countries like Turkey and Qatar the opposition has no opportunity to exert influence outside the control of the host country. It was no surprise, therefore, that the Turkish authorities in 2021 asked the owners of the opposition channels that broadcast from Istanbul to amend their editorial line and refrain from attacking the regime of Abdelfattah Al-Sisi.

This chapter has also explored the idea that political division in modern Egypt has its roots in the nationalist movement which grew from the time of the 1919 Revolution and continues today along the same political spectrum. During the 1919 Revolution, there was intense polarization between Islamists (who insisted on close ties with Turkey, or the Ottoman Caliphate) and secularists/liberals (who had pragmatic orientations and aimed at complete autonomy for Egypt). Today, political division takes the same shape (particularly the divide between the Muslim Brotherhood and the secular/liberal opposition). On the other hand, nationalist thought surely has an impact on the economy and society, but with the dominance of liberal rhetoric and the added issue of human rights. These issues have become prominent among the exiled opposition, particularly in the work of human rights groups, many of whom have had to relocate outside Egypt.

---

99. The documents on which the reviews based are: (1) national report—information provided by the State under review; (2) information contained in the reports of independent human rights experts and groups, known as the Special Procedures, human rights treaty bodies, and other UN entities; (3) information provided by other stakeholders including national human rights institutions, regional organizations, and civil society groups. See https://www.ohchr.org/en/NewsEvents/Pages/DisplayNews.aspx?NewsID=25261&LangID=E (accessed March 6, 2022).

Chapter 9

THE GREAT THEFT OF HISTORY

THE EGYPTIAN ARMY, THE FIRST WORLD WAR, AND THE 1919 REVOLUTION

Khaled Fahmy

On November 11, 2013, the Military Research Department of the Egyptian Armed Forces staged a big celebration commemorating the ninety-ninth anniversary of the First World War. Major General Amīn Ḥusayn, assistant to the Minister of Defense, delivered a speech in which he extolled the participation of the Egyptian army in the Great War and highlighted "the heroic sacrifices of the Egyptian army in that war and its magnificent deeds which changed the course of military history, and which contributed to preserving the lofty principles of human civilization." According to the Facebook page of the official spokesman of the Armed Forces, the celebration consisted of a photo exhibit that used recently released documents from the British and French national archives pointing to the participation of the Egyptian army in the war. In addition, the Facebook page added, the celebration included an exhibition of rare photos illustrating "the sacrifices of the oldest standing army in the world, and how that army maintained the stability of the Egyptian state and upheld Egypt's cultural heritage passed down from the time of the pharaohs till the present day." The Facebook page ended by explaining that the celebration also entailed screening a documentary film that illustrated how during the First World War the Egyptian army fought with the Allies in three continents: in Asia, where it repulsed an "Ottoman attack from the east [in Sinai] and fought in Syria, Iraq and . . . in the Arabian Peninsula"; in Africa, where it repulsed a Sanusi attack from the west and a Darfouri attack from the south"; and in Europe, where 100,000 Egyptian soldiers fought alongside the Allies in four countries: France, Belgium, Greece, and Italy. These soldiers, we are told, were a major factor behind the Allied victory in the First World War, and many of them were subsequently decorated with the Victoria Cross, "one of the most prestigious medals that is awarded to military leaders who enrich the history of humanity."[1]

---

1. https://www.facebook.com/EgyArmySpox/photos/a.394602110670777/394602790670709/?type=1&theater, accessed June 20, 2021.

This was the first time the Egyptian army marked this important occasion. For ninety-nine years, Egypt never commemorated its army's participation in the Great War, neither during the monarchical period nor under the republic. However, after the 2013 popular coup that brought General Abdel-Fattah El-Sisi to power, and over the following four years, November 11 became a day of military pomp and circumstance. On this day, and for five successive years, the same exact speech summarized in the previous paragraph was delivered, albeit by a different general, in a big ceremony attended by government officials, members of the press, and the military high brass.[2]

Then, suddenly in November 2018 and on the centenary of Armistice Day, these celebrations ended as mysteriously as they had started five years prior. This time no festivities were held, no speeches were delivered, and no pictures were taken. The only article that appeared in 2018 referring to the participation of the Egyptian army in First World War was a lead article in *Al-Ahram*, Egypt's semi-official newspaper, written by Cairo University political science professor Alī al-Dīn Hilāl. Hilāl's article repeated the same details mentioned in the army's speeches of the previous years, but with two noteworthy differences. The first is that instead of stating that Egypt contributed with 100,000 troops, Hilāl claimed that the size of the Egyptian force was 1.5 million soldiers. Secondly, Hilāl thanked a certain Dr. Ashraf Ṣabrī whom he identified as a specialist in military history, and who is thanked for his diligent research efforts and for unveiling to the world the size and nature of the Egyptian army's forgotten contribution to the First World War.[3]

A Scuba Diver with a Penchant for History

Indeed, back in the 2016 celebrations, Staff Officer General Muḥammad ʿAbd El-Fattāḥ al-Kashkī, Deputy Minister of Defense for Foreign Relations, singled our Dr. Ashraf Ṣabrī for his "productive collaboration" with the Armed Forces Military Research Department to "uphold the rights of Egyptians who served in the First World War." On his part, Dr. Ṣabrī gave a speech in which he explained

2. Ḥātim al-Jahmī, "Al-quwwāt al-musallaḥa taḥtafil bi-murūr 100 ʿām ʿalā mushārakatihā fī al-ḥarb alʿālamiyya al-ūlā," *al-Shurūq*, November 12, 2014, 2; Ḥātim al-Jahmī, "Al-quwwāt al-musallaḥa taḥtafil bi-murūr 101 ʿām ʿalā al-mushāraka al-Miṣriyya fī al-ḥarb alʿālamiyya al-ūlā," *al-Shurūq*, November 12, 2015, online edition: https://bit.ly/3xcEdJJ; Mahā Sālim, "Al-quwwāt al-musallaḥa taḥtafil bi-murūr 102 ʿām ʿalā al-mushāraka al-Miṣriyya fī al-ḥarb alʿālamiyya al-ūlā," *Al-Ahram*, November 16, 2016, online edition: https://gate.ahram.org.eg/News/1310035.aspx; the Official Page of the Military Spokesman of the Armed Forces, "Al-quwwāt al-musallaḥa taḥtafil bi-murūr 103 ʿām ʿalā al-mushāraka al-Miṣriyya fī al-ḥarb alʿālamiyya al-ūlā," *Facebook*, November 12, 2017, https://www.facebook.com/EgyArmySpox/posts/1175403825923931/.

3. Alī al-Dīn Hilāl, "Miṣr sharīk muhimm fī intiṣār al-ḥarb alʿālamiyya al-ūlā," *Al-Ahram*, November 11, 2018: https://gate.ahram.org.eg/daily/News/679475.aspx.

that over the previous fifteen years he had been conducting extensive research in European libraries and archives, as well as in the University of Tottenham, and that he had managed to discover a trove of archival documents that had been recently released by the British and French national archives. This newly available material, he claimed, shed light on "the heroic deeds of the Egyptian army and its role in assisting the Allies during the First World War." Moreover, it was by conducting this extensive archival research that he also discovered that many Egyptians had been rewarded with the Victoria Cross.[4]

Dr. Ṣabrī's allegations raise some serious concerns. For one thing, neither the British nor the French national archives recently released any new material in their possession related to the First World War. For another, there was no university by the name of the University of Tottenham not before, during, or after 2016. Moreover, the Victoria Cross is indeed a very prestigious award, but it is not given to those who "enrich the history of humanity." Rather, it is awarded to members of the British Armed Forces who exhibit valor "in the presence of the enemy." More importantly, there is not a single Egyptian among the 1,358 recipients of that award, assuming, in the first place, that receiving such an award from an imperial occupying power is something about which an Egyptian soldier should be proud.[5]

But who is this Dr. Ṣabrī, and what are his credentials as an expert on the First World War? Following a quick Google search, it transpires that Dr. Ashraf Ṣabrī is a doctor alright, but a doctor in undersea and hyperbaric medicine; that he owns two scuba diving clubs, one in Sharm al-Sheikh and the other in Alexandria, and that it was while pursuing his hobby off the northern coast of Egypt that he discovered shipwrecks he believed date back to the First World War. This auspicious happenstance is what triggered his interest in the history of the First World War, but this interest was not directed at studying the impact this war had on Egyptian society, a topic that, as illustrated later in the chapter, has attracted much academic interest, but at analyzing the participation of the Egyptian army in it, a subject that has somehow evaded the attention of numerous historians, Egyptians, and foreigners alike, who have been studying the history of this war for over a century.[6]

How Dr. Ṣabrī managed to convince the Military Research Department of the Egyptian Armed Forces of his spurious findings is beyond the aims of this chapter. It is worth noting, however, that since 2013, the Egyptian army has been pursuing an aggressive public relations campaign on social and traditional media to portray itself as the panacea of all ills from which Egyptians have been suffering

4. Sālim, "Al-quwwāt al-musallaḥa taḥtafil bi-murūr 102 ʿām ʿalā al-mushāraka al-Miṣriyya fī al-ḥarb al-ʿālamiyya al-ulā."

5. Kevin Brazier, *The Complete Victoria Cross: A Full Chronological Record of All Holders of Britain's Highest Award for Gallantry* (London: Pen and Sword Book, 2015).

6. Ḥanān Muḥammad, "Qarār Zaʿzūʿ bi-waqf tarākhīṣ al-ghawṣ," *al-Bawwāba News*, April 14, 2014: https://www.albawabhnews.com/518631. See also: https://www.facebook.com/groups/17016907866/permalink/10150567230842867/.

including, literally, AIDS and Hepatitis C.⁷ Of equal importance is the army's claim that it is the "spinal cord of the Egyptian state,"⁸ stressing that it is what separated Egyptian from chaos. In the wake of popular protests that swept the Arab World in 2011–13, the Egyptian military has not missed an opportunity to remind Egyptian civilians that it was the army that saved them from the fate of their neighbors in Syria, Libya, and Yemen whose countries either disintegrated into civil wars or were invaded by foreign countries, or both. In this public relations (PR) campaign, a consistent effort is made to provide a narrative in which the current army is presented in a historical continuum that stretches back to pharaonic times. The narrative is not always elegant or accurate as when the Director of the Military Museums Department within the Ministry of Defense listed in a 2016 TV interview numerous victories of the Egyptian army down the centuries, wrongly identifying each one of them. Specifically, when referring to the Battle of Hittin that was waged between Saladin and the Crusaders in 1187 CE, he claimed that it was "waged between King Ramses III and the Hittites." He added that "the Battle of 'Ayn Jalut was fought between Saladin and the Crusaders," when in fact it was fought between the Mamluks and the Mongols. And he described the Battle of Nizib between the Egyptian army under Ibrahim Pasha and the Ottomans under Hafiz Pasha that took place in 1839 CE in southern Anatolia as the *naval* battle of Nizib.⁹ Since the 2013 coup, the narrative the Egyptian army is struggling to weave about its own history has gotten more refined, with high-production films, TV series, and newspaper articles that together narrate the army's history in an increasingly sophisticated manner.¹⁰ However, the claim that the Egyptian army

7. In February 2014, and in the presence of the Interim President of the Republic, 'Adlī Manṣūr, and the then Minister of Defense, Abdel-Fattah Elsisi, an army doctor announced the discovery of a cure of AIDS and Hepatitis C. "I conquered AIDS; I can turn the AIDS virus into a kofta skewer," referring to spiced meat kababs that are common in Egyptian cuisine. For more on this fascinating claim, dubbed in Egypt Kofta-gate, see Islam Hussein, "Science Communication Lessons from 'Kofta-Gate,'" *American Scientist*, June 4, 2019, https://www.americanscientist.org/article/science-communication-lessons-from-kofta-gate.

8. The references to this theme are too numerous to list, but see, in particular, the speech given by the Minister of Defense in 2014, Major General Ṣidqī Ṣubḥī, when he made exactly this claim: Aḥmad 'Abd al-'Aẓīm Wahdī Muḥammad, "Wazīr al-difā': al-jaysh al-Miṣrī huwa al-'amūd al-faqrī lil-dawla al-Miṣriyya," *al-Waṭan*, July 16, 2014, https://bit.ly/2UXDBJP.

9. For more on these gaffes, see Khaled Fahmy, "Siyāttiliwā mudīr idārat al-matāḥif al-ḥarbiyya" (His Excellency General Director of the Military Museums Department), *Khaled Fahmy* (blog), September 21, 2016. https://khaledfahmy.org/ar/2016/09/21/ -سياتلوا مدير-إدارة-المتاحف-الحربية/.

10. Among the noteworthy, high-budget productions are the following two examples: the first is *Al-Mamarr* (The Passage), a 180-minute 2019 film telling the story of the War of Attrition waged with Israel between 1967 and 1970. Its production budget, EGP 100 million, is the highest in the history of Egyptian cinema. The second is *Al-Ikhtiyār* (The

participated in the First World War with a force of 100,000 soldiers has to be one of the most curious claims made by the army in its struggle to present itself as the prime guarantor of Egypt's stability and as the "spinal cord of the Egyptian state."

There are two central details about this curious claim that are connected to the 1919 Revolution and that require close analysis. The first is that in 1914 there was in fact an Egyptian national army and that this army fought gallantly defending Egypt's western, eastern, and southern borders. The second is that up to 100,000 Egyptian soldiers belonging to that army participated in the war effort in various theaters of operation outside Egypt, including on the Western Front.

What Was Egyptian about the Egyptian Army in 1914?

To check the veracity of these claims, and to help disentangle fact from fiction and history from propaganda, it is important to consider the nature, size, and identity of the Egyptian army during the war and on the eve of the revolution. To start with, the army that 'Urābī led back in 1882 did not exceed 13,000 men.[11] After the British had defeated that army in the Battle of al-Tall al-Kabīr, launching a 72-year-long military occupation, Britain decided severely to reduce the size of the Egyptian army and to cut it down to less than half its original size, a mere 6,000 men.[12] This was based on the recommendation of Lord Dufferin, the British ambassador to Istanbul, who had been sent to Egypt to study the cause of the 'Urābī uprising and who recommended this reduction in size to prevent the army from rising again.[13] More important than its size, the Egyptian army was in fact headed by British officers and its commander-in-chief, the sirdar, was always a British officer, even though the Khedive was technically the supreme commander of the army. Regarding Dr. Ṣabrī's claims that this army fought the Ottomans in the east, that is in Sinai, the Sanusi in the west, and the Darfouris in the south, details that most likely he pulled out of Laṭifa Salim's study on Egypt during the First World War,[14] it is noteworthy that this was done in fulfillment of British, not Egyptian, policy, and that the Egyptian army was commanded by British, not Egyptian, officers. In short, there was indeed an Egyptian army during the First

---

Choice), a thirty-episode TV drama telling the story of a commando officer killed while confronting Islamic State fighters in the Sinai city of Rafah in 2017. It was produced in 2020 by Synergy, a firm indirectly owned by the General Intelligence Service.

11. 'Urābī himself claims that the army was 36,000-strong: Aḥmad 'Urābī, *Mudhakkirāt 'Urābī* (Cairo: Dār al-Hilāl, 1953), 176. For a more credible assessment, see 'Abd al-'Aẓīm Ramaḍān, *al-Jaysh al-Miṣrī wa'l-Siyāsa* (Cairo: al-Hay'a al-Miṣriyya al-'Āmma lil-Kitāb, 1977), 43.

12. Ramaḍān, *al-Jaysh al-Miṣrī*, 33.

13. Ibid., 34.

14. Laṭīfa Sālim, *Miṣr fī al-Ḥarb al-'Ālamiyya al-Ūlā* (Cairo: Dār al-Shurūq, 2008).

World War, but this army was Egyptian in name only. It was an army that did Britain's bidding and fulfilled her imperial policy in the region.

Peasants or Soldiers?

The high brass of the Egyptian army might have been British, but its rank and file were peasants who had been conscripted according to a conscription law that allowed people to buy their way out of service. Be that as it may, might these conscripts have been the 100,000 soldiers that Ṣabrī mentioned or the 1.5 million claimed by Hilāl and who fought in Syria, Iraq, and Arabia? Or were they in fact peasants pressed into serving the British imperial army? To answer this important question, a question whose answer is intimately connected to the 1919 Revolution as explained later in the chapter, we need to go back to the very early months of the First World War and to follow British policy in Egypt as it evolved month by month.

When the war broke out in August 1914, Egypt was in a uniquely awkward position diplomatically and legally. Ruled since 1840 as a semi-autonomous province, Egypt was technically and legally still under Ottoman suzerainty and the Ottoman sultan was its official sovereign. Practically, however, and since their military victory in al-Tall al-Kabīr in 1882, the British were the effective rulers of the country. So, when the war broke out in August, the British, on August 5, forced the Egyptian government to associate itself with the British declaration of war against Germany and Austria; accordingly, the Khedival government expelled Austrian and German diplomats and seized their assets. More seriously, when the Ottomans entered the war on November 2, Britain found herself in a very precarious position in Egypt, for Egyptians, technically subjects of the Ottoman sultan, had the right to carry arms against their sovereign's enemies, that is, the British. To deal with this anomaly, Britain announced martial law on November 2, giving the commander of British troops in Egypt, General John Maxwell, power to arraign people, prevent public gatherings, and censor the press. Furthermore, Britain decided to end Egypt's ambivalent legal status and on December 18, 1914, declared Egypt to be a protectorate. On that day Cairenes woke up to read in the papers and on the walls of their city the following proclamation:

> His Britannic Majesty's Secretary of State for Foreign Affairs gives notice that, in view of the state of war arising out of the action of Turkey, Egypt is placed under the protection of His Majesty and will henceforth constitute a British Protectorate. The suzerainty of Turkey over Egypt is thus terminated, and His Majesty's Government will adopt all measures necessary for the defence of Egypt, and protect its inhabitants and interests.[15]

---

15. *British and Foreign State Papers*, CIX (1915), 436.

British officials also announced the deposition of Khedive 'Abbās, who, since his accession to power in 1892, had opposed British influence and who, purely by accident, was in Istanbul when the war broke out in Europe. In 'Abbās's place as Sultan of Egypt the British selected his uncle Hussain Kamil, regarded as sympathetic to British interests. In the words of Robert Tignor,

> In the brief span of five months Egypt had moved from an autonomous province of the Ottoman empire, temporarily occupied by British forces until order should be restored, to a British protectorate under martial law. Its Khedivate had been replaced by a Sultanate, and its ruler, 'Abbās, a promoter of nationalist and anti-British activities, had been replaced by a pro-British monarch.[16]

Most crucially, concerned about where the loyalties of Egyptians lay and suspicious of the depth of their sympathies with the sultan doubling as caliph, General John Maxwell, the commander of British troops in Egypt, issued a declaration on November 6 recognizing the religious and moral ties that Egyptians may have toward the caliphate, and exempted them from military duty and announced that it alone will carry the burden of defending Egypt. The declaration stated that:

> Recognizing the respect and veneration with which the Sultan, in his religious capacity, is regarded by the Mahommedans of Egypt, Great Britain takes upon herself the sole burden of the present war, without calling upon the Egyptian people for aid therein.[17]

However, given that the war dragged on for months on end, and given that throughout 1916 and early 1917, the British were facing serious difficulties in the Gallipoli campaign, in al-Kut in southern Mesopotamia, and, closer to home, in the Sinai/Palestine campaign,[18] British officials in London were having second thoughts about their earlier decision to exempt Egypt from the war effort. According to Kyle Anderson, the War Office wrote in May 1917 to the commander of the Egyptian Expeditionary Force—which, again, was "Egyptian" only in name, and which had been established a year prior—telling him that "It is essential that all parts of the empire should share in the strain [of the war] as far as local conditions admit . . . As regards Egypt, I am not satisfied that this is the case."[19] By June 1917, the War Office suggested that forced conscription into the British imperial force be instituted with the aim of raising 17,000 men for the war effort. But after opposition

---

16. Robert Tignor, "Maintaining the Empire: General Sir John Maxwell and Egypt during World War I," *The Princeton University Library Chronicle* 5, no. 2 (Winter 1992): 180.

17. *British and Foreign State Papers*, CIX (1915), 434.

18. Eugene Rogan, *The Fall of the Ottomans: The Great War in the Middle East* (New York: Basic Books, 2015).

19. Kyle Anderson, "The Egyptian Labor Corps: Workers, Peasants, and the State in World War I," *International Journal of Middle East Studies* 49, no. 1 (February 2017): 9.

from the Egyptian government, and from the British-led Egyptian army, the idea of forced conscription was dropped, and, instead, Egyptian peasants were to be asked to volunteer to serve in the imperial war effort in exchange for exemption from conscription. So, on October 20, 1917, the minister of war in London issued a decree modifying the Egyptian Conscription Law so that "every person liable for military service . . . shall be exempt from the obligation to such service if he shall enlist in and serve for a continuous period of one year with . . . any auxiliary service attached to the British troops."[20] Thus was born the famous Egyptian Labor Corps (ELC) to whom both Ṣabrī and Hilāl refer, insisting, wrongly, that such a corps was part of the Egyptian army.

To encourage them to enlist in this new ELC, peasants were offered a daily wage of 4 piasters, which was considerably higher than the 1914 wage rate,[21] and there seems to be some evidence that peasants "approached the recruitment effort as a financial or even entrepreneurial opportunity."[22] This put a financial pressure on the British military as, technically, it could not impose direct claims on the Egyptian government's budget. "So instead, the protectorate authorized the [British] army to make charges against a "suspended account." . . . The wages of [the] new Labor Corps . . . was billed to the suspense account. In effect, Egyptian taxpayers were lending Britain the costs of their own labor."[23]

Despite these financial incentives, and notwithstanding the fact that the entire process of recruiting men for the ELC was referred to as "volunteering," in actual practice the local officials, the governors (mudīrs), overseers (ma'mūrs), and village heads ('umdas) resorted to "sheer violence" to raise the required men.[24] The journalist and political theorist Salama Musa recounts in his memoirs his experience watching "a man [being] tied by a thick rope around his trunk and [led] behind another like him, and they marched in this state until they reached the district. There, they were put in a jail cell, and then sent to Palestine."[25] Likewise, Saad Zaghloul describes in his memoirs how

> people were sick and tired of methods deployed by administrators in forcing young men to volunteer to serve in the British army. They kidnapped people from markets, streets and alleyways, from mosques and courthouses, and then asked them to affix their seals to the volunteering forms! And whoever refused would be beaten until he added his seal. In most districts there is even a seal-

20. Ibid., 10.

21. Ellis Goldberg, "Peasants in Revolt: Egypt 1919," *International Journal of Middle East Studies* 24, no. 2 (1992): 269.

22. Anderson, "The Egyptian Labor Corps," 15.

23. Aaron Jakes, *Egypt's Occupation: Colonial Economism and the Crises of Capitalism* (Stanford: Stanford University Press, 2020), 248.

24. Anderson, "The Egyptian Labor Corps," 12.

25. Salama Musa, *Tarbiyyat Salama Musa* (Cairo: al-Hay'a al-Miṣriyya al-'Āmma lil-Kitāb, 2012 [1947]), 112, quoted in Anderson, "The Egyptian Labor Corps," 12.

maker who makes seals for those who refuse to volunteer. This resulted in many incidents ... [in which] many were killed or wounded.²⁶

A popular song from the period movingly reflects the degree of animosity peasants felt toward the recruitment process and the entire service in the Labor Corps. Addressed to Reginald Wingate, the British high commissioner, it says:

> Pardon us, Wingate! But our country has had enough!
> You took our camels, donkeys, barley, and wheat aplenty.
> Now leave us alone!
> ...
> Laborers and soldiers were forced to travel, leaving their land.
> They headed to Mount Lebanon and to the battlefields and the trenches!²⁷

As hinted at by this popular song, one of the earliest deployments of these men was as transport workers assisting general Edmund Allenby's Egyptian Expeditionary Force in its 1917 campaign in Sinai and Palestine.²⁸ There, they extended railway lines and unloaded supplies from surf boats off the coast of Palestine. But they also served in Aqaba, Mesopotamia, Salonkia, Mudros, and France. Commenting on the crucial services these men rendered to the British war effort, an anonymous British observer wrote that the "Egyptian fellaheen did splendid services on at least three fronts as makers of roads, porters, drivers of transport, hewers of wood and drawers of water."²⁹

Before looking closely into the central question of whether these men were civilians or soldiers, it may be important to clarify how many men we are talking about. Kyle Anderson, relying on annual figures listed in the Foreign and Commonwealth Office (FCO), calculates that a little over a quarter million men were gathered from villages throughout Egypt and pressed to serve in the newly created Labor Corps, in addition to an extra 100,000 men who formed different auxiliary units. The total is therefore 327,000 men.³⁰ By contrast, Reinhardt

---

26. Saad Zaghloul, *Mudhakkirāt Saad Zaghlūl*, Edited by Abd al-'Azīm Ramaḍān, vol. 7 (Cairo: Al-Hay'a al-Miṣriyya al-'Āmma lil-Kitāb, 1996), 36.

27. Ziad Fahmy, *Ordinary Egyptians: Creating the Modern Nation through Popular Culture* (Stanford: Stanford University Press, 2011), 134. There are many versions of this song. See, for example, Tawwaf, *Egypt, 1919, Being a Narrative of Certain Incidents of the Rising in Upper Egypt* (Oxford, 1925), 5, and Goldberg, "Peasants in Revolt," 271.

28. Mario Ruiz, "Photography and the Egyptian Labor Corps in Wartime Palestine, 1917–1918," *Journal of Palestine Studies*, no. 56 (2014): 52–66. Ruiz says that the first deployment of the ELC was during the military operations associated with the Gallipoli Campaign of 1915, 57.

29. Tawwaf, *Egypt, 1919, Being a Narrative of Certain Incidents of the Rising in Upper Egypt*, 8.

30. Anderson, "The Egyptian Labor Corps," 6.

Schulze comes up with an aggregate number of 1.5 million peasants recruited between 1916 and 1919, "approximately one-third of the male population between seventeen and thirty-five."[31]

From what has been said so far, it should be clear that the claim by the present-day high brass of the Egyptian army that that army served in the First World War is historically inaccurate. It is true that hundreds of thousands of Egyptians served in the war, but these men were civilians, not soldiers. The members of the Egyptian Labor Corps were never given military ranks and they never received military training, despite the fact that they were subjected to harsh military discipline. Secondly, the Egyptian Labor Corps into which these men were volunteered was part of the British, not the Egyptian army.

"I Want to Go Back Home"

Beyond the question of how the hundreds of thousands of peasants were recruited, little is known about their combat experience or how they interacted with the men and officers of the British army along whom they served. Despite the recent growing interest in the history of nonwhite soldiers of the British and French imperial armies,[32] the experience of Egyptian peasants in the First World War has largely been ignored.[33] Two important exceptions are the work of Mario Ruiz and Alia Mossallam. Ruiz relied on the official photographs of the Egyptian Expeditionary Force kept in the Imperial War Museum in London and the Australian War Memorial in Canberra. Reading these photographs critically, he contrasted the sanitized officers' account of how the Egyptian peasants "cheerful[ly] work[ed] to whistle signal under their own officers," with what the photographs reveal about "inadequate rations and exposure to rain and bitter cold combin[ing] to cause

---

31. Reinhard Schulze, "Colonization and Resistance: The Egyptian Peasant Rebellion of 1919," in *Peasants and Politics in the Modern Middle East*, ed. Farhad Kazemi and John Waterbury (Gainesville: University of Florida Press, 1991), 185.

32. For two recent studies on the imperial dimension of the Great War, see Roger D. Long and Ian Talbot, eds., *India and World War I: A Centennial Assessment* (London: Routledge, 2018), and Heike Liebau, ed., *The World in World Wars: Experiences, Perceptions and Perspectives from Africa and Asia* (Leiden: Brill, 2010).

33. The main exceptions are Alia Mossallam's work cited later in the chapter; Ruiz, "Photography and the Egyptian Labor Corps in Wartime Palestine, 1917–1918"; Kyle J. Anderson, *The Egyptian Labor Corps: Race, Space, and Place in the First World War* (Austin: University of Texas Press, forthcoming); Amīn ʿIzz El-Dīn refers to service in the ECL as "*al-shughl fiʾl-sulṭa*," Amīn ʿIzz El-Dīn, "Al-shughl fiʾl-sulṭa: Qiṣṣat faylaq al-ʾamal al-Miṣrī wa faylaq al-jimāl," *al-Muṣawwar*, March 7, 1969, 24–7; Goldberg, "Peasants in Revolt: Egypt 1919," and Schulze, "Colonization and Resistance."

illness and death."³⁴ He also quotes from their commanding officers who admit that the "British army used the ELC as nighttime decoys on constantly moving boats to fool Ottoman forces."³⁵

On her part, Alia Mossallam used songs instead of photographs to get at the wartime experience of the peasants who served in the ELC.³⁶ In London, Mossallam consulted British documents preserved in the National Archives at Kew and the Imperial War Museum. There she located diaries of British officers in charge of the men, and through a careful, critical reading of these diaries, she juxtaposed British officers' description of the members of the ELC as "willing helpers of British troops," with Egyptian peasants' feelings of estrangement from their officers and from the entire alien enterprise in which they found themselves enmeshed. Central to her analysis is a particular song that the men used to sing during their long marches and while performing their arduous manual tasks. The song in question is "Ya ʿazīz ʿainī" (Oh Apple of My Eye) that was originally sung by Naʿīma al-Masriyya (1892–1976) in the early years of the war.

> Oh apple of my eye, I want to go back home!
> Oh apple of my eye I want to go back home
> Oh apple of my eye, your absence is beyond me
>
> My darling arose ready to depart,
> and he came to bid me farewell
> He wept, drenching his handkerchief, and I asked
> "Why do you do this?"
> "Is crying your sport, or are you teasing me?"
> "Crying is neither my sport nor am I teasing you"
> The talk of the ʿawazil is bitter and painful
> Oh, apple of my eye, how I feel sorry for myself.
> Oh apple of my eye I want to go back home
>
> Oh morning star, sway back and forth between us,
> send my love to those who have captivated my soul
> I have the cure for all ills, but none for my soul
> Oh apple of my eye I want to go back home
> My aches are so strong, I can't get a hold of myself

---

34. Ruiz, "Photography and the Egyptian Labor Corps in Wartime Palestine, 1917–1918," 52, 59.

35. Ibid., 57.

36. Alia Mossallam, "'Ya ʿAziz ʿAini Ana Bidi Arawwah Baladi . . .': Voyages of an Egyptian Tune—from Estrangement at Home to Longing on the Fronts of the First World War," in *Cultural Entanglement in the Pre-Independence Arab World*, ed. Anthony Gorman and Sarah Irving (I.B. Tauris, 2021), 51–70.

> A good evening to you, oh flower of the nation
> we are the ones who suffer while they are as they are
> while others meet your fancy, embittered we become
> May God ease your path, and may He grant us patience
> Oh apple of my eye, your absence is (despite?) me

Mossallam studies a particular recording of the song made in Alexandria between 1913 and 1915. At that time, Na'īma was active in Upper Egypt, specifically in Asyut where she might have picked up the song. She might have also "witnessed people being taken away by force, as related in memoirs of . . . Salama Musa's description of events in Minya [mentioned earlier], and the judge 'Ismat Saif el-Dawla's descriptions of Asyut [discussed below]."[37] Mossallam also found a reference to the same song going all the way back to 1901.[38] This places the song in very close temporal proximity to another song, "Fi'l-jihādiyya," which was recorded down by French Egyptologist Gaston Maspero (1846–1916) in his collection of popular songs gathered while conducting excavations in Upper Egypt between 1900 and 1914.[39] In that earlier song, a mother laments the fate of her son who was snatched by the army. "Oh son, hide the rosiness of your cheeks / The Cheikh el-Béléd marked down: Fit for service." In commenting on that song, Olga Verlato remarks that it carried the living memory of conscription in Mehmed Ali's army and the widespread practice of mothers assisting their sons in evading conscription.[40] It seems plausible therefore to assume that "Ya 'azīz 'ainī" belonged to a rich tradition of folk songs going back to the nineteenth century and reflecting popular opposition to military conscription.

Mossallam argues that "Ya 'azīz 'ainī" is layered in format. It sways back and forth between the experience of those who were sent to the war in the refrain (O Apple of my eye I want to go back home), and the bitterness of those left behind (Is crying your sport, or are you teasing me?). Crucially, Mossallam remarks that in later versions of the song, versions contemporaneous with the war, the words of the refrain changes to "My home country, My home country, and the authorities (al-sulṭa) have taken my son." Reflecting the themes of estrangement and loss, one can see why "Ya 'azīz 'ainī" resonated with thousands of peasants recruited to the ELC. On the front, the song appears mainly as a work song. "In some cases . . . the song is used in a confrontational way, where complaints about work being elaborated upon to the tune of the song. Lyrics were tied to the motion of the faas (adze), and often presented as a warning from one worker to another of an

---

37. Ibid., 55.
38. Ibid., 66n35.
39. Gaston Maspero, *Chansons populaires recueillies dans la haute-Egypte de 1900 a 1914 pendant les inspections du service des antiquités* (Service Des Antiquités de L'Egypte, 1914).
40. Olga Verlato, "'Even If the Sons of Rum Are Not like Him' the Spatial and Temporal Journey of a Late 19th Century Egyptian Song," *Middle East—Topics & Arguments* (2018): 95–107.

officer spying on them or passing by."⁴¹ These British officers considered the men's occasional singing as a "quaint feature of work." For Mossallam, by contrast, the singing "plucks at chords of estrangement in Upper Egypt prior to and during the First World War."⁴²

Radicalization on the Western Front

Far from being something that Egyptians boasted about, or something that Egypt should have pride in, as argued by the present-day Egyptian high brass, serving in the Egyptian Labor Corps was a dreadful experience that peasants avoided at all costs. This repugnance had its roots in the manner in which men were gathered from their villages, and it might have also been connected to the older hostility to military service that goes all the way back to Mehmed Ali's army, as hinted at above.⁴³ Above all, it was informed by the stories the peasants brought back home recounting not only the mortal dangers they faced, but also the humiliation and alienation they felt throughout their service in the various fields of operation—in Palestine, in Gallipoli and in France. The men's experience along these fronts is yet to be written, but Alia Mossallam, in yet another pioneering study titled "Strikes, Riots and Laughter: Al-Himamiyya Village's Experience of Egypt's 1918 Peasant Insurrection," offers one of the most compelling accounts of the peasants' experience not in Palestine, but on the Western Front in France.⁴⁴ What makes "Strikes, Riots and Laughter" particularly relevant to the question at hand is that in addition to describing life in the trenches, it provides a credible link between the peasants' war experience and their radicalization on the front, on the one hand, and on the other hand, the subsequent nationwide peasant revolt which broke out in Egypt in 1918 and which Mossallam argues marked the true beginning of the 1919 Revolution.

Key to Mossallam's analysis is the word "*sulṭa*," which as mentioned earlier, can simplistically be rendered in English as "authority," but which, Mossallam argues, is multilayered and assumes different meanings as it travels, like the songs, with the men from Egypt to Palestine, to Beirut, and to Boulogne, and from there back to Egypt.⁴⁵ Mossallam's study offers a close reading of the memoirs of ʿIṣmat Sayf

---

41. Mossallam, "'Ya ʿAziz ʿAini Ana Bidi Arawwah Baladi . . .,'" 58.

42. Ibid., 54.

43. On the hostility of Egypt's peasantry to Mehmed Ali's army, see Khaled Fahmy, *All the Pasha's Men: Mehmed Ali, His Army and the making of Modern Egypt* (Cambridge: Cambridge University Press, 1997).

44. Alia Mossallam, "Strikes, Riots and Laughter: Al-Himamiyya Village's Experience of Egypt's 1918 Peasant Insurrection" (London: LSE Middle East Centre Paper Series, 2020).

45. In his landmark article on the history of the ECL, Amīn ʿIzz El-Dīn refers to service in the ECL as "*al-shughl fī'l-sulṭa*," Amīn ʿIzz El-Dīn, "Al-shughl fī'l-sulṭa: Qiṣṣat faylaq al-ʾamal al-Miṣrī wa faylaq al-jimāl," *al-Muṣawwar*, March 7, 1969, 24–7, 61.

al-Dawla published in two volumes in 1995[46] and 1996,[47] only a few months before the author's death. Given the importance of this source, offering unique insights into the peasants' experience in northern France and their subsequent participation in the wave of revolts that erupted throughout the Egyptian countryside in 1918, it is worthwhile following Mossallam's summary of it.

Sayf al-Dawla was a renown Egyptian lawyer and pan-Arab thinker, and his *Memoirs of a Village* shows a perceptive observer of village life with a keen interest in recording the habits and mores of peasants in his village, al-Himāmiyya near Asyut in Upper Egypt. But what concerns us here is his description of his own father's experience in the Egyptian Labor Corps, which he includes in the second volume of the memoir. The entire volume, moreover, can be read as an extensive gloss on the key term "*al-sulṭa*," the combined imperial military and local administration during and after the war.

One particularly poignant tale that Sayf al-Dawla relates and that Mossallam follows closely is that of one of the villagers, Yūnis, and his relationship with his uncle, Shaykh 'Abbās, the author's father who was also the village intellectual. Shaykh 'Abbās, realizing that volunteering is exactly this, *volunteering*, concludes that it has to be based on consent. He therefore makes a subversive suggestion: peasants from his village, al-Himāmiyya, who refuse to be pressed into the Labor Corps should sign a petition stating their objections. Anticipating the petition gathering tactic of al-Wafd in late 1918, 'Abbās pursues a legal tactic that would challenge *al-sulṭa* by *al-sulṭa*. After collecting signatures of peasants from his village who objected to being volunteered into the Labor Corps, he struggles to present his petition to the authorities, *al-sulṭa*. But then, and in Mossallam's words, just when he thought he tricked the law by the law, he found himself outsmarted by it.[48] For when he attempted to use the logic of the law to opt out of the war, and when he approached the Asyut police station after many unsuccessful attempts, his petition was finally given the attention that he had requested for months. The *ma'mūr* of the station asked him if he could testify orally, and in writing, that every villager mentioned in the petition did indeed object to volunteer for the war; and also that any villager that was not on the petition would by implication be willing to volunteer. Having made sure that this included all forty-five men within the mentioned criteria, Shaykh 'Abbās testified and signed to this, not realizing that he had forgotten to include his own name in the petition. As soon as he signed, Shaykh 'Abbās was arrested, on account of the fact that, according to his own testimony, those villagers whose names were not in the petition would not object to being volunteered for the war.

At this point Yūnis, 'Abbās's nephew, steps in. Seeing that his uncle was dragged to the Labor Corps after his attempt to spare his fellow villagers had failed, Yūnis steps forward and offers himself as a replacement to 'Abbās, and his account is the

---

46. 'Iṣmat Sayf al-Dawla, *Mudhakkirāt Qaryah* (Cairo: Dār Al-Hilāl, 1995).
47. 'Iṣmat Sayf al-Dawla, *Mashāyikh Jabal Al-Badārī* (Cairo: Dār Al-Hilāl, 1996).
48. Mossallam, "Strikes, Riots and Laughter," 17.

only one we have of any peasant who served on the Western Front and returned alive. Yūnis's account, as told by Sayf al-Dawla, is the most compelling account we have so far of the experience of Egyptian peasants in the First World War. Yūnis provides graphic details of the brutal existence these men faced in the trenches: the meager clothes they were given, the hostility of the locals, the bad food, the cold, the mud, the stench, and the disease. And all of this because *al-sulṭa* decreed to send them to "a crazy war [that had] erupted in Europe [which Europeans] called the 'World War'—while it was actually their own."[49]

As miserable as the men felt, they also soon realized that being sent as workers meant that they possessed a key asset that they can use against *al-sulṭa*, namely their own labor. In their camp near Calais, one of them, Thābit, is appointed as their leader, *rayyis*, and they are assigned to a Moroccan sergeant, Khalīfa, who acted as their translator and overseer.

Soon Rayyis Thābit gives them an important lesson.

"What matters most to the French," he tells them, "is that we don't stop working. So every time we needed something, we would sleep in a little longer; so the French would come and shout in their language, and the Moroccan would tell them that we didn't want to work because the food was too little, and they would provide us with more. Everything we needed, even the heavy tea, even tobacco, even red meat, we would never ask for. We learned that if we 'asked' we would never get what we requested." We learned that they are people who "*khaf ma yekhtushuh*—have fear but no shame." Our weapon was ready. We stop working and Thabit would say "The men want this . . ." and they bring it straight away.[50]

This audacity, however, soon attracts the wrath of the French military authorities. Yūnis explains how, when winter set in, one of his fellow laborers, Qubaysī, already sick and malnourished, literally froze to death. The men ask for hot water to cleanse his body and a blanket to use as a shroud, but the French authorities refuse both and rush to snatch the dead body, pile it on a wooden carriage and take it away. The group was thrown into panic. To die away from home, in *ghurba*, is one thing, but not to be buried properly meant another degree of loss; it meant oblivion. The group therefore decided to go on strike, to stand as one, and to demand to go back home. The strike of food and work went on for five days at the end of which a French general dubbed as "Jinn el-nar" (Jinn of fire, a pun on general) comes to negotiate with the men. His negotiation fails so he ordered them to stand in the rain. In defiance, they sit down. The general returns; an argument ensues; al-Rayyis Thābit loses his temper; attacks the general and kills him. At this point, the French soldiers fired at point blank killing Thābit and the entire group, with the exception of Yūnis, who feigned death and lived to tell the story from his veranda, *al-mandara*, back in al-Himāmiyya.

49. Sayf al-Dawla, *Mashāyikh Jabal Al-Badārī*, 16. All translations are Mossallam's.
50. Ibid., 13.

What is noteworthy about Sayf al-Dawla's memoir is that it does not stop at offering this unique account of the ELC peasants on the Western Front. Rather, the last-third of the second volume takes us back to al-Himāmiyya and follows a particularly brutal power struggle over land, land owned by absentee landlords who reside in Cairo, and which the peasants consider to be rightly theirs. When Yūnis returns from the front, in 1918, the countryside is already teaming with rebellion. After four long years of hardship during which time peasants saw their cattle snatched, their crops confiscated, and their men dragged to serve in a war that meant nothing to them, they finally had enough. Already in summer and autumn of 1918, a good six months before the official outbreak of the revolution, the countryside is seeing acts of sabotage, of arson, and of murder. As was the case elsewhere in the world: in Algeria, in West Africa, and earlier in Russia, peasants rose against *al-sulṭa*. In Egypt, this peasant revolt, which Ellis Goldberg and Reinhardt Schulze have dubbed the largest peasant revolution in modern Egyptian history,[51] is the true beginnings of the 1919 Revolution. The *sulṭa* that these peasants rebelled against was at once that of the British military authorities who occupied their country, the authority of the Egyptian government who did their bidding by requisitioning their produce and snatching their men, and the authority of the landlords who counseled moderation in hopes of wringing concession after the war.

The War, the Peasants, the Wafd . . .

The fact that peasants played a decisive role in the 1919 Revolution was never contested. For example, in his account of peasant activities during the revolution, Schulze gives a vivid description of subversive activities undertaken by peasants.

> [They] ransacked a police station. . . . They looted granaries and cotton silos, burned down the buildings, and stole the harvest. . . . In the province of Daqahliyya almost every *'izab* [sic, i.e., latifundia] was destroyed. The [peasants] sabotaged the irrigation system, drove away the cattle, and robbed local bank branches. Instead of planting cotton [they] inundated the cotton fields . . . and planted rice.[52]

Most prominently, peasants attacked the rail system that was the backbone of the transport network. They burned down railway stations and damaged tracks throughout the country.[53]

---

51. Goldberg, "Peasants in Revolt"; Schulze, "Colonization and Resistance."
52. Schulze, "Colonization and Resistance," 192.
53. Goldberg, "Peasants in Revolt"; Joel Beinin, *Workers and Peasants in the Middle East* (Cambridge: Cambridge University Press, 2001), 87; John Chalcraft, *Popular Politics in the Making of the Modern Middle East* (Cambridge: Cambridge University Press, 2016), 209.

What is being contested are the timing and purpose behind this peasant revolutionary activism. Most commonly, peasant mobilization is understood to have taken place *after* the British authorities had arrested Sa'd and his colleagues on March 8, 1919, and ordered them to be exiled them to Malta. Goldberg sees the peasant contribution to the 1919 Revolution as a last stage of a chain reaction that started with the arrest of the Wafd leadership followed by the student strike, then the strike of the Egyptian bar which resulted in a breakdown of the court system. "At first, the state was paralyzed and the court system rapidly broke down, and it was then that peasants began to play a significant role in the revolt."[54] The insurrection, accordingly, is seen initially as an urban phenomenon which peasants joined only later on.

British observers typically attributed the sudden upsurge of peasant activism to be the result of cynical manipulation by the Wafd cadres after seeing their leaders exiled. "Tawwaf," the anonymous author of the pamphlet *Egypt, in 1919*, puts it clearly when he argues that:

> the deliberate way in which the destruction was directed at vital points of communication and the skill shown in destroying the railway, reveal unmistakably the workings of an intelligence far ahead either of the fellah or of the type of young effendi who certainly acted as the intermediary between the ignorant instrument and the brain of the plot.[55]

In explaining the causes of peasant activism, the British could never accept that such activism was anything but an instinctive response to economic hardship. Peasants were seen as incapable of rational political reasoning, and their activism accordingly could be explained only as a result of manipulation, intrigue, or simply as a reaction to hunger. "That the Egyptian peasantry was incapable of genuine political thought or action had been the single most enduring axiom of [British] rule since its inception."[56] Goldberg, on his part, sees that "Egyptian peasant unrest had more to do with hunger, threatening starvation, apportioning the cost of was-induced inflation, and forced servitude than the foregone opportunity costs or cultural dissonance."[57] The widespread attack on railways, therefore, was informed by the peasants' desire to suspend "the transport of edible commodities to the cities, which had little to offer the countryside in exchange."[58]

By contrast, Schulze offers a complex picture of peasant community which he sees being divided between landowners who saw their interests represented by the Wafd, sharecroppers and agricultural laborers, and small-scale farmers. For

---

54. Goldberg, "Peasants in Revolt," 274.
55. Tawwaf, *Egypt, 1919, Being a Narrative of Certain Incidents of the Rising in Upper Egypt*, 3.
56. Jakes, *Egypt's Occupation*, 251.
57. Goldberg, "Peasants in Revolt," 262.
58. Ibid., 272.

him, this heterogeneous agrarian society was at variance with the Wafd nationalist leadership:

> Within the rural community . . . the three concepts [of] *istiqlal* [independence], *huriyya* [freedom] and *'adl* [justice] indicated a reality other than that perceived by the afandiyya. When a nationalist representative from Cairo came to a village and delivered an impassioned speech about Egypt's freedom, the fellahin in the audience applied these concepts to their environment. They understood such a speech as a challenge to liberate their district from the aggression formed by the restrictions and repression of colonization [abetted by the Egyptian government and the local elites].[59]

Like Schulze, Mossallam understand peasants' political imagination to be complex and multilayered. But, crucially, she sees this peasant political imagination and the attendant activism as preceding Saad's arrest on March 8, 1919. Like Jakes who argues that throughout 1919 peasants were "reactivating solidarities they had forged [a decade earlier] in 1909,"[60] Mossallam considers that peasant political activism was not triggered by the arrest and exile of the Wafd leadership. Moreover, she reads the numerous reports of "criminal activities" that bombarded the Public Security Office of the Ministry of Interior throughout 1918 as indicative, not of criminality, but of complex revolutionary activism.[61] And more clearly than any other student of the 1919 Revolution, Mossallam links peasant activism throughout 1918 and 1919 not only to the privations witnessed throughout the war years, the forced recruitments of hundreds of thousands of peasants into the ELC, or their subsequent experience in the war on different fronts but, most importantly, to their radicalization on the Western Front. Above all, what makes Mossallam's account of the peasant contribution to the 1919 Revolution truly exceptional is that she avoids slipping into simplistic causal explanations to account for the remarkable sophistication of peasant political imagination. For revolutions are never neat, rational phenomena, and they can never be firmly controlled by any one faction. Once the peasants' defiance of *al-sulṭa* spilled over from a mutiny against their European military commanders on the front into a revolt against their own landlords as well as the local civilian and the British military authorities, there was no stopping the peasants from revolting against the revolution itself. "The peasants see the revolution building, and consider the possibility of rising against it once it is over, to make sure they are ruled by [themselves]. . . . [T]he villagers' concerns are foremost in the revolution, and do not relate to nationalist interests, which they perceive to be almost as oppressive as imperial interests."[62]

---

59. Schulze, "Colonization and Resistance," 188.
60. Jakes, *Egypt's Occupation*, 250.
61. Mossallam, "Strikes, Riots and Laughter," 7.
62. Ibid., 20.

. . . and the Army

Like all revolutions, the Egyptian Revolution of 1919 is a complex historical event, and despite attracting much scholarship, we still lack a detailed account of the ideas and actions of the multitudes who participated in it. Recent Egyptian historiography of it has been shaped in no small degree by the latent hostility that the 1952 regime had always had toward it, and in particular to the Wafd and the liberal democratic principles that it represented, no matter how faulty this representation might have been.[63] Far from being a coherent or comprehensive account of this mammoth event, the previous quoted text is a brief summary of some of the more recent critical engagements with the revolution that invite us to locate its origins not on March 8, 1919, when Saad was arrested, but in a much earlier period, in the summer and autumn of 1918 when the countryside was teeming with insurrection, and not to restrict the revolution to Cairo and other cities, but to look for the origins in the countryside among peasants who saw their livelihoods destroyed after four years of war.

The sacrifices Egyptian peasants endured during the First World War are part and parcel of the complex reasons that prompted the peasantry to lead city dwellers in the big revolt that became the 1919 Revolution. A key factor in this hardship was being "volunteered" in the Egyptian Labor Force. Hundreds of thousands of Egyptian peasants were dragged into serving in this dreaded force that was part of the British imperial war effort. The months they spent in the different fields of operation—in Sinai, in Palestine, in Gallipoli, and on the Western Front—hardened them and threw into sharp relief the injustice from which they suffered back home. While most were eager to return to the comfort of their loved ones, few must have also been radicalized on the front. Upon returning home and upon finding that their compatriots had fared only slightly better due to what *al-suḷta* had subjected them to, the situation was then rife for a nationwide revolution to erupt.

However, the present Egyptian army is now making spurious claims that distort the historical record. By relying on a scuba diver with a penchant for history, the high brass have convinced themselves that the Egyptian Labor Force was composed of soldiers, not of peasants; that this force was part of the Egyptian, not the British army; and that the sacrifices endured during the war were endured by the military, not by the civilian population. Behind these claims is not the desire to point out a long-forgotten chapter in the nation's history or to recognize the untold sacrifices of thousands of Egyptians, but rather to have the opportunity to

---

63. 'Abd al-'Azīm Ḥammād, "Fī Dhikrāhā Al-Mi'awiyya: Limādhā Kariha Rijāl Yulyū Thawrat 1919? (On Its Centenary: Why Did the July Men Hate the 1919 Revolution?)," *al-Shurūq*, November 16, 2018, https://www.shorouknews.com/columns/view.aspx?cdate=16112018&id=87fe258a-a3f5-40f0-aeb2-2603adbe4c59&fbclid=IwAR0LqkhnzIsRrjG-dbOqssq6RH_sX9BVHu3a_AK8Ed6egCqUPpOZq6qy01Q.

"raise the Egyptian flag in London and in Greece next to the mightiest armies of the world."[64]

The army can have its flags and it can enjoy its photo ops. But the sacrifices of thousands of peasants who were recruited to serve in the First World War, and the inspired activism of many more Egyptians in cities and in the countryside in the 1919 Revolution will continue to be studied and analyzed with the care and respect that they deserve.

---

64. https://www.facebook.com/EgyArmySpox/photos/a.394602110670777/394602790670709/?type=1&theater, accessed June 20, 2021.

CONCLUSION

Robert D. Springborg

This volume begs the question of what parallels, if any, exist between the two great popular uprisings in Egypt's modern history—1919 and 2011. In broad terms they were remarkably similar. Smoldering discontent, fueled in 1919 by wartime sacrifices imposed by the British, and in 2011 by a self-indulged ruling family seeking to hand its power down to the next generation, suddenly exploded in mass demonstrations, with Cairo the epicenter but with reverberations elsewhere in the country. Protests were initially met with repression, which proved insufficient to quell them, thus inducing incumbent regimes to offer concessions: limited independence from Britain in the case of the former; removal of the Mubarak family and those closely associated with it in the latter. Both uprisings were reflections of regional, even global trends in which Egypt was at the forefront: anti-colonialism in 1919 and the Arab Spring version of spreading worldwide discontent with globalization and neo-liberalism in 2011.

Neither was a revolution either in form or consequence. Commencing less than two years after Russia's October 1917 Bolshevik revolution, Egypt's 1919 "revolution" was not sparked nor led by a Leninist party. Indeed, this spontaneous protest was cross-class: its leadership composed of landowners and the emerging urban middle class, or *effendiya*. Occurring thirty-two years after the Islamic revolution in Iran, Egypt's 2011 uprising was similarly cross-class, inclusive of both Islamists and secularists, and not led by clerics or a vanguard party. Objectives in 1919 and 2011 in Egypt were more limited than their temporal counterpart uprisings in Russia and Iran. Protesters in Egypt were not seeking to empower revolutionaries to destroy existing orders and construct entirely new political economies, but to replace the actual and symbolic regime leaders with new elites who did not profess agendas of transformative change. Both 1919 and 2011 were protests, not revolutions.

Their political, economic, and social consequences were accordingly more limited than those in Russia and Iran, to say nothing of France post 1789 or China post 1949. Although 1919 led to Britain's Unilateral Declaration of Egyptian Independence in February 1922, followed by the issuing of the 1923 constitution and holding of elections to the new parliament, the British occupation continued, legitimated by several reserve clauses in the declaration. It was only finally ended in June 1956. British political and economic influence, exercised primarily through the monarchy, was not unlike that it had been under the so-called veiled protectorate terminated by the British at the outbreak of the First World War. The most popular political organization associated with 1919, the Wafd Party, led primarily by members of the landowning class, suffered from ever diminishing political power from 1924 until being dissolved by the new military government in 1952.

In the wake of the 2011 uprising the core of the Egyptian regime, the military, succeeded first in dividing the protest movement, primarily by permitting the Muslim Brothers to take a leading political role, and then in grabbing absolute power by staging a popularly supported coup in July 2013. Protester demands for political, economic, and social changes were thus frustrated in the wake of 1919 and 2011. Both thereby demonstrated the limited structural changes that typically flow from popular uprisings absent effective political organization and facing reasonably well-institutionalized regimes that have control of the means of coercion. By contrast, Lenin and Khomeini understood that if the incumbent regime's vital base of coercive instruments was not divided and overcome, the regime would reassert its power. Consequently, these revolutionaries believed that armed force, rather than unarmed protests, was the key to success.

This, however, does not mean that 1919 and 2011 lacked serious consequences, both good and bad, even if those consequences were not manifested in profound and lasting institutional changes, as in Russia and Iran. But as Edmund Burke so eloquently observed for the French Revolution, dramatic changes, most especially the destruction of sociopolitical institutions and replacement of them by "revolutionary" ones, can have extremely costly results.[1]

Balance sheets for the 1919 and 2011 "moments of enthusiasm" have entries in three columns: macro/global, mezzo/national, and micro/sub-national. At the highest, global level, they both strongly signaled that Egyptians rejected existing arrangements then commonplace in the Middle East or even much of the world. In 1919 those "arrangements" were imperialism, while in 2011 they were dictatorial rule supported by external powers. In both 1919 and 2011 the Egyptian uprisings were globally newsworthy events with significant reverberations elsewhere where nationalists were struggling against colonial rule or, in 2011, where oppressed populations were seeking dignity as manifested by true citizenship and fairer distribution of national wealth. Paradoxically the dramatic events in Egypt may have had more profound impacts elsewhere than in Egypt itself.

At the national level the balance sheet is mixed and more positive for 1919 than 2011. The dramatic events of 1919 definitively commenced decolonization, even if that process played out for another generation. It marked the onset of national governmental institution building, including the drafting of a liberal constitution, formation of a popularly elected parliament, demands to nationalize the Mixed Courts that were completely realized by 1949, creation in 1925 of the first public university in Egypt, intensification of pressure to Egyptianize the military, which in 1936 opened the doors of the military academy to citizens, two of whom—Gamal

---

1. Edmund Burke, *Reflections on the Revolution in France* (London: J. Dodsley, 1790).

Abd al Nasser and Anwar al Sadat—were subsequently to become presidents. It also contributed to support for bringing under Egyptian ownership significant parts of the economy, such as by Talat Harb's Bank Misr, which rapidly expanded its industrial activities post 1923. The impact on inter-religious relationships, as described in this volume by Mark Bebawi and Philip Marfleet, was mixed. It stimulated both the growth of Islamism, especially in its Muslim Brotherhood variant and Coptic identification. But the conscious effort by the 1919 leadership, especially that of those who became the leaders of the Wafd Party, to present the uprising as a joint Muslim, Christian, and Jewish undertaking, left a legacy of at least the ideal, if not necessarily the real state of inter-religious relations. The flowering of those relations occurred over the following twenty-five or so years and contributed to much of the dynamism of the economy at that time.

But it must also be noted that the exuberant 1919–24 period contributed to the "counter-revolution" successfully engineered by the tripartite alliance of the British, the monarchy, and monarchial allied political elites, especially landowners. In other words, that moment of enthusiasm stimulated a backlash which its protagonists were incapable of withstanding. In that regard it signaled what was to occur post 2011.

Claims for positive national effects of the 2011 uprising are contentious, especially among Egyptians. The military regime has gradually shifted its interpretation of events, initially aligning itself with them but now contending that the "chaos" posed a threat to the nation, a threat only averted by the military seizing power. Among those opposed to military rule this is tantamount to political heresy, as they believe they rather than the military represent the national will and have the capability better to implement it. In their view, their "revolution" was stolen by army officers. But even in these circles there are few regrets about the actual "moment of enthusiasm" of 2011. They believe it has residual symbolic power, as attested to by the military regime effacing any and all symbols of it, such as graffiti and memorials, of which the overhaul of Midan al Tahrir is but one example. It presumably was also a practical learning experience in popular mobilization, which given favorable circumstances might recur.

The rewards of 2011, to the extent they exist for the nation, tend to be intangible. The costs, by contrast—key of which is greatly enhanced military control of the polity, economy, and even the society and its collective official memory—are real. Khaled Fahmy's expose' in the preceding chapter of the military's rewriting of Egypt's contribution to the First World War is illustrative of history being rewritten by the victor, in this case to glorify the armed forces. The military's subordination of all institutions of government—whether courts, parliament, local government, or the executive administration—has undermined civil governance now and into the indefinite future. Egregious violations of human rights and civil liberties not only are tragic for those concerned but sow seeds of resentment that may ultimately have violent political repercussions, further debilitating both governance and national solidarity. That these costs are recognized and lamented by many Egyptians is suggested by remorse over the replacement of Mubarak by Sisi.

The overall balance sheet of positive and negative micro/societal level changes resulting from 1919 and 2011 also favors the former. The chapters in this volume by Beth Baron and Mohamed Elsayed illustrate how 1919 contributed to the development of professional health services for Egyptian women and national consciousness among Egyptian Suez Canal workers, respectively. In the latter case that consciousness helped propel subsequent development of skills that made possible Nasser's nationalization of the Suez Canal Company in 1956. Taqadum al-Khatib's chapter on opposition activists in exile draws direct parallels between the two eras, noting that other countries, especially those hostile to the incumbent regime in Cairo, are happy to provide sanctuary and sustenance to those exiles. These nodes of external opposition played a role in 1919, whereas contemporary Egyptian political exiles are increasingly marginalized from both Egyptian and their host countries' politics as the latter, notably Turkey and Qatar, seek reconciliation with the Sisi regime.

Structural, situational, and ideological factors account for the more positive impacts and legacies of the 1919 as opposed to the 2011 uprising. Although brutal and repressive, British colonial rule was a softer target in 1919 than the military regime in 2011. Losing some power in Egypt was less threatening to the British than that prospect was for the Egyptian military in 2011. The former could play a long game even after granting formal independence, as the British did. The military, on the other hand, fears the game might end abruptly were it to cede substantial power to civilians. For one thing, the self-perception by the armed forces that the nation is but an extension of the military would no longer square with reality, thus weakening it ideologically as well as through possible internal divisions. For another, newly empowered civilians, like those in Argentina or Chile, might well seek retribution against political, economic, and other abuses by the military since it seized power in 1952. In 2011 the Egyptian military felt it had its back to the political wall, whereas for the British 1919 was but a battle in what they perceived would be a protracted struggle. The British could thus be less violent and more conciliatory than the Egyptian military. One might also add the ideological factor of liberal imperialism which Jamie Whidden and Zeinab Abul-Magd describe in this volume as having counter balanced more diehard versions of Britain's appropriate role and behavior in the colonial world, including in Egypt in 1919. British decision makers were thus more divided between reformers and hardliners than were their Egyptian military counterparts in 2011. It was those reformers who ultimately played a vital role in determining the British reaction to the 1919 uprising, as attested to by the granting of formal independence. Colonialists, despite in many cases imbibing of racism as Kyle Anderson describes in Chapter 7, had less at stake and were more divided than today's national military officers, whose contempt toward civilians resembles the earlier era's racism.

The other side of the 1919 and 2011 equations, meaning the protesters, also led to the more favorable outcomes of the former year's uprising. In a word, the 1919 protesters were less divided. Islamism as an organized political force did not emerge for almost another decade as Philip Marfleet's chapter describes. In 1919 the unity of the nation, meaning that of Muslim, Christian, and Jewish Egyptians, could be presented as a believable motivating slogan. While antagonisms between those of different faiths existed, they did not take organized, divisive political form. Class divisions, which were more profound in 1919 than in 2011 primarily because of the profound gaps between peasants and landowners and secondarily between newly emerging industrialists and workers, were ameliorated by traditional clientelistic ties that tied the underclasses to the owners of the means of production through reciprocal relationships. "Egypt for the Egyptians," the slogan of the ʿUrābī movement that began almost half a century before 1919, reflected the primary division, which was between Egyptians and British.

By contrast, in 2011, many Egyptians believed they shared more in common with the military regime than with even other protesters, a feeling that intensified when the Muslim Brotherhood won control of both parliament and the presidency in 2011–12. The year 1919 was basically a two-player game—colonialists versus nationalists—whereas 2011 rapidly became a three-person game—military, Islamists, and others—in which the military was far the strongest actor. The momentum generated by the 1919 uprising propelled the course of establishing constitutional, nominally independent government, before being overwhelmed by the British and monarchial led, political "counter-revolution" that culminated in the abrogation of the 1923 constitution some seven years later. In 2011, by contrast, protester momentum and coherence began to abate before the end of that year because of latent internal divisions within the movement and because it faced resolute, manipulative opposition from a military willing to deploy lethal force.

It is tempting to conclude that these two moments of enthusiasm are akin to unconsummated political romances, in which Egypt flirted with profound if not revolutionary change, but then lost its nerve. Unlike France in the late eighteenth century, Russia in the early twentieth century, China in the mid-twentieth century, or Iran in the late 1970s, Egypt's "revolutionary vanguard" was too irresolute, deployed too few organized cadres, and, in 2011, too divided to permanently tilt the balance of power away from colonialists and their "running dogs" in 1919 or the military and its supporters in 2011. Even substantial, permanent political and economic reform could not be won because poor leadership coupled with inadequate organization faced skilled incumbent actors who maintained control of the means of coercion, whose importance the opposition insufficiently appreciated and failed adequately to counter.

But this negative view may be too dialectical. Edmund Burke's critique of the French Revolution is also applicable to subsequent ones in Russia, China, and Iran. They too destroyed institutions, imposed reigns of terror on their citizens, militarized, and engaged in costly wars. Egypt avoided these outcomes in 1919 and largely again in 2011. Possibly the balance of power between opposition and incumbents, coupled with the internal divisions of the former and strength of the latter, by rendering revolution impossible, saved the nation from worse calamities.

But while that balance was not so unfavorable in 1919 to also prevent substantial reforms, it was in 2011. Far from facilitating reform, the Egyptian version of the Arab Spring ultimately polarized rather than united the nation and provided the opportunity for the military to further entrench its rule, which, although dictatorial, is not as calamitous as that by Napoleon, Stalin, Mao, or Khomeini. But given its reliance on repression, the prospect that military rule will stimulate a third uprising in modern Egypt is not fanciful. The next, if there is one, has a better chance of falling into the dialectical revolutionary category than the previous two. Failures in 1919 and again in 2011 by opposition forces to institutionalize effective, accountable, civilian-led governance led to the 1952 and then to the 2013 coup. The latter in particular is now producing the thesis that could stimulate a revolutionary antithesis in classical dialectical fashion.

CONTRIBUTORS

Beth Baron is distinguished professor of history at the City College and Graduate Center at the City University of New York and director of the Middle East and Middle Eastern American Center at the CUNY Graduate Center. She is a former editor of the *International Journal of Middle East Studies* and past president of the Middle East Studies Association of North America. Her books include *The Orphan Scandal: Christian Missionaries and the Rise of the Muslim Brotherhood*, *Egypt as a Woman: Nationalism, Gender, and Politics*, and *The Women's Awakening in Egypt: Culture, Society, and the Press*.

H. A. Hellyer is visiting fellow at the Centre for Islamic Studies at the Faculty of Asian and Middle Eastern Studies at the University of Cambridge, and scholar at the Carnegie Endowment for International Peace. A scholar and author in politics, international studies, and religion, particularly in the West and the Arab World, he is also senior associate fellow at the Royal United Services Institute and visiting professor at the University of Technology's Centre for Advanced Studies on Islam, Science and Civilisation in Malaysia. He previously held academic posts at Harvard University and the University of Warwick. His seven books and monographs include *A Revolution Undone: Egypt's Road Beyond Revolt*, *Muslims of Europe: The "Other" Europeans*, and *A Sublime Way: The Sufi Way of the Makkan Sages*. The author of some thirty book chapters and articles, he is widely published in various international media outlets.

James Whidden is professor of history at the Acadia University. He holds a PhD from the School of Oriental and African Studies (SOAS), University of London, and has taught in England, Canada, and the United States. Other publications include books, *Monarchy and Modernity: Politics, Islam and Neo-colonialism between the Wars* and *Egypt: British Colony, Imperial Capital*. He has also written encyclopedia entries, journal articles, reviews, and short stories.

Kyle J. Anderson is the author of *The Egyptian Labor Corps: Race, Space, and Place in the First World War*, along with journal articles and encyclopedia entries on the history and historiography of labor, race, and the First World War in the Middle East. He has presented at conferences on topics related to the intersection of rural labor, politics, and race in colonial and post-colonial Egypt. His research has been funded by the Social Science Research Council and the American Research Center in Egypt. He is fluent in Arabic, and teaches classes about Muslim History, the modern Middle East, World History, and historiography at SUNY Old Westbury.

Mark Bebawi is a published author, photographer, and media content producer. He has lived on three continents (Africa, Europe, and North America), speaks three languages (English, Arabic, and French), and holds three university degrees (from Exeter, Rice, and Oxford). Between 2002 and 2018 he hosted and produced a syndicated weekly radio show for the Pacifica Network, with guests such as Noam Chomsky, Richard Wolff, Seymour Hersh, Joseph Stiglitz, Daniel Ellsberg, Robert Fisk, Hellen Thomas, Gore Vidal, Howard Zinn, Chalmers Johnson, Abdullahi Ahmad An-Na'im, and many others.

Mohamed Elsayed is a history researcher and informal educator in the arts and culture working on projects in Egypt and the United Kingdom. His core mission is to work on decentralizing and democratizing access to social science and humanities knowledge and knowledge production in Egypt. He regularly contributes to initiatives focusing on humanities education and public history in Cairo and the Suez Canal Zone, and runs an educational tourism initiative. He earned his MA in history from the School of Oriental and African Studies at the University of London. His research typically focuses on labor studies, memory studies, and urban history.

Philip Marfleet is emeritus professor of social science at the University of East London. He has published widely on social and political affairs in the Middle East, on global migrations and on refugee affairs. Publications on Egypt include (with Rabab El Mahdi) *Egypt: the Moment of Change* and *Egypt: Contested Revolution*. He is editor, with Keiko Sakai, of *Iraq since the Invasion: People and Politics in a State of Conflict*.

Robert D. Springborg is research fellow of the Italian Institute of International Affairs, Rome, and adjunct professor at the Simon Fraser University, Vancouver. Formerly he was professor of National Security Affairs at the Naval Postgraduate School; the holder of the MBI Al Jaber Chair in Middle East Studies at the School of Oriental and African Studies, London, where he also served as director of the London Middle East Institute; the director of the American Research Center in Egypt; university professor of Middle East Politics at Macquarie University in Sydney, Australia; and has also taught at the University of Pennsylvania, the University of California, Berkeley, the College of Europe, the Paris School of International Affairs of Sciences Po, and the University of Sydney. In 2016 he was Kuwait Foundation Visiting Scholar, Kennedy School, Harvard University. His most recent books are *Egypt* and *Political Economies of the Middle East and North Africa*; and with Hicham Alaoui co-edited *The Political Economy of Education in the Arab World*.

Taqadum Al-Khatib earned his PhD in 2019, as part of a program exchange between Princeton University and the Free University of Berlin. He is now a postdoctoral fellow at the Free University of Berlin, and nonresident fellow at the Arab Center for Research and Policy Studies in Qatar. With his main research interests in history, cultural studies, and Middle East politics, he published his first book on the history of Egyptian Jews during the period of 1915–52.

Zeinab Abul-Magd is Professor of Middle Eastern history at Oberlin College. She received her PhD in history and political economy and MA in Arab Studies from Georgetown University, Washington, D.C., and BA in Political Science from Cairo University, Egypt. Her latest books include *Militarizing the Nation: the Army, Business, and Revolution in Egypt* (2017) and *Imagined Empires: A History of Revolt in Egypt* (2013). She published several books and book chapters in Arabic, including "Allenby wa-Thawrat 1919...Qira'a fi Daw' al-Arshif al-Biritani" in Naser Ibrahim (ed.), *al-Thawara wa-l-Tarikh: 1919 Ba'd Ma'at 'Am* (2019). She published reports at *Foreign Policy*, Carnegie Endowment, the Atlantic Council, Middle East Institute, *Jadaliyya*, and *Mada Masr*. Furthermore, she wrote occasional Arabic columns for many Egyptian newspapers, including *al-Masry al-Youm/Egypt Independent*, *al-Tahrir*, *al-Badil*, and *al-Manassa*.

Khaled Fahmy is Sultan Qaboos bin Sa'id Professor of Modern Arabic Studies at the University of Cambridge. His research interests lie in the social and cultural history of modern Egypt and his publications include a book on the social history of the Egyptian army in the first half of the nineteenth century (*All the Pasha's Men: Mehmed Ali, His Army and the Making of Modern Egypt*, 1997), a biography of Mehmed Ali (*Mehmed Ali: From Ottoman Governor to Ruler of Egypt*, 2008), and, an award-winning book on the intersection of law and medicine in nineteenth century Egypt (*In Quest of Justice: Islamic Law and Forensic Medicine in Modern Egypt*, 2018). Since the outbreak of the January 2011 Revolution, he has been a regular contributor to Egyptian and international media.

INDEX

Abbas, Raouf 32
Abdel-Nasser, Gamal 74
Abugideiri, Hibba 10
Abul-Magd, Zeinab 5
al-Afghani, Jamal al-Din 90
African Americans 136, 156, 158
African slave trade 139
Ahmad, Muhammad 140–1
Ahmed, Jamal Mohammed 31
Aini, Kasr El 13
Ali, Muhammad 3
Allenby, Edmund 5, 39, 46, 106, 113–33
   as colonizer 113–15
   on eve of February 28 128–32
   force and 1919 Revolution 119–21
   meets Egyptians 116–19
   overview 113–15
   and Pasha, Saad relation 124–8, 132–3
   supports Arabs 122–4
American Civil War 139
Amos, Maurice 19
Amos, Sheldon 19
Amraḍ al-Nisa' (Diseases of Women) 17–18
anarchism 41–4
Anderson, Benedict 56
Anderson, Kyle 5, 189, 191
Anglo-Egyptian army 141
Anglo-French employees 40
Anglo-Ottoman relationship 138
"ANZAC" battalions 148
"Arabi and His Companions" 29–51
Arab Revolt army 122
Armanious, Febe 57
Armstrong, John 56
Arshyiat El-Abeed 47
Ashur, Muhammad Badrawi 109
El Ayat, Mohamed 35
Aydin, Cemil 137

Baer, Gabriel 139–40
Baker, Samuel 139
Bakhtin, Mikhail 87
baladi 98–9
Balfour, Andrew 19
Balfour Declaration 122–3
Bambouties 30–1, 30 n.4
Barakat, Ali 150
Baring, Evelyn 75
Baron, Beth 6, 69, 86
Battle of 'Ayn Jalut 186
Battle of Hittin 186
Battle of Nizib 186
Bayly, C. A. 62
Bebawi, Mark 4, 205
Beinin, Joel 32–3, 41, 74, 77, 85–6
Bey, Clot 20
Bey, Grant 30
Bey, Shukry 9
al-Bishri, Tariq 6, 60–5
Black Africans 138, 145–57
bolshevik movement 42
Bonaparte, Napoleon 3
Bonin, Hubert 39
Boutros-Ghali, Mirrit 55, 59, 63–4, 68
British responses to Egypt's revolution of 1919 93–112
   constitutional reform 94–5
   cultural nationalism 99
   educational reform 97–8
   Egyptian nationalism by 1919 96–100
   imperial reforms 104–8
   reaction 100–4, 108–11
broke barriers movement 84–5
Brown, Nathan 78
Brubaker, Rogers 57
Burke, Edmund 2
Burton, Richard F. 140

Cairo Maternity House 20
Camel Corps 80

Camel Transport Corps 117
canal workers 29–51
  and colonial company towns 46–8
  communities 33
  Egypt's revolution of 1919 in *L'Etat du Canal de Suez* and 30–1
  histories of 31–4
  SCC and its workers 34–5
  strike 35–6
  transnational solidarity in age of nationalism 36–43
  urban experience of 43–4
Chalcraft, John 32
Chatham House Version and Other Middle Eastern Studies (Kedourie) 95 n.7
Christian-Muslim Egyptian identities 53–71
  and 1911 Congresses 61–9
  and 1919 Revolution 61–9
  and feelings of national unity 59–61
  of internal "other" 54–9
Church Missionary Society (CMS) projects 58
class-based solidarity 34
coalition 4
Cole, Juan 32
colonial company towns 46–8
colonial health-care system 6
colonial hierarchies 15–19
colonial power 75–6
colonial racism 135–58
  global color line in First World War 145–9
  of Muslims 138
  petition to French Embassy, March 20, 1919 135–7
  racial caste system in Egypt 138–44
  and slavery 150–6
color line 136–7
Coloured Labour Corps 137, 149
commission of 1918 19–22
communism 41–4
Communist Party of Egypt (CPE) 88
Congresses (1911) 61–9
consumerism 97
Cooper, Frederick 57
Copts 53–71, 54 n.2
  Arabic in tenth century, adoption of 56–7

communal identity 59
  as Egyptians 57–9
  identity 53–71
  Muslim relations 60–1
  political identity 59
  religion 56
  religious ideas and practices 57–8
corporate identity 39–40
cosmopolitanism 43, 49–50
CPE; *see* Communist Party of Egypt (CPE)
Cromer, Lord 75–6
cultural nationalism 99

Davis, Stephen 57
el-Dawla, 'Ismat Saif 194–6
al-Dawla, Sayf 196
dayas 20
Deeb, Marius 78, 82–3, 89
Department of Public Health 16–18, 24
de Tocqueville, Alexis 2
al-Din, Amin Izz 32, 150
divide-and-rule policy 61
Dobbin, Roy 11, 15–19, 25
domiciliary model of delivery 11
Douglass, Frederick 156
Du Bois, W. E. B. 156
Durrell, Lawrence 153

Ebeid, Makram 4
EEF; *see* Egyptian Expeditionary Force (EEF)
effendiyya 96, 97 n.19, 98–9, 104 n.39
Egypt as a Woman (Baron) 69
Egyptian Armed Forces 183–202
  in 1914 187–8
  in First World War 183–7
  participation in Great War 183–4
  peasants/soldiers 188–92, 198–202
  radicalization on western front 195–8
  Ṣabrī collaboration with 184–7
Egyptian Conscription Law 190
Egyptian diaspora 160–1
Egyptian Expeditionary Force (EEF) 115, 119–21, 192
Egyptian Labor Corps (ELC) 117, 146–53, 157, 190, 193, 198, 200
Egyptian National Party (ENP) 161
Egyptians in exile during two revolutions (1919 and 2011) 159–81

diaspora youth politics in times of political turmoil (post-2013)   178–81
diasporic activity, efficacy of   162
Egyptian diaspora, definition of   160–1
Germany and nationalist movement   165–70
host countries, motivations, methods, and consequences   162–4
methodology   159–60
research questions   161
Switzerland and   159–62, 167–8, 171–8
tools and methods   170–8
Egyptian Socialist Party (ESP)   43, 88
Egyptian unity   59–61
Egypt: Old and New (Martin)   142
Egypt's revolution of 1919   3–4, 203–8
Egypt's revolution of 2011   159–81
  Allenby, Edmund and   5, 39, 46, 106, 113–33
  British responses to   93–112
  canal workers and   29–51
  Christian-Muslim relations and   53–71
  colonial hierarchies   15–19
  and colonial racism   135–58
  commission of 1918   19–22
  "complete independence" (*istiqlal tamm*)   94
  historiography of   74–7
  impact on British   5, 93–112
  impacts on Egyptian social consciousness   6
  and its aftermath   22–6
  in *L'Etat du Canal de Suez*   30–1
  mass movement and   5, 73–92
  medical doctors and   10–27
  medical sovereignty   19–22
  midwives   19–22
  as moment of unity   53, 59–61
  as multifaceted historical event   7
  from nationalism to Islamism   89–92
  versus revolution of 2011   159–81
  women's maternal health and   10–27
  and worker's strike   35–6
ELC; see Egyptian Labor Corps (ELC)
Elgood, Bonté   11, 19–22
Elgood, Percival   19

El Lenby   44–6
Ellis, William T.   87
Elsayed, Mohamed   5
Elshakry, Marwa   58
El-Sisi, Abdel-Fattah   184
El-Enani, Khalil   90
ENP; see Egyptian National Party
ESP; see Egyptian Socialist Party (ESP)
ethical duality   92
ethnicity   56
European nationalism   31

Fahmi, 'Abd al-'Aziz   83
Fahmy, Khaled   7
Fahmy, Ziad   74
Faisal, Emir   122
Fann al-Wilada (The Art of Childbirth)   17–18
Fanus, Akhnukh   62–3
fellahin   96–100, 100 n.25
"Fi'l-jihādiyya," song   194
al-Fiqi, Mustafa   61
First World War   3, 38, 68, 149, 154–5, 183–202, 204
French Revolution   2, 6
From Mission to Modernity (Sedra)   58
Frontier of Loyalty: Political Exiles in the Age of the Nation-State, The (Shain)   162
Fu'ad, Ahmad   22–3

Gallup Organisation   5
Gardner, Brian   126
al-Ġayyātī, Shaykh 'Alī   161
Gender and the Making of Modern Medicine in Colonial Egypt (Abugideiri)   10
George, Lloyd   130–1
Germany
  involvement in 1919 Revolution   169–70
  and nationalist movement   165–9
Gezirah Sporting Club   142
Ghali, Butros   85 n.62
Ghali, Butrus   23
Ghali, Wasif   4
global color line   136–7, 145–9
Goldberg, Ellis   74, 80, 198
gonorrhea   10

Gordon, Charles 139
Gorst, Eldon 61–2, 66, 105
Grey, Edward 61–2

hakimas (midwives) 11, 20–2
Halls, Katherine 135
Hanafi, Hasan 60
Hanley, Will 49
Hanna, Milad 59–60, 69
Hanna, Sinut 4
Hannaford, Ivan 150
Hart, William 55
Hatina, Meir 60
Hawliyyat Misr Siyasiyya (Shafiq) 152
Haydar, Ali Bey 12
Haykal, Mohammed Hasanayn 55, 59–60, 68
Hilāl, Alī al-Dīn 184
History of Medical Education in Egypt, The (Mahfouz) 11
Hizb al-Watani 64, 85
Hourani, Albert 31, 70
Housri, Helmi 38
Husayn, 'Adil 60
Ḥusayn, Amīn 183
Hussein, Sharif 122

Ibrahim, Ali Bey 23
Ibrahim, Vivian 61, 63, 69
Ibrashi, Zaki Bey 108
identity 57; *see also* Christian-Muslim Egyptian identities; Copts
imperialism 55–6
Imperial War Museum 192–3
independence 97
internationalism 38–9
International Worker's Union of the Isthmus of Suez 42
Islamism 43
Isma'il, Khedive 139
Al-Ismaily 44–6
Isthmus
  nation's symbolism in 44–6
  radical ideologies within 41–3
Izzat, Muhammad Bey 23

jallabiyya 96, 96 n.13
Jellett, Henry 13
al-Kādī, Mansūr 161

Kamil, Mustafa 64, 68, 97–8, 97 n.19
al-Kashkī, Muḥammad 'Abd El-Fattāḥ 184–5
Kashkul 96, 96 n.13
Kasr el Aini 20
Keatinge, Henry 19, 22–4
Kedourie, Elie 95
Khadduri, Majid 114
Khalid, Khalid Muhammad 60
al-Khatib, Taqadum 5
Khedivate of Egypt 3
Khedive 3
Khedivial Sporting Club 142, 157
Khuri, Ilham 42
Kitchen, James 121
Kitchener, Herbert 19–20, 105, 142
Koch, Robert 12
Krämer, Gudrun 90–1

labor movement 74
Lady Cromer Memorial Home 24–6
Lawrence, T. E. 122
Lehita, Aly Bey 38
Lenin, Vladimir 3–4
Le Phenix 35
Liberal-Constitutional Party 94–5, 106–8
liberty 94
Lockman, Zachary 32–3, 74, 77, 85–6
Loewen, Jim 68
Lonely Minority, A (Wakin) 70
Lord Allenby 5

McMahon, Henri 122
Madden, Frank Cole 12–13, 17
Maghraoui, Abdeslam 75
Mahdist Wars (1885-98) 141
Mahfouz, Naguib 9–12, 9 n.1, 19, 24–7
  and Dobbin 15–17
  relationship with imperial doctors 16–19
  from student to young doctor under British rule 11–14
Mahmood, Saba 62–3
al-Majalla al-Tibbiyya al-Misriyya (Egyptian Medical Review) 23
Malcolm, Ian 39
al-Malik, Balsam 'Abd 25
Malititos, George 38

Mangin, Charles   146
Marfleet, Philip   5, 205
Marsot, Afaf Lutfi Al-Sayyid   114
Martin, Percy F.   142
Marxism   32–3
Maspero, Gaston   194
Al Masry   44–6
Al Masry sports club   44
mass movement   5, 73–92
  broke barriers   84–5
  massive   78–9
  from nationalism to Islamism   89–92
  in new forms of public politics   84–6
  peasants and   80–2
  revolutionary process   92
  soviets and   80–2
  spontaneous   78–9
  Wafd and Left   87–9
  women to fore   86–7
  workers and unions support   79–80
Masters, Bruce   56
maternity hospital   24
Maxwell, John   189
medical doctors   10–27
medical sovereignty   19–22
Mediterranean Expeditionary Force   118
Mehmet, Haci   139 n.9
Memoirs of a Village (al-Dawla)   196
midwives   19–22
Mikhail, Kyriakos   62–8
Milner, Alfred   75, 125–7
Milner-Zaghloul Agreement   126–7
Milton, Frank   12, 17
Mitchell, Richard   90
Mohammed Ali Street   30
Mossallam, Alia   192–6, 200
Mubarak, Hosni   1
Muhammad, Ali Fahmi   63
mumaridda (female sick nurses)   21
Munson, Ziad   91
Musa, Salama   194
Muslim Brotherhood   43, 73, 89–92, 204
Muslim-Christian solidarity   4, 61
  and 1911 Congresses   61–9
  and 1919 Revolution   61–9
  and feelings of national unity   59–61
  of internal "other"   54–9
Muslim-Coptic unity   59–69
Muslims, racialization of   138

Muslims and Copts in the Framework of a National Society (al-Bishri)   60
mutamassirun   86

Nash'at, Hasan   107
al Nasser, Gamal Abd   204–5
nation   56
nationalization/nationalism   29, 31–4, 56
  British responses to   96–100
  corporate/urban identity   39–40
  European   31
  histories of   31–4
  movement   32–3
  precursor for internationalism   38–9
  radical ideologies within Isthmus   41–3
  transnational solidarity in age of   36–43
  urban experience of   43–4
  workers *versus* employees   40–1
National Party (*al-Hizb al-Watani*)   64, 85
Nation's Party (*Hizb al-Umma*)   64
nativism   55
non-registered workers (*du tâcheron*)   34
Nuqrashi, Mahmud Fahmi   108

One People and One Nation (al-Fiqi)   61
Orientalism   55
Orientations (Storrs)   142
others of culture   55

Palestine   18, 113, 115, 118–19, 122–4, 148, 189, 191
Pasha, Adly Yakan   127
Pasha, Mahmoud Shoukry   13
Pasha, Sarwat   128–9
Pasha, Tewfik   68
Pashas in Paris   30–1
Pasteur, Louis   12
peasants   80–2
  in Egyptian 1919 Revolution   198–202
  Egyptian Armed Forces and   188–92
  in mass movement   80–2
people of colour nationalists   137
petition from Shadi   135–7
Philosophy of the Revolution (Abdel-Nasser)   74
public activism   5

al-qabda al-hadidiya 89
Qasr al-ʿAini Hospital 10, 13, 16–18, 24–7
Qurʾan 153
Qureishi, Zaheer 84

Raafat, Samir 142
racial caste system in Egypt 138–44
racism 5
radical ideologies within Isthmus 41–3
RAF; *see* Royal Air Force (RAF)
al-Rafiʾi, ʿAbd al-Rahman 150
Ramdani, Nabila 74
al-Raziq, Hasan ʿAbd 64
registered workers (*inscrit*) 34
Reid, Donald Malcolm 31
religion 55–6
Religious Difference in a Secular Age (Mahmood) 62–3
revolutions 1–2
Revolution Undone: Egypt's Road beyond Revolt, A (Hellyer) 1
Reynolds, Nancy 49–50
Richards, Owen 23
Rosenthal, Joseph 42, 88
Rotunda Hospital, Dublin 15
Royal Air Force (RAF) 81
Royal College of Obstetricians and Gynaecology 15
Ruiz, Mario 118–19, 148, 192–3
Russell, Thomas 76, 79–80, 79 n.33, 141–2
Ryad, Umar 61

El-Saadawi, Nawal 86
Ṣabrī, Ashraf 184–5
al Sadat, Anwar 204–5
Safran, Nadav 31
Said, Edward 55
Salim, Muhammad 118
Sayce, Henry 62
SCC; *see* Suez Canal Company
School of Midwifery 20
Schulze, Reinhardt 191–2, 198
Sebesta, Edward 68
secularism 56, 71
Sedra, Paul 54–9
self-determination 93
Sergius, Qommus 69

Seven Pillars of Egyptian Identity, The (Hanna) 59
Shadi, Abu 135
Shafiq, Ahmad 18, 24, 152–3
Shain, Yossi 162
Shaʿrawi, ʿAli 154–5
Sharkey, Heather 58–9
Al-Sharq television channel 161
Shepheard's Hotel 157
Sidqi, Ismail 89
Simsimeyya 29
sirdar 141
Skouphopoulos, Alexandre 42–3
slavery 140, 150–6
Smith, Anthony 56
Smith, Charles D. 31
Social Movement Theory 91
sovereignty 97
Soviets 80–2
Stack, Lee 109
State Council (*Majlis al-Dawla*) 60 n.28
Stoler, Ann 49
Storrs, Ronald 142
strike, workers 35–6, 79–80
Suez Canal Company (SCC) 29–30, 34–5
  clerical workers 34
  manual workers 34
  technical staff 34
  workers strike 35–8
Suez crisis; *see* Tripartite Aggression in Egypt
Suez family 39–40
Sulayman, William 61
sulṭa 194–5, 198
Switzerland 159–62, 167–8, 171–8
Sykes-Picot of 1916 122
syndicalism 41–3
syphilis 10
Syria 113–24

tawqilat campaign 78
Thābit, Rayyis 197–8
Tharwat, ʿAbd al-Khaliq 107
Thawrat 1919 (al-Rafiʾi) 150
Toledano, Ehud 139
training school 22–4
Tripartite Aggression in Egypt 29

Trotsky, Leon 84
trusts (*awqaf*) 3
Turkey 159–64, 167–8, 175–81, 188

umm al-misriyyin 86
unions 79–80
'Urābī, Ahmad 68
'Urābī revolt 141
urban identity 39–40

Van Doorn-Harder, Nelly 54
Venables, E. K. 146
Verlato, Olga 194
Victoria Cross 185
violence 6
Vitalis, Robert 153

Wafd 4, 78–9
al-wafd al-misri 77
Wafd Party 4, 78–9, 94–5, 95 n.7, 107–8, 125–6, 204
Wakin, Edward 70
al-Wardani, Ibrahim Nasif 64
Al-Watan newspaper 63
Wavell, Viscount 125
welfare capitalism 39
Wendell, Charles 31
Whidden, James 5
white supremacy in Egypt 139

Wickham, Carrie Rosefsky 89
Wilson, Woodrow 3–4, 77, 125
Wilsonian principles of self-determination 93
Wingate, Reginald 104, 124, 154, 191
Wintringham, John 149
women
  doctors 22
  in mass movement 86–7
  maternal health 10–27
  rights 6
"Women's March" of March 16 6
workers 79–80
"Workers on the Nile" by (Beinin and Lockman) 32
worker's strike 35–6
workers *versus* employees 40–1
working class, engagement of 5

"Ya 'azīz 'ainī" 194
yawm al-jihad 77
YMCA 148

Zaghlul, Saad 4–6, 30, 38, 68, 69 n.79, 74, 78, 94, 96, 102–12, 124–8, 132–3, 152, 155–6, 173, 190–1
Zaghlul, Safiya 6
Zizania 38
Zubaida, Sami 49, 84–5, 91

www.ingramcontent.com/pod-product-compliance
Lightning Source LLC
Chambersburg PA
CBHW062223300426
44115CB00012BA/2188